OUR EARTH AND BEYOND

A MESSAGE FROM THE
UNIVERSE TO 21ST CENTURY EARTH
BOOK I

SATURN

JUPITER

EARTH

UFO ESCORT   COMET SHIP

VENUS

COLLECTORS'
FIRST EDITION

JAN ROSAMOND ADLER
With Ron J. Oberon

May you let your Love and Light shine for all to see!

Solon, a High Director of the Universe from the 25th Plane, wrote about the cover design of the Universe's Book I, *Our Earth And Beyond*: "We want to have Saturn, Jupiter and Earth with Pluto below the Earth; then Venus and the lime green-glowing Comet Ship coming to Earth escorted by UFOs. This will make an eye-catching cover for our Book for all of Earth's Souls to read."

Planetary Photos courtesy of NASA

Publisher: Ron Oberon & Associates, LLC   ronjoberon@sbcglobal.net
150 S. Glenoaks Blvd., #9342   Voicemail: 888-294-8778
Burbank, California 91502   Fax: 888-230-2272

Recommended reading: The "Conversations With God" series by Neale Donald Walsch and Dannion Brinkley's "Saved By the Light."

Represented by Italia IP, James A. Italia
Patent Trademark Copyright Attorney
3500 W. Olive Ave., Suite 300
Burbank, California 91505
italia@italiaip.com

Publisher's Cataloging-in-Publication Data (Provided by Quality Books, Inc.)
Adler, Jan Rosamond
    Our Earth And Beyond: a message from the universe to 21st century Earth. Book I / Jan Rosamond Adler with Ron J. Oberon.
p.cm.
LCCN 200790453
ISBN-13: 978-0-615-13526-7
ISBN-10: 0-615-13526-9

1. Spirit writings. 2. Automatism. 3. Spiritual life. 4. Self-realization. 5. Conduct of life

I. Oberon, Ron J. II. Title
BF1290.A325 2007   133.9'32
                       QB107-600169

If unavailable in your local bookstores, copies may be purchased singly or in quantity from the publisher via any of the contact methods listed above. Use the Web site to request healing or books. All healings are free of charge. www.ronsgiftofhealing.com

Collectors' First Edition Printed July 2007. Printed in the United States of America

Prelude to Book II, "Many Planes Above"

Cover art by Janice Wynne

IN LOVING MEMORY OF MY SISTER, JAN ROSAMOND ADLER

November 3, 1936 – April 22, 1996

In Loving Memory

Jan Rosamond Adler

November 3, 1936
April 22, 1996

Touched by an Angel

A poem in Celebration of the Life of Jan Adler

Many friendships are special, but none quite the same,
As this beautiful one I'm about to explain.
When I needed a friend, a friend indeed came,
So I'll keep coming back to this truthful refrain,
I was touched by an Angel.... and Jan was her name.

Once when I thought that I couldn't get through it,
She gently but firmly said, "Yes, you can do it!"
Lifting me, pushing me, I'd hear her say,
"Everything is gonna be okay,
Let the universe guide you and wisdom you'll gain!
Meditate everyday and you'll soon see a change."
These affirmations shall with me remain,
I was touched by an Angel.... and Jan was her name.

I'll remember the classes and healings at Ron's
How Todd was so close to Jan, his dear mom
And her daughter who bears a resemblance so strong
All her lovely grandchildren - what a legacy long.
And the love we all shared that transcends this Earth plane
I was touched by an Angel.... and Jan was her name.

When asked of world problems she said, "We must love!
Love from the universe - Love from above.
Love, she said, is what life's about.
God wants us to love from the inside out"
These teachings I'll keep so they'll not be in vain.
I was touched by an Angel.... and Jan was her name.

May she soar like the birds she so very much loved.
May the white light surround her - That light from above.
May the love of God keep her - For love she proclaimed,
I'll remember this Angel.... Jan was her name.

Written 23 April, 1996

by Gail Green

To the Family and Friends of Jan Adler;

Jan was like a second "Mom" to me. She was encouragement,
strength, teacher, confidant and more. We will all miss her
so but knowing that she is at peace and "at work" helps me
greatly. In spirit we are never apart.
Jan, my dear friend, I love you and I wish God speed!

Gail

CONTENTS

A NOTE TO READERS

My Sister, Jan Adler, with my help, wrote Two Books, "Our Earth And Beyond," Book I, and "Many Planes Above," Book II, for the Universe. She completed this labor of love before returning home to work from the Universe, 11 years ago on April 22, 1996.

Both Books are built around questions or comments from me or from Jan. Throughout both I've presented those questions or comments in italics. I've also presented my own Inspirational Writing in italics.

In addition, I've emboldened, capitalized and/or underlined key words and phrases to underscore their importance, and liberally spaced the text on each page to make it easier to read.

These books warranted this unique formatting because it is the First Time this Truthful and Special Information has been given to Earth.

Ultimately, we want the reader to pause and reflect over what is presented in each of these Books, and to fully understand the Universe, and how Life really works.

Finally, I have asked most all of the Questions and Highlighted text to Stress the way things on Earth are, and what needs to be done to Change.

Ron J. Oberon

I

PREFACE

Both Books are meant to Open Minds and Teach that there are things which Exist Beyond our Present Understanding and that there are New Ways of looking at Things.

This is how we grow. We grow through gaining Knowledge.

"You know in your **Search** for **Knowledge**, you can keep **Only True Friends**. All others <u>will leave if they</u> <u>do not grow with yo</u>u. Just a bit of **Wisdom**."

Jennifer, "Mary Todd Lincoln"

"I do not claim these as my Books. These Books belong to the Universe."

All the information received in these Books came from High Teachers of the Higher Planes of the Universe; bringing their Knowledge and not ours.

It is their intention to present this Truthful Knowledge in layman's terms to the entire World for each Soul to Change Its Ways and accept the Universe and Life as it really is, but not to offend anyone.

It is your God-given Free Choice for you to accept and Open Your Minds, or reject this and remain the same as you are at this time of your Life.

Jan R. Adler

Jennifer, I hope Earth Souls will Open Their Minds to accept the Wisdom and Understanding in these Books!

I, Ron, said this after already receiving so much Truthful Information, which made such common sense to me. Jennifer, who is "Mary Todd Lincoln," wrote in a large hand the following response.

"RON…IT IS NOT YOURS TO WORRY WHO ACCEPTS OR REJECTS WHAT WE SAY."

"You only make things better for yourself when you think of someone else. We in the High Universe are so Grateful for you and Jan; presenting this Higher Knowledge for all Earth Souls to Choose, to think for themselves about what we say."

Jennifer, "Mary Todd Lincoln"

"With this Book we will Teach you the Best, and the most Knowledge, Truth and Accuracy, ever taught on Earth."

High Teacher of Teachers, Conier

In some places we explain further the information received for our own understanding as we discussed it with the Teacher writing.

This is because for much of this information, it was the first time these answers to our questions have ever been given to anyone on Earth.

We were so surprised and so many of you will be, but the answers do make sense and are quite interesting.

Before 1985 we were not aware of any of this information.

Many automatic writing sessions were taped. We then added some of our comments on the subject for Clarification, which many times brought forth the next question. Sometimes when we were talking together the Teacher's explanation would just come through Jan's pen.

You will see where many subjects are clarified, often including examples given by the High Teacher who is writing. This all transpired as a personal two-way conversation, with material for these Books coming from each High Teacher, which we were so privileged to have in our presence.

You will never read Books with such Important Messages and with answers to the many Questions you may have.

These Books also have Information given to impact and Change every Soul on Earth, which will affect the outcome of the entire Earth Plane.

We all must Change Our Earth Lives away from all of the Corruption, Ignorance and Negativity, to realize Our Purpose for Progress as a Spiritual Soul Being.

The answers to the Questions you'll find here are not mine. They are from High Teachers of the Universe, who feel Earth Souls are now ready to receive this Knowledge.

*They were originally to be published one year prior to the arrival of a **"High Holy Spiritual Color Comet Ship"** on **January 17, 1988**.*

See the Chapter of the same name.

This Special Happening was to bring many High Teachers from the High Universe with Messages to all Earth Souls to Change Their Ways.

This was meant to put a Stop to All the Corruption, Ignorance and Negativity on Earth, and to bring Final Proof of Life after Death.

There is much Information on the Comet Ship in this Book I.

However, due to the Importance of the Mission and Messages, the High Teachers changed their plans. They felt that Earth Minds were not Open Minded enough to accept and receive the Comet properly.

They wanted to have Worldwide Impact and needed more Earth Souls' Attention and Co-operation; better control of Negativity and to eliminate any Interference. So even though they did arrive, they never Landed or Materialized.

They did temporarily Materialize over England to test the response they would receive from Earth Souls. You can read more about this event further on in this Book.

After 20 years I have been strongly impressed to now finish the work my Sister and I started so long ago. The timing is now getting better for the Earth Souls to receive this Information.

Therefore, I should now Publish the Books for the Universe, hopefully to be available at least One-year prior to the arrival of the Comet.

Many More Souls need to Change Their Ways before the possible return of the Comet in late 2007, or 2008, to evaluate the Progress Earth Souls have made.

If the Minds on Earth do not begin to Open to accept this Information and Change their Ways to a more Spiritual Way of Life before arrival, this date will be once again postponed.

More and stronger Disasters will continue happening as long as it takes to get Our Attention. We must Change our Corrupt, Selfish Ways.

If this does not happen even after the Great Disasters, the High Holy Spiritual Color Comet will further delay its Landing.

We have been told they wanted the Earth Plane to be much more Spiritually Advanced for their Mission to Succeed. This may even take another 10 years to accomplish.

Jan and I were just the Messengers for this Comet. We were stunned and amazed, as we were Learning all of the new Information, as we went along.

I feel there are more Open Minds today than there were in the 80s, and that Many More Changes will now occur toward a more Spiritual Life on Earth to accomplish this Special Mission.

With these Books I and II, the Universe will Teach you, and all Earth Souls to Open their Minds to the Truth and Accuracy of Life on Earth. Learn how to prepare yourself for your continued Soul Life on the Planes Above.

The Universe's main concern is that Earth Souls Change their Ways to Better Themselves, and Progress with much more LOVE for their neighbors and All Earth Souls Around them.

Only then will the High Teachers works' succeed. This will bring Peace and Happiness for the Betterment of All Mankind.

I am a Universal Healer and Teacher of the High Universe. I Volunteered when the Master Directors of the Round Table of the Very High Universe asked me to bring my much-needed Healing to Earth at this time.

My Sister Jan also Volunteered. Then we were placed together for this Very Special Mission. However, Minds were not opening and Earth Souls were not co-operating for the Mission to be accomplished. Jan was then called back to the Universe. She now works with me from there. This Mission will be completed before I am called back Home.

See the chapter, "My Life's Mission" as a Healer and Teacher, which begins on page 238, followed by the chapter explaining my Healing Progress.

We all have different Missions of Our Own while here on Earth to Accomplish before it's Our Time to return Home to the Universe.

Ron J. Oberon

INTRODUCTION
By Jan R. Adler

Automatic Writing and Art

A Direct Connection to the Universe

I do not claim these as my Books. These Books belong to and come from the Universe.

How many of us are really aware of the Universe? Or how many even give a thought, to Our Purpose in the Universe!

These Books will answer these questions and many, many more about Our World and our purpose for being here, and where we go from here.

There are Many Planes and Dimensions that do Exist. They are a Real part of Our Great Universe.

Through Automatic Writing, I have been given Great Knowledge and Wisdom from the Higher Planes of the Universe, some of which has never been given to the Earth Plane before. Prior to 1985, I was not aware of any of this information.

Through the writing I have answered many questions for Thousands of Individuals, Personally helping them move forward in the right direction with their Lives – answers to many of the Questions we have all been curious about in Our Daily Lives.

Their Lives have been turned completely around, with the help they received because of this Direct Connection to the Universe.

They are usually given the Direction they should take to make a Change In Their Lives to get back on the Right Track. As the Universe would put it, "to help them get on with their Lives and make Progress."

Some people receiving Personal Automatic Writing do Not Always Accept the answers to their questions given by the Universe, but nevertheless, what they receive is Truthful and Accurate.

VI

The challenge and the opportunity for them is to Open Their Minds and exercise their Free Will; make a Decision or a Change, or take a Stand with a Situation in order to Learn their Lessons and Progress.

It is said everything in Life has a Purpose, nothing is Wasted, be it so called Accident or Injury, Illness or even Death. All is for the Learning of Lessons and Correcting Mistakes from Past Lives.

Everyone must Change Their Ways to Stop the Corruption on Earth, and earn their way to Higher Planes when it is their time to return Home to the Universe.

This all began for me one day a few years ago when a Psychic Reader told me I could do Automatic Writing and that I had a Protecting Guide assigned to me; I could ask my Guide for help, for whatever I needed.

Not quite fully understanding this at the time, I thought, what do I have to lose if I try? But I was unsure what Automatic quite meant.

Would it mean that the pen should move by itself, or should I guide it by holding it in my hand?

Then I thought to call on my Guide, and ask him if he could make the pen move, while I was holding it in my hand.

Suddenly the pen started moving and my Guide started writing to me. I was so excited that for a moment I didn't know what to do. So I began asking him questions.

He told me that he was my Protecting Guide, "Antony," who was "Marc Antony," and he and I were together in a Past Life.

I was "Cleopatra," and he was assigned to me at birth for us to work together to correct Lessons from our Previous Life together.

So he answered many questions for me Personally that proved to me he was a real Personality, that he Loved me Very Much, and that he has been with me all of my Life.

He then proceeded to write and tell me that I had been Chosen by the Universe to write Two Books and then he asked me if I would be willing to do so.

I would be Honored to do this, I answered, but I was not a writer and would need some help with the writing.

Immediately the writing changed, reading, "I have been chosen to be your first Automatic Writing Teacher, and I will help you understand Automatic Writing to write "Our Books."

Through the continued writing, I learned that I would have Many Teachers and each one would contribute to their Books until the work was complete. We would repeat the process for the Second Book.

The names of both Books were given; the first to be called, "Our Earth And Beyond" and the second to be called, "Many Planes Above."

They would contain True Information about the Universe, some of which has never been brought through to Earth before; information they felt Earth Souls are now ready to know and understand.

As we continued, I couldn't stop asking questions. The more questions I asked the more answers I received, always in Simple Plain English that I could easily understand. Most surprisingly, all the answers seemed to make sense.

I learned that my first Teacher was a Woman during her time on Earth. That she lived in England, wrote Many Books, and called herself "Cormeir," her chosen Dimension name.

She started writing through my pen with Information about Our Life on this Earth and about a "Color Comet Ship" being sent to Earth which was to arrive in 1988. It would bring Messages to Earth about a "New Dimension" which they have Created for Peace and Happiness.

The Information continued to come for the start of their first Book. I hope you will enjoy reading it again and again because I feel it could be picked up whenever you feel a need for a Spiritual Lift or some Universal Help in Your Life.

These Books will be Your Direct Connection to the Universal Power, and provide all the Strength you will ever need in this "Your Earth Life" or Your Continued Life on the "Many Planes Above."

I bring these Books to you to Open Your Hearts and Souls. As an Automatic Writer, these Books have been given to me from my High Teachers of the Universe. In reading them you will realize there are Important Messages to Learn.

I am self-taught through God and the Universe. All of my Beautiful High Teachers have brought me Wisdom, Patience and Knowledge beyond the Earth's Availability.

What is Automatic Writing? This is what I asked, when I was told I could do this. Well it's just what it says.

The pen moves Automatically writing Information that is not mine. It is a direct connection to the Universe.

Before you start to work, you must always ask for the Divine White Light of Protection to be placed around you and your Aura, in order to receive High Spirit Guides and Teachers. Always ask for the Highest and the Best to come and help.

When this happened to me, and through my Protecting Guide's direction, I was able to connect with the High Teachers of the Universe through my pen.

These Books each contain direct messages from my High Teachers. I was told in the beginning that I was Chosen with this Special Gift to write Books for the Universe to make the World aware and allow people to understand more about their Purpose in Life on this Earth.

As we go through Our Life, it is a Difficult Process. We all should search Our Inner Souls to make the time we have here on Earth more Successful, Happy and Peaceful for Ourselves. This will also happen for all of those around us.

The High Teachers of the Universe say that they are there to help each and every one of us at anytime we may need Guidance and Reassurance.

Why not ask for the help you need in your everyday Life?

God cares and Loves us all,

Jan R. Adler

JAN'S HIGH WRITING AND ART TEACHERS

Jan worked with 12 Writing Teachers and Eight Art Teachers. Each Teacher possessed a different personality, though they were all Knowledgeable, Accurate, kind and loving, and possessed a great deal of patience. I've provided samples of her Art on page three.

On the next several pages I have presented a list of both sets of Teachers. Each list identifies each Writer or Artist by his or her Earth or High Dimension name and includes the dates they wrote or painted with her, how long they worked with Jan and when they moved on to a Higher Plane.

Page four begins a brief account of each Writing Teacher during their time on Earth, including who they were and what they did. We start with information received from the first Teacher, Cormeir, and continue with information left by each Teacher as the work Progressed.

Jan did create paintings for individuals, and then wrote for them to explain what the design and colors meant to them in their lives. These private writings cannot be shared.

However, I've included a sample of this kind of writing on Page three. Aristotle wrote this about the painting that Jan created specifically for me that hangs in my office. I did not include a photo of that painting.

Jan's Art began to develop late in 1986. The Ancient Minoan Artists said they wanted to give their art as a gift to the Earth Plane; art that was destroyed in 1900 B.C.

Each Art Teacher contributed their talents and over the next 10 years Jan's skill as an Artist continued to progress. Each one earned a Higher Plane or Planes when they completed their assignment working with Jan.

They were also assigned to continually elevate Jan to Higher and Higher Planes as she co-operated with their Universal Work. Jan's Universal Work continued for 11 years, writing for Our Books, Art Works and answering all of my questions. She also wrote privately for thousands of individuals.

Jan was called back Home to the Universe on April 22, 1996, to continue her work from there in the High Universe. Note: Book II contains a brief account of the Art Teachers during their time on Earth.

WRITING TEACHERS

03-16-85 to 05-08-85	1 month & 3 weeks	**Cormeir**
05-09-85 to 05-30-85	3 weeks	**Michel "Michelangelo"**
05-31-85 to 07-01-85	1 month & returns in 9 days	**Marylin**
06-15-85 to 06-16-85	1 day	**Mauy "Moses"**
07-02-85 to 07-08-85	1 week	**Samuel**
07-09-85 to 07-10-85	1day	**Sornia**
07-10-85 to 08-30-85	Returned for 1 month & 20 days	**Marylin**
08-31-85 to 01-12-86	4 months & 2 weeks	**Conier**
01-13-86 to 04-13-86	3 months & 1 day	**Jennifer "Mary Todd Lincoln"**
04-14-86 to 09-28-86	5 months & 2 weeks	**Teddy Roosevelt**
09-29-86 to 01-14-87	3 months & 2 weeks	**Mara**
01-15-87 to 08-23-87	5 months & 1 week	**Solon**
08-24-87 to 04-27-88	7 months & 3 days	**Markus**
04-28-88 to 04-22-96	7 years 11 months & 22days	**Aristotle**

Jan passed on April 22 1996

ANCIENT MINOAN ART TEACHERS

Ancient Minoan Art

10-28-86 to 02-02-87	3 months & 5 days	**Mina**
02-03-87 to 02-22-87	20 days	**Conar**
02-23-87 to 12-31-87	10 months & 7 days	**Thuis**
01-01-88 to 05-28-89	1 year 4 months & 29 days	**Palora**
05-29-89 to 01-06-90	7 months & 9 days	**Mithus**
01-07-90 to 09-14-91	8 months & 7 days	**Monique**
09-15-91 to 04-02-92	7 months & 18 days	**Thor**
04-03-92 to 01-29-93	Returned	**Monique**
01-30-93 to 04-22-96	3 years, 2 months & 23 days	**Andreas**

These are photos of two paintings that Jan made for separate clients. Jan wrote about each, explaining the meanings for each client behind the symbols, colors and designs. The Universe would start helping each individual get on with their lives the moment the painting was hung in their home.

5-8-88

Aristotle is here oh Yes This painting is given to you so that your house will be well protected and it will give you a lot of healing its also will help the financial situation to get better and its is a very High Teacher of healing that stands guard The Birds is the highest of all in The Universe & its your Good Luck for carrying on our Work. In the next few months nice things will be happening to you as to get you more stabilized and there will be less pressure. July is a Special month for you of much Happiness Very good news will come that will make you happy. The fall is also very good more money comes in More healing work & talk about the future for your healing work The pink is Love for all that you give so truly. Next year brings a change in Your life more like you wanted You will get your wish by next Spring The energy from this picture will help your house kept all negitivity out You have it almost cleansed & to stay cleansed We here in the Universe Wish You Great Healing Powers to Carry On Your Work for Us & Thank you very much for all you have done We send Good Health Happiness a lot of miracle healing powers & Prosperity for you Thank you Aristotle

4

Cormeir is here to tell you, Jan, about Our Books you must write for us in the Universe. You are A Chosen One, chosen to tell Earth people about Life After Death.

When your Earth time is finished, and you leave your body, Our Teachers tell your Doorkeeper or Guide to bring you to them, on the Astral Plane.

All who arrive must Listen to the Teachers who tell them what Work they must do to Correct all Earth Mistakes.

You must not refuse to Work, as you will stop your Progress, and not be allowed to come to Our Planes.

If you refuse to Listen and Work, you will be sent to a Cold Dark Corner to sit until you decide to Work Off Your Mistakes.

I am called Cormeir, and you and I will be the Connection to the Knowledge for the Entire World to read.

I am not just a Comet Courier; I am a High Teacher from a Higher Plane. I am Most Happy to answer all your questions, as much as I can, and Truthfully, too, as you are asked to write for others.

Future events we bring will happen for you and your friends, and those that come to you for Guidance, through your Automatic Writing.

Our only significant problem in sharing this with you will be with time and dates, as there is no time in Our Spirit World.

I will help with the first Book, "**Our Earth And Beyond**," for a while, and then Michael, a Higher Teacher than myself, will come and contribute to Our Book.

The second Book, called "**Many Planes Above**," will be written by much Higher Teachers yet to come.

There was not much more to add on Cormeir except that her name was a Dimension name. I was not sure in what year, but she was a writer of many books when on Earth and Lived in Nottingham, England.

In the beginning she was confused on times and dates. Also at that time, we did not know how long a Teacher would remain with Jan.

Cormeir paved the way for the much Higher Teachers to come in, as did each Teacher that followed. Cormeir left after only one month and three weeks, before we could ask her to clarify her Earth Life.

Cormeir started writing the first Book 10 days after she arrived, and finished her contribution to the Book six weeks later.

Then in May 1985, Michelangelo came through in the middle of the page, and wrote the following.

The Second Teacher: Michael "Michelangelo" – May 9, 1985

I am your New Teacher, Jan; my name is Michael. I am of a Higher Plane and was sent to help you write this Book for Our Teachers, who feel Earth people should know about the Universe at this time.

Yes, Jan, I am here beside you to help you all that I can. Michael is my Earth name, and I spent time on Earth as a Teacher and Writer of much Great Learning to Earth Souls.

These Learnings were like a Script to Teach Earth Souls at that time about Our Future on the Earth Plane.

Many of my Teachings are still found carved in Rock in the city of Rome, and they represent Much Knowledge for all Earth Souls.

I am Roman and lived a long time on the Earth Plane Teaching, 1475 – 1564 A.D., and you will still see my carved Rock Sculptures and Paintings in Rome.

This is when the Rulers of Rome were a powerful group, and this was when many Good Earth Souls were sent early to Our Planes from the Earth.

I lived in a Grand House in Rome with many Servants, and I learned to write from a Servant of mine called Colitus.

6

Colitus was a Holy Believer, and taught me to believe there was another World beyond Earth.

My writings from my days on Earth are what my Teachers told me to write, just like you write, Jan. All that I wrote when I was on the Earth Plane remains on Earth.

You must someday see my Writings in Rome; when you go I will tell you where to find them.

I received information from the Higher Teachers that this is what we in the Universe want you to do, Jan.

Yes, I am Michelangelo, and I am now a Teacher of Very High Knowledge, which I learned from Teachers of the Higher Planes. Michelangelo was my Earth name, but you may call me Michael.

I created Writings in Stone, and I wrote about the Earth, and what was coming. My Paintings <u>tell many</u> <u>stories and my</u> Sculptures are <u>the finest</u>. My Teachers gave me this work for all Earth Souls to remember.

Jan, do you like to travel, and go places? I used to like to travel, but when I was on Earth I walked everywhere and sometimes we drove Carts pulled by Mules. It was a lot of fun; you would have liked it. Look at the difference today on Earth!

When you travel to Rome you can see my work all over the city. When all is done with the needed Changes on Earth, there will no longer be a need for my Writings anymore.

I want to Teach you all my Knowledge, so that Our Book will be the best ever written.

You, Jan, will be a Very Good Writer after my Teachings and work with you. You are Special and your Knowledge from us is going to make you famous.

When this Book is finished, we must work on another. "**Many Planes Above**" will be the next Book for you to write.

This information from Michael is sifted from Jan's personal writings, and the following is the last I found written on the day before he left. He was only with Jan a short three weeks. The following is a personal writing about himself and his family to Jan.

Michael is here Jan. I was born in a small Village, Caprese, in 1475 A.D., and then we moved to Florence in Northern Italy. My birth name was Michel Angelo Buonarrot.

I was the oldest Boy, one of four children, and my Parents were Italian and German mixed. We were a poor Family.

My Parents didn't have much at all; that is why I worked so hard to take care of my Family, which I did for many years from a young age. Once I started working I changed my name to Michelangelo.

In the year of 1496 I was 21 years old and working in Rome. Later, in 1501, I was commissioned to Florence to sculpt David for the City. At this time I was 26 years old, but it took me three years to complete the Statue.

I was a Great Worker, and did much Painting and many Sculptures on Earth in that time, including the Sistine Chapel in Rome, where I eventually earned a nice home with servants. You will find my works from over many years all over Rome for all to see.

I lived on Earth for 89 years, until 1564. I accepted my last assignment for the Pope as Chief Architect for St. Peter's Basilica at age 75, years old, in 1546. * I still wanted to do more but my Teachers said I had done enough.

I am entering Michelangelo's response to the Pope's comments as he accepted the assignment.

*"Many believe...and I believe...that I have been designated for this work by God. In spite of my old age, I do not want to give it up; I work out of Love for God and I put all my hope in God." * www.Michelangelo.com*

On page 54 we've entered an actual page of Michelangelo's writing and signature.

The Third Teacher: Marylin – May 31, 1985

Marylin is Jan's next Teacher. She told Jan she was an old Teacher from a Very High Plane and came to the Spirit World in the year 1902.

She wrote many Books, which were called Special Books when on Earth. Marylin listed 12 Titles published around 1890 for me to check out at the Library. They tell us about the Dimensions and the Earth Plane.

She was born in 1860 as Marylin Smith, and lived in the State of Maryland, near the water where she wrote her Books.

She writes, I am a wise Chinese Lady, and my Family came to the United States as slaves in the year 1823 from China. We were brought to help Americans and as Our Generation grew we became Independent and my Father became very wealthy.

I never married, as it was not my thing and against my Father's wishes. I wanted to write Books and when he passed I spent the rest of my Earth Life writing.

In my first Life on Earth, I was a man from Greece and I wanted to travel to China, so they sent me back as a Descendant of China. I did visit China in that Life twice.

I am a High Teacher of Writing, and was sent to write for you, Jan, to help people, and for you to write Our Book.

I was Chosen to Teach you to write, and now my Lesson is to Learn to Help Others. I was a Good Soul, so therefore I am able to Learn on this Plane through you to help people on Earth. We are both Learning together.

There is also a page that I asked Marylin to write about herself, that we entered in Our Book on Page 69.

When it was Marylin's time to leave during her writing – in the middle of the page – the text changed to large scripting.

"I would like you to know that I am going to leave you soon, and there is a nice man here, who you will really like, and I want you to know that I will be near if you need me."

His name is Mauy and he is a Very High Teacher with Very Thorough Knowledge, who is not going to write for Our Book, because I am your Teacher of Writing.

This Teacher, Mauy, was not meant to be one of Jan's writing Teachers, but had just finished a long rest, and was allowed to come through to help him adjust to working once again with Earth.

NO, Jan and Ron, I WILL TELL YOU AGAIN, so you will understand.

He is a High Knowledgeable Teacher. He will be here only for a short time to answer only questions on the Book. You will need this Knowledge and you have him because I am Learning and working to Help People. There is a Very Special reason for this. Henceforth, I will still write every time you write for people or the Book.

Mauy will help from behind the scenes on Our Book, and I don't want you to get upset because it will be all right.

You are a Chosen One and will be sharing much of his Knowledge and Information with Earth people.

You have all three Teachers – Marylin, with Mauy and Michael, who is working behind the scenes with you at this time.

We may send more Teachers because we all are instructed to contribute to these Books.

At this point the writing returned to normal size. Marylin's message about Mauy was so important that she wrote in a much larger hand; so large that it filled three pages. Now Mauy is allowed to write only once, briefly about himself.

I am your New Teacher for a short time. My name is Mauy, and I am Honored to be able to work with you, Jan. I made up this name. It's an odd name. I chose it because nobody else has it.

10

I am from the Earth Plane so many years ago that I don't remember when. I have been resting for many years on a Very High Plane and now want to get back to work again.

All of the Teachers have Chosen me to share my Knowledge of Our Dimensions. I am a Very Old Soul and lived Three Lifetimes on Earth before my last incarnation…now I'm remembering; it was around 1450 B.C., and my Earth name then was Moses.

Now I'm trying to remember how to write, as I haven't written for nearly 3,500 years. It's difficult for us to remember dates and time.

I am a High Knowledgeable Writer, and my original writing on Earth is still to be seen. I wrote the Tablets of the Old Testament given to me by the Universe at that time.

Yes that was I, Moses; I am from Egypt and Israel, and I wrote many Tablets. I still see these Writings all over the Earth Plane.

I wanted to meet you and tell you something about myself. As we said, Marylin will be doing all the writing, and Michael and I will be here helping her with Our Knowledge to answer all questions and assist when needed.

Marylin is back, and we are all going to prepare you, Jan, for the coming of much Higher Teachers, one at a time. Everything we do is for that Important Purpose.

This was a great help to Mauy. It helped him to readjust to working again after resting for so long. I want you to know we Love you. Remember, Mauy and Michael, who is still with us, are here to help.

We have two more short time Teachers to come; one is Samuel, and the other is Sornia.

The Fourth Teacher: Samuel – July 2, 1985

Samuel was Jan's next Teacher for a short while, and this is his writing.

11

My name is Samuel and I am your New Teacher, Jan, of Great Writings, to work with you now for a short time. My Teachers say it is time for you to move up again, as you are doing so well.

I am from Jerusalem in the days of Jesus, and I was a man of many means. I led the Jewish Army for Caesar and was a Great Warrior, a Great Warrior of the Chariots and fought many Battles. Now I am a Great Teacher.

I am working on a High Plane with much Knowledge about all on Earth. It is a Great Honor to serve you and I know this way of writing.

I am a Teacher, Philosopher and Writer and Very Knowledgeable. They called me "Samuel The Great" and I wrote Important Information on Life in the time of Caesar.

Many read my Scrolls of Writings and you may see these Scrolls someday when you visit Rome. Jan, your next Teacher will be Sornia.

The Fifth Teacher: Sornia – July 9, 1985

I am here for a very short time. I picked that name because I like it. I am Italian and have Great Knowledge from a High Plane.

I will bring Truth and Accuracy to your writings and I Love to help people. I stood beside Samuel to learn your works. I am ready to work with you on Our Book and write for all your friends today.

I am a Petite Lady and I Love to write. I have been working in the Spirit World many years now helping people.

I am very romantic, with dark hair and blue eyes and a pretty woman like you, Jan. I was married to a man who was very much in Love with me. We had a beautiful Love Life on Earth.

Sornia was the last of Five Teachers. They all stayed a short time: Michael for three weeks, Mauy for one day, Samuel for one week, Sornia for one day, Cormeir for one month and three weeks, and Marylin for one month.

Marylin later returned for another month and 20 days. We were also told of another Lady Teacher, Someri, who was also there to help.

The next Teacher was Marylin, who had been our 3rd Teacher. She returned on July 10, 1985, for a month and a half. She wrote the following just before she left on August 31, 1985.

I have completed my extended stay, and I must move on now, Jan. Because of you I have Progressed significantly, and <u>I thank</u> you. You also have Progressed Rapidly to a High Plane of work, and you have now earned another New Teacher.

The Sixth Teacher: Conier – August 31, 1985

He is a man named Conier and he is a Very Knowledgeable Teacher that comes for Special Reasons. He will use his Mind Healing and Teaching to improve your writing. I will be around for a while to help Conier adjust to writing again. Michael will also help from time to time.

My Teachers tell me it is time to rest for a while. We need rest after we work with an Earth Soul and before we move on to our next Pupil.

Each Teacher made their Earth contact and contributed directly to the Books. They also remained for varying periods of time assisting in the background to quickly move Jan up a Plane or two, to prepare her for the Higher vibrations of much Higher Teachers to come.

There was a reason for everything that came through her pen and for all these beginning Teachers that visited her. As Jan moved up so did each Teacher to a Higher Plane. Conier comes in now to write.

I am your next New Teacher, Jan. My name is Conier, which is a Dimension name and I will be writing for you for quite a while. I am a Very High Teacher and one of the Highest so far to help you Learn and to Teach you much more of Our World and Dimension.

I am a man and a Very Old Soul of much Knowledge from a place called Saturcon, which is a different Planet in another Universe.

I have been <u>resting for a long time</u> and I must learn to Write again and in English, which I have never done before.

13

All of his writing first came through for Jan personally in strange symbols used on his Planet Saturcon or in Ancient Greece, and Jan had to ask him to get help to write in English. I am entering it here followed by his writing for our Book, so some of it is repeated in "Our Earth And Beyond." His words follow.

Sure I'll write in English. As I said with my <u>symbol writing</u>, you are Beautiful like a Greek Goddess and I LOVE You Very Much, Pretty Lady. The memory of writing is returning quickly with the help of Marylin and Michael. I am fine; don't worry, we will write very well together.

I Lived on Earth in 297 B.C. and was a High Priest of Greece. Now I am a High Teacher of all Guides and Teachers here in Our Dimension. I was a Writer of many Tablets, and wrote many of the Laws of Greece in that time. The people of Greece followed my writings.

I was called John Samitez, but they addressed me as Father Corren. This was my Third Reincarnation on Earth in 297 B.C. I also remember being an Influential man, and Very Strong Willed. I now need to Learn to Lighten Up

I wrote the original Greek Tablets that all existing World Religions came from, and also studied all the Planets of the Universe.

All Earth Religions were started from these Tablets. I spent my time on Earth Teaching Souls Progress for all Souls, for all Mankind.

I accomplished so much Progress while on the Earth Plane that I have been Teaching here in Our Dimension ever since I returned, helping all Teachers and Directors.

I Guide the work of many Dimension Teachers and help all Directors.

I was asked by Our Dimension Teachers to contribute to Our Books, and work with Earth Souls for Progress and Development of their Souls on the Earth Plane.

It is an Honor to contribute to Our Books, and to help Earth Souls to Progress for the Betterment of All Mankind.

Kindness and Love to all. This will bring Earth's Peace.

When Jan started writing with Conier, I was fascinated with his name so I asked the following question. "Conier will you write and explain how you received your name?"

Hello, Conier is here. OK, let's go, yes. It's a Dimension name and Our Teachers give us these names. But we have to earn them.

Once you work hard and earn the right, you may have a Dimension name. This name is only allowed when you come from a Very High Plane.

I am one of the Teachers who have worked Teaching Spirit Teachers for many Earth years. My name stands for a High Priest of Spirit Teachers.

I teach much Knowledge about all subjects. Some only teach just one subject. I teach many subjects.

Will you contribute your Knowledge to Our Books?

Yes, I will contribute to Our Books as many others have already written and others will.

May I read this material already written by Jan, and ask questions?

Yes, Ron. You <u>may</u> <u>read what has been written so far</u>, and yes, you may ask Questions. What would like to ask?

Not right now, Conier; let me read through the material, and note my Questions to ask later to be entered in other Chapters of Our Books.

OK. You will read Our Book, Ron, and it will tell all Our Messages. Then all of your questions will be answered correctly; then you and all others will learn about Our Planes.

Our first Book will be named **"Our Earth And Beyond"** and the second Book, **"Many Planes Above."**

I thought this was proper to enter into the Introduction of Teachers, demonstrating that I always asked permission to ask Questions and receive answers on different subjects for the Chapters of Our Books.

On page 97 is printed what Conier wrote about himself for Our Book with a copy of his actual writing following on page 98.

Next is when Conier was leaving after we received much of his Knowledge and Wisdom, Jennifer "Mary Todd Lincoln" arrived.

The Seventh Teacher: Jennifer "Mary Todd Lincoln" – January 13, 1986

Conier is here, Jan, and I wish to tell you that I am leaving soon because my work is finished.

I am going to a Higher Plane, and you are getting a New Teacher. Her name is Jennifer. She is a Beautiful Lady and is a Very High Teacher with a Special Connection to you.

You have progressed to the Sixth Plane to work with her, and she will teach you much Knowledge.

My Teachers wanted me to leave you now, but I asked to stay one more month before Jennifer takes over. They have allowed me to do so.

She is here and I will let her write for you, as I have been training her to take my place and write for you.

Conier allowed Jennifer to write for the first time. She wrote the following.

Jennifer is here, Jan, and I will tell you about myself. When I lived on Earth, I was a hard worker and a Very Spiritual Woman. I taught Earth people all about the Spiritual Planes and now I am a High Teacher.

I am so excited that we are going to work together and I will Teach you much Knowledge about the Planes of Our Dimensions, and also Politics on the Earth Plane.

I was "Mary Todd Lincoln" in my last Life on Earth. My first Life found me on Atlantis. You and I then met in a Previous Life, my second Reincarnation, when you were Cleopatra.

I was your First Lady and <u>best friend</u>. I will tell you all about this someday, and my shortened Life between as Mary Queen of Scots, where I was assassinated in 1587.

I Love to write Jan, and I wrote all of Abe's Speeches when I was First Lady at the White House, in my last Incarnation on Earth. I will start working with you very soon, and until I start I will work with Conier, and help him with his extended work. We All Love you very much for working with us.

Mary Todd Lincoln, 1818-1882. First Lady to the 26th President of the United States, Abraham Lincoln, 1861-1865

Jennifer wrote the following for Our Book. More of her writings appear in Book II, "Many Planes Above," in the Chapter entitled, "Jennifer – Mary Todd Lincoln," along with writings from Abraham Lincoln.

Concrete Proof <u>is now being</u> <u>established</u> so Earth will fully recognize that we do Exist.

For as each day passes we try to identify <u>the wants and needs</u> of Earth Souls to <u>prove that we do hear</u> the Souls asking for our help.
<u>Keeping</u> <u>in mind always</u> that you must <u>earn the right to benefit</u> on the Material Level.

On the other hand, there are <u>unearned</u> Souls that take for Granted all that they have received in this Life.

They have forgotten <u>why they were allowed</u> to attain Material Wealth <u>in the first place</u>.

These Souls with Great Material Possessions <u>were allowed to attain this wealth</u> because of Past Life works; but now <u>they</u> <u>feel there is no need</u> for Spiritual Progress.

Until these Souls return to the right path, we will Stop their Material Gains.

We are in the process of balancing Earth Souls; these Souls have many Lessons to Learn and must develop the patience and strength necessary to Learn those Lessons.

Jennifer, are there Higher Teachers still to come through Jan's pen?

Yes, the High Masters will appear in Our Next Book, "Many Planes Above."

Oh! Do you mean from the High Council of Master Directors, which Control the Universe?

Yes, but the High Council of Master Directors, will speak for themselves at that time.

Jennifer, after all of her wonderful Knowledgeable contributions, announces her departure and her replacement.

The Eighth Teacher: Theodore Roosevelt – April 1, 1986

Jennifer is here; my work <u>with you is about finished</u>. Jan, you have given me so much more Recognition than I ever had on Earth.

Thank you so much for doing these things for me; I will now move to the Twelfth Plane.

I Love you very much, Jan; your New Teacher is coming from a Very High Plane – the Thirteenth Plane, in fact – and is Very Knowledgeable in all Important Matters.

It is his first contact with Earth since he left and first time coming through the pen. I am now helping him to write with you, as he needs practice just as I did.

Teddy is here. I am your New Teacher of the Thirteenth Plane. I will be able to write for myself soon; right now it is difficult for me to get through your pen. Thank You, I do appreciate this. I am Theodore Roosevelt.

I was President of the United States when I lived on Earth. My job was Very Difficult, and I am assigned to help because of my Earth experiences in Worldly Affairs.

I have stood beside Jennifer for a while now and have been Learning to come through your pen. Jennifer and I together, Thank you.

TR in his Rough Rider dress

Theodore Roosevelt (TR) 1858-1919
Twenty- Sixth President of USA, 1901-1909

On Earth I led the Rough Riders up San Juan Hill, in the Spanish American War in 1898.

I told the Soldiers it was Important to the United States for us to all band together. I used to say this all the time to the men; "Right, you got it," and we did get it. I am a strong person and I know where it was always; I had it all under control.

I was aware of the Universe by my Inner Voice. I did not understand at the time, but I was fully aware that the help was coming from above, for my Drive, Determination and Guidance.

I therefore always felt I never was alone in any of my Decisions; I made those decisions in the form of a Meditation.

When I was traveling in the Dakotas, I was searching my Soul for Inner Strength and Peace, and Guidance to tell me the way to go.

My Guide, Samson The Great, was always with me. I knew this as he came to me in a dream when I lay in the Outdoors in the Badlands of the Dakotas.

This is where I got My Strength and the Will to move forward. My Ranch is still there; it's a Museum now and you can go there to visit.

When I visit now I always <u>sit in a chair on the porch</u> as I always did <u>when I was not working</u>.

Now I am on a Mission for the Universe but we have all access to any place on Earth.

Normally we don't bother with life-on-earth pastimes, but it is a memory from my past and there is where I also find Comfort and Progress.

Yes, Ron, I died in that chair because I knew my body was finished and my work was completed. The Universe asked me to return Home and Teach.

Franklin D. Roosevelt tried to follow in my footsteps. His wife Eleanor held the Country together.

My work on Earth was Important and I am where I am today because of all the Good I did on Earth.

Franklin Roosevelt was a scared rabbit. He did know and didn't know, what to do, but the credit goes to his wife, Eleanor.

I was the best President the United States ever had; the next best was Truman. He accomplished much and made better decisions than I did. Franklin D. Roosevelt was OK, but he could have done better.

Now Reagan's successor – George Bush, Sr. – will be a very active man for the people, and will make many changes.

Jan we have been moving you up very quickly; you are now on the Eleventh Plane, and soon to rise to the Thirteenth Plane. We are programming you for even Higher Levels.

When we reach the Thirtieth Plane it is no longer required to refer to them by numbers.

We have been and will keep trying to obtain the co-operation of those certain Earth Souls to arrange contacts with Very Influential people. You will write with these people about a host of Worldly Affairs, which must be changed.

Many World Affairs need answers and I am well qualified to provide those answers when you write for the top Political Leaders.

I am Honored to be with you and I will do all I can to help World Affairs at this time if we can convince these Souls around these Leaders to Listen to our impressions.

I am upset at what has happened to the United States since I left. There is much that must be corrected.

The Universe is working hard to straighten out the Earth, but there is so much more to do. Slowly it will become more Peaceful for all to enjoy.

I will also start the Next Book with you Jan, "Many Planes Above," which will explain the order and works of the Universe.

You Jan, are working on the Eleventh Plane now and moving up fast. When your journey is complete you will arrive at much Higher Planes to work with one of Our Directors of the Round Table.

I am pleased to have learned – now that I have returned to the Universe – about my Connections with my Life when I lived on Earth.

Alice was my First Love and my Soul Mate from the Universe. She was taken from me early in my Life. She was the one I always loved.

Edith was my Second Wife in what were my Last Life, and Mother of my children. She was a good woman and gave me a Good Life. I loved Edith; she was my Sister in a Previous Life, and I loved her very much as we grew up together.

However, today I am with Alice once again as we are Soul Mates working together now for Eternity in Love and Progress.

In my Previous Life I was a Very Influential person; I was Julius Caesar in the days of Rome and our paths crossed, Jan, for a time when you were Cleopatra.

The connection of Souls Progressing through Lives of Reincarnation is so beautiful.

When I was President, I only wanted to help Earth get on the right track. I come to you now, Jan, to help and Guide you in the right direction for the Universe as well. You are one of us and I need to help you Accomplish Your Work on Earth.

After writing over a five-month period with Teddy, including Book II, "Many Planes Above," and answering so many of my questions, it was time for him to leave.

Remember they leave when their work is finished and after rising Jan up to a much Higher Plane – in this case, from the Tenth Plane to the Fourteenth Plane – to prepare her for her Next Teacher.

The Ninth Teacher: Mara – September 29, 1986

Jan, your Next Teacher is a Greek Princess and a Very Beautiful Lady. She also is well known all over the Earth from the early days of Greece.

Plato is her High Master and she will ask him to help you carry on Our Work. Her name is Mara and she is from the Twentieth Plane; she is Very Influential and Wise, and she knows Business to the hilt and can foresee more than I.

I am Mara and I come from the Twentieth Plane. I am your New Teacher, Jan. All of us here in the Universe are so pleased to have you working with us and it is Our Pleasure to work with you now.

I am a Princess of Greece and I was Very Spiritual when I lived on the Earth Plane. I am also a Very Influential Teacher here in the Universe.

I am with you mainly because your Knowledge is now required to advance and I will bring you Higher Knowledge, which far surpasses Earth Knowledge.

I lived in Athens, Greece, in the year 1900 B.C., as part of the early civilization of Greek people.

I want you to know that in our day on Earth we had updated Plumbing, Electrical and two-story houses; many things of today existed then.

It has taken the Earth this many years to reclaim what it had in 1900 B.C. This was taken away from them because of all the Selfishness and Greed.

My Father was King Himona of Greece; one of the country's Very Important Kings. History remembers him.

23

I worked with my Father in business and helped with all the New Inventions we gave to the World at the time. As Princess my job was to help the people. Don't worry, the Greek people worked hard. They were much like the Americans today.

My Father, King Himona, was a good King. But when Greed set in the people toppled my Father's Kingdom and he died.

Before he died, he ordered everything we had around us to be burned and I was saved temporarily. But it soon became apparent they were to find me.

I went into hiding and carried on my Father's work with a group of his faithful followers. We buried all the Treasures that were created.

Those Treasures have never been found to this day because the people wouldn't appreciate all that we created. I'm sure those Treasures will be found someday.

Jan, you have moved to the Fourteenth Plane and I reside on the Twentieth Plane. I work there helping the Universe.

I came to work with you here to raise you up to the Twentieth Plane, and you, Jan, are then going to be so open to the Universe.

Mara, could you describe your looks for me?

Yes. Jan, I am quite pretty and very tall. I wear White always with Gold, and I have dark hair.

Thank you. Mara, updates Jan's Progress to Higher Planes.

November 29, 1986 – Mara is here, Jan. I want you to know and be aware that you are on the Eighteenth Plane now, and I am on the Twentieth Plane.

This is because of your efforts, you have done so much for me and I am So Grateful. Thank you; we are making Great Progress.

24

January 14, 1987 – Mara is here, Jan. I am not going to be able to work with you much longer as you have now advanced to the Twentieth Plane. I am going to move on to someone else. My work with you is almost finished.

Mara, announces Jan's next Teacher a day later.

The Tenth Teacher: Solon – January 15, 1987

A New Teacher is coming now and you will be pleased; this Teacher is a sharp businessman who will help you advance to the Twenty Fifth Plane.

I will remain for a while yet until he adjusts to your vibration. I will miss you. But you are advancing so fast you need a Higher Teacher.

His name is Solon and he is a Universal Director from the Twenty Fifth Plane. A Powerful Man who will advance you to Higher Knowledge that will give you a clearer picture of the Universe.

He is much in tune with Earth's problems of today. He is with you for three reasons: for his Wisdom in Business, to provide direction, and to encourage speaking, which will also be required.

Therefore the Universe feels that this Director will be able to complete these tasks more quickly.

All Directors are from the Twenty Fifth Plane or Higher, and from now on you will work with Directors.

When he lived on Earth he was a successful businessman who helped many Earth Souls advance.

A Wise and Knowledgeable man, he is also a Greek, and has an Intuitive Mind. Solon and is going to speak with you momentarily.

I love you, Jan, and am going to miss you Very Much. Thank you for working with me and advancing me to this Higher Level.

Thank you, Mara. You're so Welcome, Jan.

Mara left and Solon wrote.

I am a New Director and your first Director of the Universe. Solon is here, Jan. I am here to work directly with you to make Immediate Progress for all to see.

The last time I lived on the Earth Plane was around 500 B.C., about 2,500 years ago. My Life on Earth was very productive.

Since then I have been working hard in the Universe to Teach and Make Progress here for the Betterment of All Souls.

Solon was The Lawmaker of Athens, a Poet and a Merchant. He wrote the Constitution that spurred the Growth of Democratic Institutions in Greece, 640 - 560 B.C. Source: Wikipedia.

I have entered some of Solon's Poetry to Honor him and to acknowledge his work with us. What a great pleasure it was to work with him.

The man whose riches satisfy his greed,
Is not more rich for all those heaps and hoards,
Than some poor man who has enough to feed,
And clothe his corpse with such as God affords.
I have no use for men, who steal and cheat,
The fruit of evil poisons those who eat.
Some wicked men are rich, some good men poor,
But I would rather trust in what's secure,
Our virtue sticks with us and makes us strong,
But money changes owners all day long.
If now you suffer, do not blame the Powers,
For they are good, and all the fault was ours,
All the strongholds you put into his hands,
And now his slaves must do what he commands.
True you are singly each a crafty soul,
Each day grow older, and learn something new,
Such power I gave the people as might do,
Abridged not what they had, now lavished new,
Those that were great in wealth and high in place,
My counsel likewise kept from all disgrace,
Before them both I held my shield of might,
And let not either touch the other's right

Excerpts, "Solon The Lawmaker of Athens" by Plutarch
Internet Classics Archive

Thank you, Solon, for all of your contributions of Poetry for Earth Souls to now enjoy.

Jan asked Solon, "Could you give me an idea of the comparison of Earth years to Universe years?"

Yes, Universal years are <u>much longer</u> than in Earth time. For example, 100 Universal years equals one of your Earth years.

Solon is correct now; that's true, I am Very Knowledgeable of all Earth Laws, as <u>I am a creator of them</u>. Thank You.

Very well, Jan, you will be writing with <u>influential people</u> and you are going to start soon. I have come with you to start this process and to see that all Earth Souls Pay Attention. I am here to straighten them out once and for all.

You have Progressed <u>rapidly</u> and the Universe is pleased with your Progress. But I will see that you will make even Faster Progress with Our Work.

The Knowledge you will be receiving is Accurate and True. This will make the Earth Souls Pay Attention to Our Work.

Our Work serves the best interests of Earth people, who <u>don't understand what it's all about</u>. But many will Open to the Universe now and realize there is Life After Death.

At this time Solon announces the next of Jan's Teachers on August 23, 1987.

The Eleventh Teacher: Markus – August 23, 1987

Solon is here, Jan. Don't be sad that Our Work is <u>almost finished now</u>; I love you, too, but you have earned this High Master Director and he will <u>help you so much with your growth and learning</u>.

He will bring you Strong Power to Advance so much Higher that it will surprise you.

He is a King of Egypt from the days of Atlantis. He is Wise and Knowledgeable, and his name is Mark, though it was Markus during his time on Earth. But you can call him Mark if you like.

He has worked hard to reach this High Level. He is a Very High Master Director of the Universe and comes from about the Fiftieth Level.

He is here to raise you above all Earth people with Knowledge, Wisdom, Love, Understanding, Truth and Accuracy, so the Earth Souls will become aware of the Universe.

He was a Wise Emperor of Ancient Egypt in the days of Atlantis before Corruption set in and it disappeared under the water.

His Wisdom was the connection to the beginning of the World, as you know it today; connecting the people of Atlantis to Egypt, which created the Earth Plane Civilizations.

Markus is here. I am so happy to be working with you, Jan, and it's a pleasure to be here. OK, you like my name. Well let me describe for you how I look.

My face is young. I'm tall and handsome, with dark hair. You, Jan, and I, are going to set the Earth on Fire. Jan, please, rest assured that we are going to make a significant amount of Progress.

My name is popular. It's mostly Italian in origin, but I was an Egyptian Emperor. I am the High Director of Our Comet Ship, and my purpose is to see that we gain the Co-operation of Earth Souls so the Landing near Santa Paula, California, will go smoothly.

Markus, after contributing all of his Higher Knowledge and the Comet delayed, announces Jan's next and final Teacher on April 27, 1988.

The Twelfth Teacher: Aristotle – April 27, 1988

Jan, I understand you are getting a New Master Director now. You will be Happy with this Director, just like I am. He is Very High, Very Smart and a Very Kind Advanced Soul.

He comes to you with my blessings to Advance Our Work with you. My work is finished so I am called back to the Universe. I will still work with you from here to manifest the Comet more quickly.

His arrival means that you are raising much Higher now, more than you realize. He knows a <u>great deal more than</u> I and he is a Very Special Director.

You are a Chosen One who we placed on the Earth to <u>carry</u> <u>on the work</u> and he is a Very Important Master Director of the Universe.

He comes to work with you to manifest Great Changes on the Earth Plane, Changes, which <u>will even surprise</u> <u>you</u>.

His name is Aristotle, and comes from Greece. He is a Wise man, born on Earth in 384 B.C.

As a young man he studied under Plato in Athens, which then was the Intellectual Center of the World. Aristotle became a Great Lecturer and Philosopher.

Later he became Alexander the Great's Teacher.

Jan, your New Director, Aristotle, is now here and will begin to write for you. He will also help with the Art, but remember, Palora is still the Artist.

Aristotle begins to write for the first time and remains with Jan for eight years.

Aristotle is here Jan, and I am your New Director of Life. I am very happy to be with you. You <u>will like working with me because</u> I am Very Knowledgeable with everything all around. I want to thank you for <u>allowing</u> <u>me</u> to be your Teacher, as I have not worked on Earth for a long time now.

The Earth Souls will recognize me quite easily as <u>I left many</u> <u>of my works and writings</u> on Earth, which are <u>still studied today</u>.

The Entire Universe is there to help us Progress. When that happens the Universe's Teachers also Progress. Like us, they <u>are working constantly</u> <u>to better</u> their own Soul's Progress.

It is much harder to work from the Universe than the Earth Plane. Progress is so much slower there, compared to how much we can accomplish here on Earth.

Jan, I am from the Round Table. It's the Highest Dimension and because you are accomplishing the work we want done here in the Universe you will reach this Level very soon.

You understand that the Master Directors of the Universe made their decision not to land Our Comet Ship at this time because of the Closed Minds of the Earth Souls and their lack of Co-operation.

The Comet was ready to land on Earth on the date and time we had planned. However, Earth Souls were not ready or willing to receive it properly.

Therefore, we would not allow the Books to be published at that time. We ask you to leave the information about the Comet in Our Books because it is Critical and it absolutely will still come.

Maybe it will arrive now in 2007, or at least in 2008. We will tell you Ron, when to Publish the Books.

In 2006 I started working with Book I, "Our Earth And Beyond," which was written in 1985. It is now June 2007 and I have now been given permission from the High Universe to go-ahead and publish these Books.

Book I begins here.

OUR EARTH AND BEYOND

Book I

High Writing Teacher Cormeir

March 6, 1985

Welcome, my name is Cormeir and I am a High Teacher from a New Dimension, and I will teach Truthful Knowledge about Our Spirit World.

Our Dimension exists on a Plane in Space, where we all are learning about a Comet Ship, which will soon be sent to Earth.

This Comet Ship when it arrives on Earth will not be new to Earth as we have visited there before.

In 1982 a couple saw us land on a farm in Kansas. We tried to explain about Our Ship and our Purpose but they didn't understand because we speak with Thought Language, which is different than an Earth voice.

Now we will explain through you, Jan, with the writing of Our Books, – Our MESSAGE – We want all Earth Souls to <u>read and re-read again and again</u> until they understand this Message from The Universe, until they understand how Important it is for all on Earth today.

We want to tell you and all Earth Souls what we are about. We are Spirit, or Souls who live on High Planes in the Universe.

Our Dimension is far beyond the Earth Plane. We are living in Our Dimension now and forever, and you will live there, too, someday, when your time on Earth has passed.

In this Dimension we work at improving Our New Life and we want all Earth Souls to know that <u>they</u> <u>must</u> go to <u>work also,</u> as soon <u>as they</u> <u>arrive here</u> in order to improve themselves and Progress to Higher Planes.

Right now we are Learning from Our High Teachers about another New Dimension and also a great deal about this Color Comet.

31

It is a big Spiritual Spaceship from Our Higher Planes, which will be sent to Earth soon on a SPECIAL MISSION that will have on board many Old High Spirit Teachers.

These same Teachers select from among us those who will journey to Earth on our Comet to give messages to Earth people, and those who will not.

Only Old High Spirit Teachers are selected to go, as we are now Teaching new things. We need at this time to Open Minds on Earth and prepare Earth Souls for the coming of our Comet.

Since we work through your own individual Guides, it would also be Wise for you to listen to your Guides or your Teachers to learn these new things.

This will help you when the time comes for you to pass on to Our Dimension. This will enable you to arrive on a Higher Plane.

We want you to Open your Minds, and learn from these Books, what must be done to straighten out your Lives. That way, when you pass on, you will Listen to your Teachers, and then immediately begin to work and Progress to Higher Planes.

Opening Earth Souls' Minds will help you to arrive on Higher Planes, which will now be a New Accomplishment for us because most of Our Attempts earlier in Earth's history have failed.

It is now time for Earth Souls to Open Up, Listen and learn their Lessons, as we must all reach this point, no matter how long it takes.

Some never learn and after they pass on they must remain in Dark Corners for many years. Once there, no one can help them but their Teachers, and then only when they are ready and willing to Listen.

Our Greatest problem is that Earth Souls do not Listen while on Earth and then still don't Listen when they arrive here in Our Dimension.

When you pass to Our World, the first thing you must do is Pay for all of your Mistakes. You will see all that you have done during your Earth Life and must make Right or correct each and every Mistake.

You will meet with your Teachers and they will explain and show you the <u>work you must do to straighten out</u> your past Mistakes.

The Teachers will find an Old Soul on Earth in a troubled state <u>for you to work with. You will teach them to straighten up their</u> Life.

This is not an easy task, because most Souls on Earth are not aware of what is happening and <u>do not</u> Listen <u>to the impressions they are receiving.</u> This makes Spirit's Work so much harder.

Nevertheless, Spirit must persist and continue trying to teach these Old Souls where they went wrong and convince them to Change their Ways.

Our Comet is coming to tell the people of Earth to Change their Lives and <u>way of living</u>. They must try and do more Good for all Mankind and then we will be able to Change the Earth for the Betterment of All.

There is too much Unkindness and Corruption on Earth, and those Bad Earth People are the ones that must Change their Ways.

They should not Lie, Cheat, Steal and Hurt <u>their fellow man</u>, or <u>decide when to send another</u> Soul <u>out of his or her</u> Earth <u>body</u> to Our Dimension. <u>This has never been right</u>, and we are now taking Control of Earth in order to Change all of this Selfishness.

If Corrupt Earth Souls <u>don't listen and change</u> there will be another Comet Ship coming in the year 2007 or 2008. It will rain much Destruction on these Old Souls, removing them <u>from</u> the Earth and placing them in the Dark Corners of the Universe.

Their Teachers will <u>not be very</u> patient with them because Teachers are <u>too busy to waste time</u> with Souls that <u>do not</u> listen.

These Souls must wait in the Dark and Learn that they cannot just Selfishly take everything they want, whenever they feel like it or Hurt Others.

They must wait in Darkness until they learn they were wrong and are willing to <u>work to correct their</u> Mistakes.

33

It could take <u>thousands</u> of Earth years before they come to realize that this is why they are there in the Dark and what they must do to emerge from the Dark Corners.

This is because the High Spirit Teachers are tired of these Souls not finishing their work of Correcting Mistakes from Previous Lives, which is the reason they were sent to Earth <u>in the first p</u>lace.

There is no Progress made when a Soul arrives on Earth and <u>refuses to</u> Listen to his Guide and Correct Past Mistakes, but instead creates more Mistakes.

We are giving them a Chance to Change, to get back on the Right Path in <u>the next</u> 20 to 30 years, or we will remove them all and place them into Dark Corners.

Then Our Work, that is the work of the High Spirit Teachers, will cease on the Earth Plane when these Souls <u>are removed</u>.

All the Good Souls' will be reborn through Reincarnation in Our New Dimension, which we are now Learning about. The Good Souls Minds will be cleansed of all Corruption that existed in their memory of the Earth Plane.

With no Memory of Earth they will live in Peace and Harmony, for there will be no Money or Governments, or <u>any</u> reminder of the Earth World as it now exists.

There will be plenty of everything to meet everyone's needs, and there will be Calmness for all Good Souls to enjoy.

This New Dimension <u>now exists</u> and we are Learning more and more about its Beauty and Harmony.

It's like another Earth in another Universe, only all is Peaceful where Souls work together free of Corruption.

It is where all New Souls or all Good Souls are now presently born, as we have <u>stopped</u> New Souls from coming to Earth for many <u>hundreds of years</u> <u>now</u> and all Good Souls have been <u>stopped from returning</u> to Earth for some 50 to 60 years now.

That is why there is such Disharmony and Corruption on the Earth today, because we are tired of the Good being Victims of the Selfish.

We have therefore created Our New Dimension for the Good Souls to continue their good work there, instead of returning to Earth, thus creating this Imbalance between Good and Corruption on the Earth Plane.

I feel you are tiring, Jan, so this will be enough work on Our Book for today. We will be explaining more about what is to be done to straighten up the mess that the Earth is now in as we go on.

April 5, 1985

Cormeir wants you to tell the World what it must do to improve the Earth before 2007 or 2008.

You must Change your Lives to Live a Better Life. You must be more Considerate to all around you and more careful of what you are giving out to others.

You must be a new and changed person and consider your next-door neighbor and those around you.

You must also try to care more for You, Yourself, and how you act to bring the good person in you forth for others to see and for you to begin to see the Good in Others.

To change for all of us in the Higher Universe to see – as we can see every Soul on Earth at all times as they really are in their Hearts – you must,

CULTIVATE THE GOOD WITHIN.

You can never hide your true intentions from us and we are always testing you so you can prove your intentions.

We want you and All of Mankind to know that when the new High Holy Comet leaves from another Universe on its journey to Earth it will take three years to arrive.

We advise all Earth people about this Comet because it brings ultimate proof of all Life After Death.

35

You will understand what we mean after our arrival and you have met all of us High Teachers and Couriers. Then we will give you more Information and Messages to tell all Earth People.

This Comet will bring proof beyond a doubt, as the Comet Couriers and High Teachers it carries will materialize, as they existed on Earth for you to recognize, thus proving that Life does continue After Death.

We want Earth people to try and Change their Ways before reaching Our Planes of Learning. Most of us try to teach Earth Souls all the time but they are Stubborn and do not Listen. But now Our High Teachers want all to listen.

On Our Planes we teach a new way of Life – the way to Learn your Lessons and correct your Mistakes. Regardless of who you are or who you were on Earth you must keep working after the death of the physical body to better yourself.

You must try and do a better job on Earth now so that you can accomplish Higher Levels of Learning when you return home to the Universe. Many of our students Progress immediately upon arrival and others never Progress for many years.

The ones that do not Progress will stay in Dark Corners until they choose to Work and Learn.

Today, many are in these Dark Corners because they refuse to grow. These Lessons should be learned while on Earth but most people never even try, therefore they must learn all their Lessons after their Earth Lives are finished.

It is much easier to teach you Lessons on Earth, because to Learn the same Lessons in the Spirit World is a difficult and slow process that could take Centuries.

April 8, 1985

Cormeir is here writing through Jan, and I want to tell you over and over again about Our Comet Ship that we will send to Earth.

The date has been postponed, and has not been confirmed by Our High Teachers, The Master Directors of the Round Table of the Universe.

36

We will tell you when it will come to Earth for you to meet us.

Some Couriers and Very High Teachers will be on board, and each one will make themselves known for you to recognize.

So all that we tell you should be included into Our Books for all the Earth to Read, and to tell the Younger Generation about Our World.

This will become Important for the Destiny of Souls on Earth and a Special Event in the Earth's history because many people will Listen to the Messages we bring.

The ones that do not listen will perish. Therefore, you all have much work ahead of you and we will help you all that we can.

We are telling all on the Earth Plane that we mean business and that we are in Control of the whole Earth.

They must Listen to what Our Teachers say, especially about how the Earth Must Change or you will see how Disastrous it will be for all people who do not Listen.

All Evil and Corrupt ways of the Earth's people Must Change.

They must Learn to care more about each other and we will repeat this often, otherwise all who are Selfish and Greedy will perish, as we have already said, and be placed into Dark Corners for many thousands of years with no help or comfort.

Our Teachers are too busy and have no more time for Selfish people, so they must wait in Darkness until we have many more Teachers to teach them, and that may take a long time.

These Books will be Truthful and Highly Knowledgeable, and are written for those who wish to Pay Attention. Listen to what we say, and then try to Learn from reading it over and over again.

We must explain about Life After Death. It's important to understand that you are in your physical body on Earth for just a short time period compared to the life span you'll encounter in the Next Dimension, which is an extremely long time.

The right and the privilege of Reincarnation to Our New Dimension will exist for the Good Souls only after leaving their physical body. They will then be Reincarnated there if they choose, with no memory of their past Life on Earth.

The New Dimension is a better existence in which we live forever. We have no Body and we do not need to sleep. We have no Money and no real needs, except to Learn and Teach for the Betterment of All around us.

Teaching and helping others less fortunate is most satisfying for us in the New Dimension. We in the Universe are always Happy. And we are hoping that this will become the Way of Life for many in the near future who come here.

All will live in Peace under Our Teachers' Laws because we have no Material things, Corruption or Selfishness, and all Souls will share equally.

When these Good Souls arrive here their every need is furnished. They lead a simple existence enjoying Nature and because their minds work with their Souls, it creates for each and everyone a most Happy existence.

April 11, 1985

Again, we repeat with these Books that Our Comet when it arrives will warn Earth that all Souls must Change their Ways, for they are mostly all on the wrong track, and must change.

Our Highest Teachers will give Messages, which the entire Earth must know to accomplish these changes.

They will find out the Earth's Destiny and also what they all must do to Change the Earth, which is being Destroyed by Man.

When all of the Earth knows and complies with our rules as they are given only then will all things Change for the Better, but if they do not comply, many more Disastrous things will continue to happen.

These happenings will remove Souls, which are not Paying Attention to Our Messages, leaving only the good to remain.

My Teachers are continually telling me that you all must Learn more about Our Dimension before it is your time to leave the Earth, which is when everything changes.

You are expected to be <u>ready to straighten out all of the things you did wrong to others</u> or all the Mistakes you made while on Earth.

First, you are <u>asked what it is that you feel you did wrong</u>, then <u>what you feel you did right</u> by Our Teachers, even though Our Teachers already know this.

You then, as we have already said, must <u>begin to work</u> and <u>make up for all of your mistakes and wrongdoings</u>. We will repeat ourselves many times for you to know that we mean business.

Again, each one is then shown <u>what it is that they must correct</u>. Some do not want to correct their mistakes, so then they are placed, as we said, into Dark Corners, to wait there until <u>they decide to rectify their</u> Mistakes.

Those that want to correct their Mistakes once they are shown how, start Learning Immediately. As they Learn and make Progress they advance to a New Plane.

As you advance to each Plane you expand your Knowledge, which makes it easier for you to Learn. When you have worked hard enough, or long enough to Pay for all Mistakes, you are then ready to Teach.

Some Souls will teach on the Planes, only while others Teach Earth people. There is plenty room here for everyone and Our Work <u>is never done</u>.

There is <u>no sleep</u> and <u>no one gets tired</u> because it is <u>all just working</u> Souls with <u>no body</u>, unless they want to take on their <u>previous</u> Earth <u>form temporarily</u> to look like Earth people.

Everyone can choose how he or she would like to <u>look for identification</u>, maybe as they looked when they were <u>young</u> and sometimes a form can be taken to Earth <u>for recognition</u>.

This happens sometimes for Identification to Other Souls on Our Dimension or could happen with Our Teachers' permission on Earth for a special purpose.

I could materialize with my Teachers' permission, and I will ask if this can be done. However, I feel they would say it is unimportant at this time.

Materialization on Earth must be for a very special mission like when Our Comet Ship arrives and Our High Teachers will temporarily take on their former Earth forms so the people of Earth will recognize them.

I will now tell you more about Reincarnation so you will better understand. Reincarnated Souls are Old Souls taking on a new Body.

Not everyone is Reincarnated back to Earth, but rather only those Souls who must make up for Previous Life Mistakes.

When they arrive they will feel only a slight sense of familiarity with their Previous Life such that they cannot tell for sure or remember much about that Life.

The Teachers have control when a Soul Reincarnates back to Earth. But because of Free Will, when they return to Earth, these Reincarnated Souls sometimes do not listen to their Teachers.

Then they make the Wrong Choices that entangle them with Material Corruption and therefore make more Mistakes.

Then the Soul, when finishing its Earth time, returns to Dark Corners for many years waiting for Teachers to once again work with them when they have time.

If Earth people would Listen and make fewer Mistakes there would not be as many Souls in Dark Corners feeling Lost and not knowing why they are there.

Sometimes, Our Teachers feel it is better to be Reincarnated back to Earth to Learn faster than it is to stay in Darkness waiting for Teachers to teach them. When Teachers do decide to return Souls to Earth to Learn, they are still the same Souls with almost the same personality.

Sending them to Earth helps them arrive back in the Spirit World on Higher Planes if while on Earth these Souls corrected all of their Mistakes.

Again, unfortunately some Reincarnated Souls are not Listening to Our Teachers while in their Earth body. So they are brought back and must wait again in Dark Corners until Teachers have time to spend with them.

Many times they are sent back again to Earth, and these Souls will be sent back time after time, until they learn their Lessons.

However, several hundred years will always pass between Reincarnations, and when Souls get old and still never learn they are left in Dark Corners for Thousands of years.

Lessons are hard to Learn for many Souls because of the Millions of Souls already sitting in Darkness. The Teachers are exhausted from all the work with these Souls and again hope that Earth Souls will Change before more end up in the Dark.

We repeat this message because of its importance. The reason the Comet is coming is to tell the Earth people to Change their Way of living and become better people.

Our Teachers will warn Earth people that if they do not listen there will be no more Earth as they know it, and when this happens each Soul will be put in their own dark place.

They will remain in the Dark until there are enough Teachers with the time to Teach them on a one-by-one basis and advance them far enough along so they may begin to work and pay for all their Mistakes on the Astral Level.

All Earth Souls will be evaluated and placed to one side or another.

April 14, 1985

As much as possible, we try to reunite Soul Mates on Earth to Learn Lessons to make Faster Progress.

Mostly these are the ones that Teachers feel will not have to come back again. But sometimes a decision must be made and they are returned to Earth to Learn Again.

There are only two kinds of Souls that are not Reincarnated back to Earth. Those that Lived a Good Life while on Earth and with little teaching could advance to Our Higher Planes.

Then there are some Souls that also did advance, during their Earth Life, which made enough Progress to become Couriers to Teachers or Guides to Earth Souls.

Only Souls with Mistakes to Correct are Reincarnated back to Earth. Each one of you is here on Earth to Correct Mistakes.

Couriers make the Teacher's job easier by serving as their Messengers and fulfilling assignments – after Courier Souls Progress and Learn they can be assigned as Doorkeeper or Guide to an Earth Soul.

Guides, Doorkeepers and Guardian Angels are all the same; we call them Doorkeepers, but you may like to call them Guides and so we will also.

When Guides are placed beside a Soul that is Reincarnated, they must have already paid for most of their Mistakes.

Some Mistakes are still to be corrected so Our Teachers give Guides this job to be assigned to an Earth Soul. They must stay with their assigned Soul on Earth trying to keep them on the path until that Soul returns home to us. Upon returning to us from Earth both Soul and Guide are asked to see how many Mistakes were corrected.

If Our Teachers feel the Guide has done his work properly then he will advance to Teach. A Guide's job is hard because Earth Souls do not always listen to their Guides.

The Earth Soul returning must also show all Mistakes are Corrected and Completed. If not this Soul could return to Earth again, in a few hundred years. If the Guide did not do his work then he will be assigned another Soul with which to work.

Until both Souls are Free of Mistakes, neither one can advance. These Souls work alone on the Astral Plane while awaiting assignments from their Teachers.

42

Earth is made up of all kinds of people, and sometimes-Good Souls have been sent back to Earth to help Teach Other Learning Souls what they must do.

However, their work on Earth is so hard to complete that this is another reason why Our Comet Ship and Highest Teachers are arriving – to try and make-work easier and better for all.

As we have already said, there will be Messages for all Earth Souls to follow, which will help make Teaching easier, for those Good Souls already on Earth.

April 24, 1985

I am a Teacher of writing. I was a writer when I lived on Earth; then when my Soul came here, I first had to learn the Ways of the Universe and I worked for a long time before I became a Teacher.

Now that I am a Teacher I must first teach the Earth people to advance to Higher Planes so that I can become a Higher Teacher.

I, Cormeir, have never since been Reincarnated back on Earth because I am a Chosen Teacher. It is not necessary for me to be reincarnated unless I was assigned a Very Special Mission.

I am Accurate with all I bring you; it is Truth and through my help writing for Our Book I will Teach Earth Souls so I may Advance Higher on Our Planes.

Our Planes of Existence are far above Earth, and each and everyone on Earth will arrive here someday.

When arriving on Our Planes, above the Astral Plane as we previously stated, we all must work to rectify Our Mistakes and each and every one of us must account for our actions in our Earth Life.

You are asked questions about your Earth Life and why you committed certain acts when knowing full well they were wrong.

Then you are asked to explain why, and after your explanations you must undo all of the wrongs you committed to make things right so that you may Progress.

Sometimes, as we said, this takes many years to accomplish. Because so many Souls are so Stubborn, when they refuse to go on they must again just sit for a long, long time.

This, we repeat, could go on for Thousands of Years for some of these Stubborn Souls.

Everyone here works and we all have Teachers to help us. When Our Teachers feel that we have corrected Our Mistakes, we then have earned the opportunity to continually advance to Higher and Higher Planes.

Each and every one of us is Progressing always. We never stop gaining Knowledge. We are always Happy and never tire of Learning and Teaching. Therefore, again we repeat this Valuable Information to Earth Souls for their benefit and for the benefit of all Our Teachers on Earth today.

Many of Our Teachers on Earth now, as well as all Teachers in the Universe, are Teaching Earth People to advance on the Earth Plane so that when they arrive on Our Plane they have already become Very Knowledgeable.

While on Earth, you all must Teach Earth People about Our Planes and what they can do to advance to a Higher Plane before it is their time to return home to the Universe. Our Teachers are busy and they need a great deal of help to Open the Minds of all Earth Souls.

If your work is completed properly on the Earth Plane and you use the Knowledge in these Books to Teach Others you will arrive on a Higher Plane to carry on your Teaching.

If Earth people, and we can't stress this enough, would make Fewer Mistakes it would make Our Teacher's job so much easier.

All who live on Earth are obligated and responsible to themselves and for their Own Actions. They can never blame another for their actions. The kind of person they are on Earth is the kind of person they will be when they arrive back on Our Planes.

We want Earth people to be more considerate of others in their actions; they then would find their Earth Life would be so much easier.

Also, you all should appreciate more what you have and be Happy with your surroundings rather than constantly finding fault with everything around you.

When Earth people find fault constantly they are bringing more Mistakes upon themselves and more Mistakes means more work for them. Everyone on Earth, as we have said, must pay for each and every Mistake, whether they want to or not.

When they come to Our World so many must sit in Dark Corners and wait for Teachers. They do not understand why they are here in the Dark.

Many are unaware that they are no longer on Earth. Our Teachers are always busy now, and we repeat this again because we want the Message to reach these Souls while still on Earth.

Until Teachers have time or until we have enough Teachers to spend with them, there will be no one to help those Souls in the Dark Corners.

They will have to just sit and wait. Most of them, as we have said, wait for Hundreds of years, because they do not know they are Responsible for their Mistakes.

We do not have enough Teachers for every one of these poor Souls at this time to Teach and we want Earth Souls to Progress to become Teachers.

This is why we want Earth people to have all of this Knowledge before passing on to Our Dimension.

Cormeir wants you to know that Michael, my Teacher of Higher Knowledge, is writing through me now after asking my permission.

As I am Jan's present Teacher and when my work with her is complete, Michael will be her next Teacher and I will move on to a Higher Plane.

Michael comes to you from a Higher Plane already and your fast advancement with me has made it possible for him to soon teach you more for Our Books.

We must try and understand what we are doing here on Earth; try to understand that all of us are in Our Learning Period. We also must realize that it will take many years before all is corrected to Change the Earth.

Right now, Our Planes really <u>need</u> <u>your</u> Complete Co-operation, in the way that we all <u>must help</u> <u>each other</u> so that all work Progresses Faster.

Our Work needs to Progress to create Tranquility for all. When <u>this is accomplished</u>, each and everyone will be Happy. Someday this will be done and then even Teachers will be able to rest.

Our Teachers work constantly to attain more Happiness for all. Happiness reigns on our Planes on Higher Levels. The Lower Astral Levels needs much more work to be done.

We need more Teachers, as we said, because the ones we have are so busy and not enough Souls are Progressing to become Teachers. We want <u>each and everyone to work hard</u> and <u>accomplish what they</u> <u>must do</u>, helping Earth people to Mend their Ways.

Also, we must keep working hard so we may help these Earth people understand that <u>it takes longer for them to advance</u> when they do not Listen to their Guides and Teachers.

The problem is that most Earth people never want to Listen and this, we repeat once again, always makes Our Work, that much more difficult. We try to Teach Earth people not to be so Mean or so Selfish with each other, not to be so Corrupt, but most Never Listen to what we are saying.

Each and everyone have a little voice inside them.

They should Listen and follow their Inner Feelings to Improve themselves because they always <u>know when they</u> <u>are doing</u> <u>wrong</u>.

Not many of the Earth people <u>care at all about these things</u>, so again: Our Comet is coming to bring these Messages from the Highest Teachers, for all the Earth to Listen.

We want Earth people to know that Our Teachers <u>mean business</u> and that you will be advised exactly when and where the Comet will be arriving, so that all Earth may Learn of this Spiritual Event.

April 29, 1985

Cormeir is here to bring my Last Information for Our Book, "Our Earth And Beyond," and then my Teacher Michael will take over for a while.

He has been <u>practicing through me</u>, as he has not written for a very long time.

He was "Michelangelo" when he was on Earth.

You should <u>all know by</u> <u>now</u> that we are all here working hard trying to get Earth people to Change their Ways.

I repeat myself again – they must start being more Kind to Each Other, more Thoughtful of Others. There are too many Souls on Earth that are so Selfish. They think only of themselves, never of the next person. Because of this Selfishness we are telling them to Change their Ways.

Most Earth people <u>choose to ignore our advice</u> and go about their Earth Life doing whatever they like. This causes so much <u>trouble for everyone</u> because of what these Souls are <u>doing to others</u>.

They have brought troubles on themselves – the price they have to pay for the harm that they are doing.

Again, they <u>must</u> pay <u>for all of these</u> Mistakes and <u>wrongdoings</u>. When an Earth Soul harms Other Earth Souls they <u>receive the same back to themselves</u> in their Earth time.

Or it will be in Spirit time. When things come back to these Souls, they always then wonder <u>why</u> <u>them</u>?

"As you give out so shall you receive."

Sooner or later, each and every one must pay for their Selfishness.

If Earth people understood this better, perhaps then they <u>would think twice before they</u> <u>hurt another</u> Soul.

Each and every Soul is sent to Earth to learn its Lessons, and if they are not learning those Lessons, again a Dark Corner is created for them to sit in when they reach Our World.

We are no longer sending these Souls back to Earth. Rather they must stay in the Dark Corners they have created for themselves and wait. We are now continually removing them from the Earth Plane.

So if each and everyone would take time to stop before they act and think that they will have to pay for their transgressions sooner or later, they may think twice before Caring only about themselves.

They are not thinking about how the Other Soul beside them feels because of their Selfish, Harmful actions.

Always things done deliberately to another Soul must be paid for in Sharp Lessons, and each and everyone will have to work twice as hard to make up for these Mistakes and Wrongdoings.

Often Earth Souls feel they can take advantage of the one next to them without even thinking about what they are doing – and the Poor Soul Suffers.

However, the Poor Soul that suffers will be Rewarded when they leave Earth and arrive in Our Dimension.

They will know that the suffering was worth it by the Progress they have made. But if the Selfish Soul knew what it had done to slow their own Progress perhaps they would not have hurt Poor Souls who didn't deserve this treatment at all.

Now, Our Teachers are working to help Earth people try and Change their Ways, to share and care about others more and to put an end to Selfishness. This can only improve the Earth Plane.

If this doesn't work the Earth Plane must stop, and the Good Souls will go to the New Dimension we have created for all Good Souls to Live in Peace.

Again, each and every Earth Soul must account for all wrongdoings and if they are not rectified on the Earth Plane they must be corrected in one of Our Dimensions, which we have created.

One is full of Dark Corners with unhappy Souls and another full of Bright Light with Happy Souls.

Again, after Our Comet arrives with Our Messages, everyone on Earth will know what we mean and why we came.

This, then, will be proved to Earth Souls so that all Souls can Change their Ways. They also must know that we are still in Control and always will be.

All of those behind the Corruption, Power, Money and Selfishness are the Earth people that must learn that we are in Control, Not them.

When the Comet arrives Earth people will take notice and some will Pay Attention, but most of the Corrupt will not.

It depends on what Changes those Corrupt Souls on Earth make that determines where they will go. Our Teachers, as we have said many times, are busy and have no time for Souls that Don't Listen.

Our Planes now have many Teachers, Couriers, Doorkeepers or Guides, and all of these Souls work diligently to help Earth people. As so many are Not Listening, this creates much more work for Our Teachers.

They just have too much work. **This is why Life must be changed for the Betterment of All who lives on the Earth Plane**.

To Summarize: we want to attain more Happiness with less work, and everyone can live together without Corruption.

These Messages in our Books are clear. We will bring Disastrous events, and Earth people must hear and understand our Messages while they still have time to Change Ways before they are all removed from the Earth.

Each Soul must learn all of its Lessons – no matter whom they are or what position they hold – as each and everyone knows within Himself or Herself what they must do.

49

We are always using our Messages to try and help Earth People, but usually they are ignored, thus again making Our Work so much harder.

You will know what is right when you give of yourself. Then you will receive guidance and direction. Only then will you know who you are and if you are on the right track.

Before I leave, I want to tell you a little more about Our Dimension, where Souls must go to atone for Past Errors – a Dimension where all of you will someday play an important role.

It is a place where much work is done, as we all will try and Help Each Other.

When an Earth Soul's Mistakes are cleared with Our Teachers, we have earned this Plane, a Plane where Helping Others is its purpose.

When this is done, we then can start Teaching Souls on the Earth Plane to better themselves from Our Side.

However, as we have said many times, so many Earth Souls just Don't Listen and then you, too, as a Teacher will see how much more difficult this work becomes for Our Teachers.

You may think we are repeating ourselves endlessly but you must tell all Earth people that we mean business.

My Teachers stress the Importance that all on Earth should know that all Souls must pay for their mistakes and No One Soul can ever escape this.

There is too much Dishonesty and Corruption on the Earth Plane and some Earth Souls think they can get away with it – but they never can. You can never hide anything from us, as we see all.

Again, we have said many times that No Soul can escape from its wrongdoings, and when you don't pay for your mistakes on Earth you must be left alone in Dark Corners.

These Corrupt Souls will again <u>remain there alone</u> with their <u>own thoughts for many</u> <u>thousands</u> of years and <u>cannot leave or see anything</u> but Darkness.

Even if they tried to <u>leave they</u> <u>wouldn't know where to go because</u> <u>the</u> Darkness goes on forever <u>in all directions</u> and there is no one there to ask; <u>they</u> <u>are all alone.</u>

Also, when Souls arrive in Our Dimension it is Important to realize that when Our Teachers ask you to work off your mistakes, y<u>ou must be</u> <u>willing to do so.</u>

Then you <u>start working immediately</u>, and <u>if</u> <u>you refuse</u> you may end up sitting in the Dark, as we hope you should by now realize, for a long, long time.

We have Intensely Repeated Our Messages because this keeps happening to Too Many Souls when they leave their Life on the Earth Plane. This has been happening all throughout Earth's history.

Our World is much different than the Earth Plane. It is a place where there is Much Happiness, we have no Money here or the need for it, and we are all working Souls Helping each Other.

GOD is Unity of All and all are part of GOD – GOD is not one person; it is Unity of All Souls as One – Working Together for the Betterment of All Souls.

When you come to the Spirit World <u>all</u> problems <u>from</u> Earth <u>are gone</u>; they are left there. Only the Mistakes made on Earth <u>follow</u> <u>you</u> and <u>must be</u> <u>corrected</u>.

Each Soul is <u>his or her</u> own Judge and <u>you cannot put off or escape</u> <u>what</u> y<u>ou did on</u> Earth; you must work and pay for all Mistakes.

The only way you pay for Your Mistakes is by working hard to help the very same Souls you hurt.

Sometimes Our Teachers assign hard, challenging tasks that you must complete.

They choose Souls on Earth, which are just like they were when they existed on the Earth Plane, to work hard with and try to convince them to Change their Ways.

However, again, most Earth people don't listen, making all of our jobs so much harder.

Nevertheless, when you are chosen to help Earth Souls you must try to convince these Stubborn Souls to Listen.

Our Teachers coming on the Comet will show Earth Souls what they must start to do.

It is time to put an end to All Corruption on Earth. We want UNIVERSAL PEACE with much LOVING and CARING for ALL.

Cormeir left and "Michelangelo" began to write to contribute to Our Books. In the following he tells us about himself as he wrote

His actual writing, and signature appears on page 54.

HIGH TEACHER MICHELANGELO

May 9, 1985

Michael is here and would like all of you to know that I am a Very High Teacher of the Universe.

I come to work with Earth Souls for their Progress before they arrive in Our Dimension.

I lived on Earth many years ago. I am known for <u>my fine works</u> of Art. <u>I also was a fine writer</u> for which I never received any recognition.

My Arts are still adored by the Earth Plane. I am glad I was able to <u>contribute these fine works</u> to all of you, to enjoy for many Lifetimes.

I am now a High Teacher of the Universe and I am working from here to help Earth Souls to Progress. I help with my <u>talents to improve the work of many artists</u> on Earth today.

<u>I always loved to write</u> and I am pleased to contribute to Our Book for all Earth Souls to read.

We all hope you will help us with Our Progress to better your Souls' Progress.

We want all Souls to have much happiness and Love of All Mankind.

Please try and improve your Earth lives. Our Book brings Important Messages for all Earth to Pay Attention.

Michelangelo

Michael is here and would like all of you to know that I am a very High Teacher of the Universe. I come to work with earth souls for their progress before they arrive in our dimension. I lived on earth many earth years ago. I am known for my fine works of Art. I also was a good writer for which I never got any recognition. My Arts are still adored by the earth plane. I am glad I was able to contribute these fine works to all of you, to enjoy for many life times. I am a High Teacher of the Universe and I am now working to help earth souls progress. I help with my talents to improve many artists work, on earth today. I always loved to write and I am very pleased to contribute to our book for all earth to read. We all hope you will help us with our progress, in order to better your souls progress. We want all souls to have much happiness & love of all Mankind. Please try and improve your earth lives. Our Book brings important messages for all earth to pay attention.

Michelangelo

Michael is here and I am your new Teacher for a while. I possess the Highest Knowledge and will bring you Truth and Accuracy.

I am a Teacher of writing. But I am also a Teacher of Knowledge, here with you Jan to teach you all that I can.

Jan, Our Teachers have chosen you to write Our Books called "**Our Earth And Beyond**" and "**Many Planes Above**."

These are **IMPORTANT BOOKS** about Earth Plane news, for all on Earth to read. They will give Earth Souls the Knowledge they have never had about Life After Death.

We will tell about the future of the Earth Plane and explain where you are going and what is going to happen if more Souls don't Heed Our Warnings.

If Earth people do not listen to what Our Teachers have to say, there will be much continued Destruction in the form of Disasters on Earth, which could bring an end to the Earth Plane as you know it and the beginning of a New Dimension.

We will share much of the same information that we feel is the most **IMPORTANT** for each Earth Soul to fully understand.

Completely understanding the Soul's Purpose on Earth and what happens when you arrive in Our Dimensions is the key MESSAGE and purpose of these Books.

We repeat information about Correcting Mistakes and the fate of Souls if they don't listen because we want every Earth Soul to Fully Comprehend this.

This way they may decide what the Future of their Own Soul will be and cannot say that they did not know.

This is why we want All Souls on Earth to read this Book.

It is most **IMPORTANT** that every Earth Soul knows the **TRUTH** so they may make their own decisions about the Earth's future.

If this Earth Plane ends everyone will be left with just their Souls and no bodies.

All Souls will gather into two groups, with none in between: the Good Souls and the Bad Souls.

Half good or half bad is unacceptable. **This will be Complete Separation**.

It does not matter what Earth Souls think because they will not have any control over their fate.

Our High Teachers will be the ones to decide who goes where and they have Control of all Souls.

When all Souls are separated to <u>one side or the other</u> <u>we will then</u> have less work to do.

The Souls that decide Not to Pay Attention or Listen and continue with their Old Ways will be called back from Earth and <u>simply</u> <u>placed in</u> Dark Corners.

There they will wait their turn to meet with Our Teachers so that they <u>can start</u> Learning what they did <u>not want to</u> Learn while on the Earth Plane.

They will all be given a chance to Work and in time Progress. However, they must learn while still on Earth. That's because Our Teachers are busy and do not have time to waste on Earth Souls who don't want to Listen or to Work.

All Working Souls on Our Planes are busy working hard trying to get Earth Souls to straighten up their Lives.

There is too much Materialism on the Earth Plane and <u>all material</u> <u>things will be left</u> behind when entering Our Dimension.

In Our New Dimension there are no Material things over which Souls need to Cheat, Steal or act Selfishly.

Once again, the Souls that Listen and Change their Ways will receive the Rewards of Our New Dimension.

This New Dimension is a <u>Beautiful Place</u> to go, and <u>we repeat, only</u> <u>the</u> Good Souls will go there if they so choose.

Upon arriving in this New Dimension these Good Souls will have <u>no</u> <u>memory</u> <u>of their</u> Past Life on Earth.

This is the same with all Reincarnated Souls on the Earth Plane; they have <u>no memory</u> <u>of their</u> Previous Lives.

However, we assure you that only Peace and Harmony <u>exists in this</u> Dimension for each Soul to enjoy.

Michael is here. I want you to know that all we write should go into Our Books even when we sometimes provide duplicate information.

This is because we want to make sure that all Souls on the Earth fully know and understand what happens after their Earth Life.

First, there is Life After Death, and when passing on from Earth to Our Dimension all Earth Souls must pass through a Tunnel accompanied by their Guide to meet their Teachers face to face.

Our Dimension is made up of Many Planes and as you work hard Helping Others you will Progress from Plane to Plane.

To begin to Progress you must first look over your entire Earth Life with your Teachers. They will show you the work that you must do for continued Progress.

Then you start your Work Immediately after you pass from the Earth. If you are not willing to work you will be sent to sit alone in Dark Corners until you decide to go to work.

Each and every one of us must work if we want to Progress.

Those that refuse to work may sit for as long as they like in the Darkness because each has the Free Will to make their own Choice. But eventually they will have to start their work.

Once we start working it is up to each one of us to decide how hard we want to work and just how fast we want to Progress.

When you leave your physical body you must be able to accept this fact that work is what you must do, the Work of Helping Others to Progress, and a willingness to start immediately.

You will leave your physical body behind, along with all other material things, as well as the Pressures and the Responsibilities of your Earth Life to be free to start your Spiritual Progress.

At that very moment when you are leaving your body a comforting feeling begins to wash over you, a feeling of Great Relief and Calmness comes over you, and you feel good right away.

You arrive on the First Plane, the Astral Plane, where your Teachers are waiting for you.

You have the option to accompany them at this time. And as we have said before, if you Choose not to you are put aside in Dark Corners until you ask for your Teachers to come and get you.

This is your GOD – given Free Choice.

Many Souls stay in Dark Corners for many years not remembering why they are there. But when they decide to call on and accompany their Teachers, only then can they start Progressing.

You must be aware of the Mistakes you made in your Earth Life. When you can admit to all Mistakes then Teachers will start working with you to begin correcting each Mistake.

You are then assigned to a job just like on the Earth Plane only we don't sleep and there is no need to eat; we work all the time without getting tired. Whatever your job is you must work at it steadily and when it is finished you will advance to a Higher Plane to continue your work.

As you advance you will eventually become a Teacher yourself. However, you must possess great Knowledge to become a Teacher and this takes many long years to Accomplish.

During this process you could be assigned as a Courier to Our Teachers or a Doorkeeper, or as you prefer to call them, a Guide to an Earth Soul at birth.

Once you advance and become a Teacher, Our High Teachers assign you your first Earth Soul. These are the same High Teachers that assign us. Each and every one has a job to complete with their assigned Earth Soul.

Our High Holy Spiritual Color Comet that will come to Earth with all of Our Highest Teachers on board bringing a Long Message for All the Earth to Hear.

58

You will be told what to do to Change your Ways, to make Life After Death much better for all of you.

When the Changes are made all the Good Souls that have paid for their Mistakes on Earth and through Reincarnation will be sent, as we have previously said, to a New Dimension of Peace and Tranquility.

Life in this New Dimension will be a New Earth-type Life. Only Earth Souls that have corrected all of their Mistakes or Good clean New Souls will reside there.

There will be no Money for Corruption or Selfishness, and all will share equally to Live in Peace from the Land.

It will be a Time of Peace for all. This Dimension is like no other Dimension we have ever created.

We created this Dimension because we feel it is time to eliminate all of the Corruption from the Earth Plane.

It is time that we stop all the Greed and Selfishness that Earth has created through all the Centuries in its history.

Our Teachers feel now it is nearly time for all of us to come to terms with ourselves and Open Our Minds to Our True Purpose: **To Progress and Advance Ourselves**.

Earth Souls must Open their Minds, get their lives together and get on with their True Purpose.

Those that Open their Minds and really want to hear Our Message so that they might Change their Ways will be the only ones to advance to Our New Dimension.

Also those that are already Good Souls will not have to worry, and those Earth Souls who will not listen, or are Not Listening, will have to pay for their Mistakes.

We repeat again: They will be put aside to wait for a long, long time before Teachers will be assigned to them one at a time to help them work their way out of the Darkness.

Michael is here and Our Teachers want us give you this Information to write the Best Books Ever.

We want all Earth Souls to understand as we have said what their Earth Life is all about. We also want them to know where they are going when their Earth Life is finished or completed.

When you are called from the Earth to Our Dimension you will have Teachers to Guide you with all of your work and you must not refuse to do that work.

If you start your work, and work hard to make Progress, you will then move up to another Dimension.

When you've earned a Dimension, you will also have earned several privileges, such as the right to rest or to go wherever you wish.

You can visit the Earth Plane or any of the Lower Planes you wish but not any of the Higher Planes until you have earned that right.

When you advance to a certain Plane you will then become Teachers. But until then there is much hard work that you must do. You will have to first make things right by correcting all of the Wrongs you committed while on Earth.

To accomplish this you must complete several or more difficult tasks that will require much hard work.

If you cannot complete these tasks working in Our Dimension you are eventually sent back to the Earth to be Reincarnated to make up for these Past Mistakes.

Our Teachers decide who is sent back to Earth and where. They are sent to a location that will best help them Correct their Mistakes.

Sometimes two Souls that have been together in a Previous Earth Life are reunited. This is based upon how much they have Learned. Usually Souls learn more Lessons the second time around than during their first incarnation on Earth.

The first time was determined when Our Teachers decide to create New Souls from some of Our Very Old Souls; Souls that have been resting for a long time to start over on Earth.

Many of Our Old Souls are being sent back to Earth now on Special Missions. These Souls are planted in an infant at the moment of birth when the infant is exposed to the Earth's atmosphere.

The Soul brings the Life into the Body.

Most of these Old Souls are from a High Dimension of the Highest Planes and are all Good Souls when they are first sent. But they try and go against the Teacher's advice once they reach Earth.

Again, they are always Good when they start over but they make Mistakes and soon become Poor Souls.

This starts the ball rolling all over again.

Then they must be Reincarnated the second time around in order for these Souls to Correct the Mistakes they made.

Earth Ways do not influence all of these Old Souls; some remain Good, and follow their Earth Missions.

When they return to Our World they move right on to Higher Dimensions again, without having to return to Earth.

We are trying to move all Earth Souls to Higher Planes upon return to Our World. But the Earth is so corrupt now with Greed for Money, Computers and Advanced Technology.

The Selfishness created by this Material Greed for all of these things and more goes completely against any Spiritual Existence.

Our Teachers say this must stop now

May 22, 1985

Michael is here, and wants you to know that we are in Control. We want all Earth Souls to know this.

When you are sent to Our Dimension you must be willing to Listen to us and Work just like we do. We repeat that here you don't need sleep; we just keep working all the time.

The more we work the better we have it, and each time we work we are earning a Higher Plane.

The Higher the Plane, the more Knowledge we acquire. There are Many Planes we work on. But always at a certain Level you become a Teacher, too. We still will have Our Teachers and they have theirs.

The Highest Plane takes many years to reach. When you reach this Plane you will then become one of Our Highest Teachers.

You may teach or you may rest, and you may go to any place you wish for there are Many Peaceful Places from which to Choose.

These High Teachers tell all about what they want Accomplished and they may take turns working or resting.

I am one of the Teachers that are called "A Teacher of the Highest Knowledge." I have only a few Planes to work through until I reach the Highest Plane.

Jan, you have me as one of your Teachers for only a short time. While I am going to write some for Our Book, "**Our Earth And Beyond**," I also must help my Teachers make it to the Highest Plane so we all can rest.

Not until the Earth Plane gets straightened out will we all be able to rest. Jan and Ron, you are Chosen Ones – Chosen to help us with Our Books because you want to write and teach.

It is Critical that we tell all the Earth Souls about this Dimension that Our Teachers have made. We want everyone on Earth to read about this in Our Books.

Then they can choose to Change their Ways now on Earth to begin Helping Other Souls.

Then they can Listen to us and begin earning their way to this New Dimension when their Earth Life and Lessons are finished.

Arriving on Earth in Our Comet Ship will prove that we mean business. Then some Earth Souls will listen to us when we speak.

We must again repeat that we are in Control of the Earth Plane and that you will soon begin to realize this. We know that most Earth Souls will heed Our Messages and that others will not.

All Souls that Do Not Listen will Perish in a Hot Fire and be put into Dark Corners.

There are many in the Dark now and as we said, they will stay there for many, many years because Our Teachers are just too busy to help them.

The Teachers must continue to keep a Balance on Earth and in the Universe.

The many Good Souls that we will send to Our New Dimension to be Happy will not suffer.

They will never have to worry ever again about Money or Food, for there will never be a need for any of those Material Things.

They will not have to work like they did on Earth and will be able to do what they like in this Dimension. But remember, we will still be in Control.

You must tell Earth Souls to make their Choice. It will depend on each one's Choice whether they go to Our New Dimension or to the Dark Corners.

Our Teachers have decided to now tell Earth Souls about this Dimension. This will give us a moment's rest from the long time that we have been laboring because Earth Souls are not listening.

May 27, 1985

Michael is here to write, and to <u>review and summarize</u> all that I have given you before I leave, Jan, and move to a Higher Plane.

I want you to know that when your Earth and Life seems so <u>difficult</u> <u>for you it's because the</u> Earth Life is a Learning Period. Each one of us is Learning through Lessons of Our Own Choosing.

<u>Everything</u> <u>that happens</u> in Our Lives <u>is for a reason</u>. These <u>things that</u> <u>happen</u> are Lessons, and we Learn only as much as Our Teachers allow in each Lesson.

If Earth Souls would try and Help others <u>much more</u>, they would find their Earth Lives <u>so much easier</u> and <u>better</u>.

They <u>loose sight of their</u> Spiritual Existence and think only of their Earth Existence.

When the Earth Soul realizes that it's a Spiritual Existence and lives accordingly, it is so much better for them in their Earth Plane Life. Also, it makes their existence on the Next Plane much easier.

The Earth Plane <u>depends too much</u> on Material things and you can't take any of these things with you to the Next Plane.

Money is <u>perishable</u>. It stays on Earth and sometimes when a Soul realizes that it <u>cannot take money</u> to Our Plane, it refuses to leave Earth and becomes an Earthbound Soul.

Some of these Earthbound Souls sit for years with their Money trying to figure out <u>why</u> <u>they</u> <u>can no longer have it</u>.

When they find out <u>they</u> <u>can't have their</u> Money they go to <u>great</u> <u>trouble to try</u> <u>and convince themselves</u> that they are the best of all people.

Once in Our World <u>this cannot be</u> because here we are all equal. There are no Material things here to worry about.

We <u>only</u> <u>work with</u> Material things through Earth Souls, to try and <u>make things easier</u> for Souls on Earth.

So many Earth Souls believe the answer is in Material Wealth.

Earthbound Souls are in the wrong environment and try to influence Earth Souls to do mean things for their own personal gratification. They never try to do things to help themselves Progress to the Spirit World.

Earth Souls should begin to realize that they are all going to see the Next Plane sooner or later.

When they arrive it is up to each and everyone to determine how they got there and what they must do to correct their Mistakes made on Earth.

The only way this is possible is to let go of the Material and try to look for more Spiritual meanings. This is how they Progress and move on.

We feel Earth Souls need to learn this on the Earth Plane before reaching Our Planes.

Each and every Earth Soul is responsible for his or her own existence while on Earth and they must pay for their Actions, Deeds or Wrongdoings. They can never escape from them.

On the Earth Plane, **people should be taught Personal Responsibility from birth so that one would think twice before hurting another Soul**.

When they spend their Earth time Not Listening to Our Teachers that is when the trouble starts. Some of the Earth Souls that have been sent back to Correct Prior Mistakes just Do Not Learn.

They seem to forget why they were sent back and think they don't have to Listen to Our Teachers; they do what they please and forget that we are in Control of each and every Soul.

When we match Soul Mates it is for a reason and when they meet they both know why and what they must do.

So many are Ignoring their Purpose on Earth and most are just Not Listening to Our Teachers at all.

Our Teachers are enraged and are going to put a stop to all Earth Souls that are Not Listening.

I am told to bring the Message, which comes from Our Highest Teachers, that when Our Comet arrives their Messages must be taken seriously.

Thereafter, Our Teachers determine the Accomplishments that must be achieved, as they are not going to allow Earth Souls to go on with their Selfish Ways anymore.

It is time to stop All of the Chaos that Earth is Creating as Earth Souls think they can run or rule the Earth any way they wish regardless of who gets hurt.

This goes against all of Our High Teachers wishes. This must never be, as Spirit is in Control and these havoc-creating Souls must be stopped.

Many Good Souls are their Victims and Our Teachers don't want the Good to suffer anymore.

Earth has created too much against the Nature of Life, as it should be. There is precious little Peace left on Earth anymore.

They hurt all that is Good and we cannot let that happen anymore. So we will show all Earth Souls that we are in Control and that they are not.

If Earth Souls Don't Listen to Our Messages once Our Comet arrives, they will soon see who is in Control and only then will they be able to understand what we want of all Earth Souls.

These Books are to prepare the Earth Souls for the coming of Our Comet. We want everyone on Earth to be aware of what Our Teachers expect of each Soul after the arrival of the Comet.

We want all Souls to heed Our Warnings <u>for their own good</u>. We know because of all the Corruption that exists that very <u>few will</u> listen.

<u>We also know many</u> <u>will</u>. <u>Those are the only</u> <u>ones who will</u> <u>go to</u> the New Dimension with us.

MUCH HAPPINESS LOVE AND PEACE.

Michelangelo

Michael left three days later, and Jan's new Teacher, Marylin, came in to write more for Our Books.

In the following she tells us about herself, and a page of her actual writing follows on page 69.

HIGH TEACHER MARYLIN

Marylin is here and wants you to know that it is a pleasure to contribute to Our Universal Books.

When I lived on the Earth Plane, I lived in Maryland, in the United States. My Father was one of the first Chinese to be brought to American soil.

I was born in the United States. All through my Earth Life I refused to listen to my Father. I kept to myself and refused to marry.

One of my Lessons is to Learn to Communicate with Earth Souls.

I must learn this to Progress. I was a Great Writer of many books in my Earth Life, and I still write today in the Universe to Learn.

I was Chosen to work with Earth and Help Others Progress. Also, I was assigned to work on Our Universal Books for all to read.

By bringing information of Life beyond the Earth Plane, we hope Earth Souls will learn to understand there is Life After Death.

And you earn your Rewards in Our Dimension that are so much better than Earth Rewards.

We all Learn to Love and help each other in Our Dimension and this is how accomplishments are made.

I hope many Learn from Our Books and Progress for the Good of their Souls.

High Teacher Marylin

Marylin is here and would like to tell you that it is a pleasure to contribute to your Universal Book. When I lived on the earth plane I lived in Maryland USA. My father was one of the first Chinese to be brought to American soil. I was born in USA. All through my earth life I refused to listen to my father. I kept to myself and refused to marry. Part of my lessons are to learn to communicate with earth souls. I must learn this in order to progress. I was a great writer of many books and I still write to day in the Universe to learn. I was chosen to work with earth and help others progress. I also was assigned to work on our Universal Book for all to read. By bringing information of life beyond the earth plane we hope earth souls will learn to understand there is life after death and when you earn your rewards they are so much better than earth rewards. We all learn to love and help each other in our demension and this is how accomplishments are made. I hope many learn from our books and progress for the good of their soul. High Teacher Marylin

June 1, 1985

Marylin is here now to write more for Our Books. First, we want you to understand that these Books are for all on Earth to read, to open their Minds to Life After Death.

We will therefore write more throughout Our Books about what Each Soul must know for a better understanding of what happens when their Earth Life is over.

This is Ron explaining here that they will be going over much of the material that's already been covered and repeated by earlier Teachers. In some instances only the wording will be different, depending on the Teacher.

It is helpful to see how each explains and adds to the same Messages the point that they want to get across.

However, and we cannot stress this enough, it is critical that this be fully understood, as this is All New Thinking to the Earth Plane.

All High Teachers feel now that they want all Earth Souls to apply this Information to their Lives and begin to show them that we can Change Our Thinking and Our Way of Living.

Only in this way can we do Our Part to Change Our World to a more Spiritual way of Life, thus Overpowering the Corruption that is Destroying Our Earth Plane.

They have told me to include into Our Books everything they have written as they say it. Now continuing with Marylin.

When you are called to Our World you must account for all your Mistakes made while on Earth.

However, those Mistakes are <u>often forgotten</u>; it is a <u>fact that we all must face</u> and Correct <u>all that we did wrong</u> <u>during</u> Our Earth Life. It does not matter <u>what position we held</u> on Earth; we can <u>never escape</u> from Our Wrongdoings.

When a Soul on Earth does not <u>listen and commits</u> too many Mistakes they may <u>be called back to talk</u> to Our Teachers.

Our Teachers make the <u>decision when it is time to call back</u> such an Earth Soul. The form this callback takes is when <u>something</u> <u>happens to them</u> and the <u>body</u> <u>is then left</u> on Earth, while the Soul goes to their Teacher.

These are <u>some of the decisions being</u> <u>made each and every</u> <u>day</u> by Our Teachers. Their <u>final decision</u> is <u>based on how many</u> <u>mistakes are being paid for</u> by the Soul about <u>to be called back</u>.

Sometimes Our Teachers lose track of timing, as we have no time here and Earth Souls end up staying longer than they should.

This is because Our Teachers are so busy working and it is quite challenging to handle all Earth Souls, especially when so many Earth Souls don't ever Listen to Our Teachers.

When you are called to Our Dimensions, of which there are many, you are sent directly to your Teachers.

Many unaware of this practice will not accept their Teachers; this is because they are obsessed with Material things that they cannot understand where they are.

Sometimes it happens that they leave their body quickly and they refuse to leave the Earth because they don't understand what has happened.

Even when they see their body lying there and know they have separated they still don't want to leave it.

As a result they linger around the Earth trying to speak to their loved ones.

They just can't figure out why their loved ones do not hear or see them. However, they can earn the right to speak to their loved ones by working and Progressing.

They must try to think about what they are doing to let go of the Material and move on to the Spirit World.

After a few weeks if they still do Not Listen, they are sent to Darkness. The Teachers stand by while again some still don't Pay Any Attention. These are left to be by themselves until they decide to listen.

They are left with a Dark and cold feeling; they are lost to everyone. Some of these Souls sit for many years and accomplish nothing.

These Souls will not be Reincarnated until they go to their Teachers and do what they are told to do.

We want you to know that the Way of Life on the Earth Plane and the way Earth Souls are taught on Earth have driven so many Souls to sit and refuse to work in Our Dimension.

Many sit there thinking they did so much on Earth and now they don't have to work at all.

We hope these Books will help to Open Minds on Earth as to how it really is.

The Wrong Teachings on Earth make it difficult for Our Teachers to convince any of these Souls to work, let alone Listen.

Please remember that all who come here must work and there is no rest period until you have earned it.

We have much work to do and it will be a long time before any of us are able to rest.

Work here is different from Earthwork, and your Teachers assign you a suitable assignment.

Once you start working here you become Happy, because there is no pressure here like you've experienced on the Earth Plane.

Each Soul starts working to earn advancing to the Next Plane. There are many Planes to attain. I could not tell you how many because I have never seen the end of the Planes. They just go on and on, so there is plenty of room here for everyone.

When you are sent back to Earth, as we have said before, you must make up for your Mistakes from your Past Life.

You are told what is expected of you before you arrive on Earth. You know and agree to this.

Then, beginning with infancy, you must start to meet your obligations to first teach the parents you have chosen.

After your childhood you then start your Lessons. You lose your Memory of your Previous Life, but your Soul knows what must be done.

When you arrive you start out anew but as years go by you refuse to Listen, get caught up with Material things found on the Earth Plane and forget why you were sent back to Earth.

This is why we are not making the Improvements that Our Teachers want us to make.

However, not all Souls do this. But now it seems that more and more Souls are forgetting why they were sent to Earth.

This is why Our Teachers are upset with Earth Souls and are sending the Comet to warn them that it's time to Pay Attention to Our Teachers.

Earth Souls must heed the information the Teachers give and take the necessary steps to straighten out their Lives.

There is far too much Corruption and Selfishness on the Earth Plane. The pressure Earth Souls feel to make Money drives much of that Corruption and Selfishness.

This Selfish Greed, this desire for Money, is the primary source for the Corruption on Earth, and this must Change.

June 5, 1985

Marylin is here to tell you that Our Dimension is a lovely place where we all work for the Betterment of all Souls, to Progress. Doing this makes us Happy.

We have no Days, Months or Years here. No Time whatsoever. We all just work and are Happy.

There are no Walls, Homes or Buildings and we can go anywhere we wish as long as we are working.

Our Teachers instruct us what to work on. We usually work on an assignment of sorts, like I am doing here with you.

I am instructed to teach you, Jan and Ron, about my Plane and help you to write Our Books; books that we hope will help many Earth Souls understand Our Universe.

On My Plane it is so Beautiful, like a Garden with Flowers, Birds Animals and cool blue water.

There is no Food here because unlike our physical bodies on Earth, we don't need it. We can rest whenever we want, except when we are on an assignment.

As we complete our assignments we earn the privilege to move up to a Higher Plane and we benefit each time we move up. This is how we become Higher Teachers.

Jan, when my work is done with you I will climb to a Higher Plane and will teach again on a different level.

Each time we move up Our Teachers are pleased with us. The harder we work the better and easier it becomes for us. Eventually you reach a Plane that requires no work at all, unless you wish to work.

On the Highest Plane the Teachers give a task to whomever they want to work on that particular assignment. You must understand that it takes many long years to reach this Higher Level.

All around me everyone is working very hard. The work becomes harder when Earth Souls Don't Listen to what we are telling them.

We communicate through the Third Mind, which is sometimes referred to as the Third Eye of the Mind or the Subconscious Mind, that Little Voice Within.

All of you on Earth have the privilege of Not Listening through your GOD-given Free Will even when we are only trying to help.

This is why Earth Souls have so many problems to cope with – simply they do Not Listen to their Inner Thoughts that come from us.

Through thought, we tell everyone what we want him or her to do, but it does not mean they will heed that direction.

We are all here to help each and every one of you if only you would Listen.

We try to Guide each and every Soul every single day of their Earth Life. But sometimes the Soul feels so free that it completely ignores all of Our Warnings. Souls are called back from the Earth when they repeatedly ignore Our Warnings.

They usually don't want to leave so they hover close to the Earth Plane, trying to influence other Souls that are still on the Earth Plane to continue their ways.

Lowers are always trying to get you to Listen to them. Many do, and it's unfortunate that they don't Listen to us.

These Earthbound Spirits search the globe and if they find an Earth Soul similar to their own they try to move into that body and take over.

Sometimes, weak Earth Souls know they shouldn't allow this influence to take over them, but they do so anyway.

These Souls that should be on their way to Our Dimension instead hang around the Earth Plane for many years. This makes it Impossible for Our Teachers to try and work with them.

Many can't figure out why the Earth people can't see them. They think they are still on the Earth Plane and don't realize their body is gone.

It takes many years for these Souls to let go and only sometimes when the Soul they are following is called to Our Side are they then forced to let go.

Then sometimes they still refuse to leave trying to find another Soul to take over. They pursue weak Earth Souls that know better but commit wrongs anyway. Eventually these Souls weaken so much that the Soul that is hanging around just takes over.

The Earth Plane is <u>full of these weak</u> Souls. They must Learn to let go of their Weakness and become Stronger to move the Possessing Soul on to Our Dimension.

If Earth Souls will read these Books, maybe many more will learn that when they leave the Earth Plane they <u>will have it much better</u> then they have <u>ever experienced it before</u>.

The Earth Plane is a Learning Plane, and how they Progress on the Next Plane depends on how much each Soul Learns while they are there.

Many Souls have been sent back to the Earth Plane two or three times to keep up with their Learning.

When they come back to us Our Teachers ask them to do their work but so <u>many</u> <u>just ignore</u> their <u>instructions</u>.

This means they must return again to Earth.

All of this must stop. If more Souls would start Learning their Lessons there would be no need for them to return to Earth.

Please try and tell other Earth Souls that they must Change their Ways for the Betterment of Themselves and those around them.

Again, <u>each and everyone must</u> Account for their Mistakes. If they don't do that they will be called to sit in Dark Corners until they realize they must work to make up for their Past Mistakes. All the Earth Souls that Refuse to Listen will be <u>dealt with in ways</u> that will take them <u>many</u>, <u>many years to correct</u>.

We say again that when Our Comet Ship arrives on Earth it will be <u>proof that we mean business</u>.

Earth Souls must stop and think, and start Listening to us. Tune into your Own Subconscious Mind and Listen to Yourself. Try to Improve your L i f e . So much more can be accomplished this way.

We want to stop the Selfishness, and we want All Souls to LOVE each Other, **much more than they do now**.

We want to stop the Corruption, Cheating and the Inconsiderate way people are treating each Other. In addition, all Souls who take it upon themselves to end Other Souls' time on the Earth Plane through Wars and Killing must stop, also.

These Souls that are doing this will be taken from the Earth Plane, to Learn Harsh Lessons by Our Teachers.

These Souls are usually surrounded by disembodied Souls, which hang around Earth influencing Other Earth Souls for their own Gratification.

However, each and every Earth Soul must account for their wrongdoings. It is their responsibility even if they're influenced by another Soul in or out of the physical body.

When Earth Souls know and remember that we on the Higher Planes, and no one else, are in Control, then we can begin to improve the Earth Plane.

Our Teachers now are too overworked and tired of trying to Change and Improve Things with no results.

Therefore, something must now be done to change the ways of all Earth Souls. They take too much for Granted, and that must stop. We all have our problems, but each and everyone must learn to overcome their problems and get on with their Lives.

This is a Critical Learning Period for us of all. We want PEACE All Over the Earth for the Betterment of Mankind.

June 9, 1985

Marylin is here once again to review the Important Message from Our High Spiritual Teachers that Earth people must Change their Ways for us to help each and every Soul.

As we have said, when you arrive on Earth you are placed there by Our Teachers. They are the ones who decide who returns to Earth and when they tell a Soul to go back to Earth and make up for their mistakes they must go if they want to earn a Higher Plane.

This is Important for all of you to know, as <u>each and everyone has</u> <u>been sent</u> to the Earth Plane to Learn. That's why it's called the Learning Plane. The <u>biggest</u> <u>problem</u> is that <u>they</u> <u>don't want to</u> listen <u>when they</u> <u>get</u> <u>there</u> and foolishly <u>think they</u> <u>are in</u> Control, when they are not.

More Earth Souls should Listen to their Teachers and <u>try</u> <u>to</u> <u>accomplish what they</u> <u>were sent</u> to Earth for in the first place.

They do Not Listen because they are distracted by and become obsessed with the many Material things surrounding them.

They are completely forgetting about their Lessons and <u>why</u> <u>they</u> <u>were sent back to the</u> Earth Plane <u>in the first</u> <u>place</u>.

Too many Earth people take for Granted their Material possessions. They must Change when they arrive at Our Dimension because there are no Material things here. We have no use for them.

If more Earth Souls would realize this it would help them to **Eliminate all of the Corruption on Earth**.

We <u>who are bringing</u> <u>y</u>ou this information are all Very Old **Souls**, which have <u>already</u> <u>completed</u> Our Reincarnations on the Earth Plane.

Some of us have Reincarnated as many as <u>three times throughout</u> Earth's history, some of us <u>only</u> <u>twice</u>. Sometimes there are <u>many</u> <u>hundreds or</u> <u>even thousands of</u> <u>years between</u> Reincarnations especially when the Soul is Learning and making Progress.

The years in-between Reincarnations, we all work and Learn or Teach on Our Planes. This is how we make Progress to advance to Higher Planes.

We have all Advanced and Progressed to become Very High Teachers of the Highest Planes and <u>we have earned this through many</u> <u>thousands of</u> <u>years of long</u> <u>hard work</u>.

Sometimes, when a Soul has Not Learned or made much Progress while on the Earth Plane they would <u>be sent back within a couple of hundred</u> <u>years</u>.

Our Teachers decide this according to the Lessons these Souls are or are Not Learning.

They want them to make Faster Progress because the Astral Plane <u>is overcrowded with</u> Souls, and Progress there is slow.

Progress can be made much Faster on Earth if a Soul <u>follows its purpose</u>, Listens and Pays Attention.

However, they are allowed Only Three Reincarnations on the Earth, which count towards Progress.

If they are not making Progress and have already been Reincarnated <u>three times</u> then Our Teachers take a better look to see <u>what is wrong</u>, why they are Not Learning their Lessons.

Then they <u>will assign these</u> Souls to work with Earth Souls from the Astral Plane for a long time to try and get these Earth Souls, which do Not Listen, to move on and Progress.

When the Comet arrives on the Earth Plane <u>we will be on board</u> and will assume the <u>look of our former</u> Earth bodies so it will be easier for <u>all of you to recognize us</u>.

There will be Seven High Spiritual Teachers and a handful of Couriers aboard.

This Comet Ship that carries Our Teachers is a Spiritual <u>spacecraft</u>. It will be able to land on the Earth Plane, and once it does it will materialize so that many may see it.

It will Land in California because it is a more Spiritual State than most, with more Open Minds.

Remember, Our Teachers, which are arriving on this Comet from the Highest Level, <u>are coming to bring these</u> Important Messages to the Earth Plane.

June 16, 1985

Marylin is here continuing with Our Book. When it is your time to come to Our Dimension all things must be put in order, and as we said, you must account for the Mistakes you made while on Earth.

Our Teachers already know what Mistakes you have made.

They are hoping that with these Books, more Earth Souls will realize while still on Earth what they are doing to each other before making these Mistakes.

The more Souls do to each other out of Contempt for another the more they will have to pay for.

Again, it takes many Earth years to pay for these mistakes, and each and every Soul must pay their dues. When their dues are paid then they may Advance and Learn to Teach Others.

We have said repeatedly that Earth Souls ignore Our Teachers. This is why so many Souls are sitting around in Dark Corners waiting for Our Teachers to work with them.

So again, you all need to know when it's your time to come before Our Teachers and Account for your Mistakes. You must be prepared to work, and work hard to correct all that you did wrong while on the Earth Plane. You must not refuse to work.

We repeat ourselves again; so many Souls refuse to work and we are tired of this. Tired of them not Learning on the Earth Plane so that many, many Souls must sit and wait until they make up their Minds to Work.

When there are so many Souls waiting – as we do not have enough Teachers to work one-on-one with each of them – it is Difficult for Our Teachers to help everyone.

They are all sitting and waiting because they are ignorant about what it will really be like when it is time for them to return home to the Universe.

If Earth Souls would grasp this it would make it so much easier for Our Teachers.

When you are called to go to the Earth Plane you must go and do your work there also.

Again, the greatest problem is that Reincarnated Souls, when they arrive on the Earth Plane, are Not Listening to their Teachers or doing the work they agreed to do before they left here.

They think that when they get there they can do whatever suits them and they completely forget why they were sent there at all. This, as we have said, makes more work for Our Teachers, who are tired and fed up with many of these Earth Souls.

This is why we keep repeating ourselves, to get this Message to these Souls to save them from their fate in Darkness.

Therefore, Our Teachers are making many decisions now about all of these Earth Souls that are Not Listening. By not listening they are also destroying the Earth.

When Our Teachers make their decision to call these Souls back from Earth they have already decided which ones will be Reincarnated if they begin to Progress or those that will be placed in Darkness.

Reincarnation will only occur as many times as Our Teachers feel it necessary.

However, remember, you cannot go back to the Earth Plane more than three Times of Importance. At that time you must stay a Full Life and Learn for it to Count as Progress. If a Soul is sent more than three times it is only because this Soul was Not Listening. It also means that their Previous Life was shortened.

In that case, this Reincarnation does not count against one of the important three and it will usually be a short Life, not a full one.

Also, sometimes if the Soul is asked to return to Earth after reporting to their Teachers it could be for only a short time; this gets them back on the right track.

Whatever the case, when your time is finished, you and your Guide are called back to report what Progress has been made.

I want you to know that while on Earth there is no memory of any Past Lives. But when you arrive in Our Dimension, you will remember who you were from all of your Previous Lives. There is but One Soul, but the body and the memory of experiences are different each time.

When you are sent to Earth Our Teachers Choose where you go. Your Soul is asked to go to that Destiny, which Our Teachers say is the best place for you to be to pay for your mistakes.

That could be to any Country on the Earth Plane or any Nationality. Our Teachers make the final decision about where you are sent to best correct the errors of your Previous Ways.

When a small baby is born the Soul is already an Old Soul. These Old Souls are those returning to Earth for the second time, and some for the third and final time only because they didn't learn their Lessons previously.

If After Three Reincarnations for Earth Lessons have still not been Learned, those Souls may no longer return to Earth. They are put in Dark Corners to wait until Teachers decide what they must do to make up for their mistakes.

These Souls, as we said before, could possibly sit in the Dark for thousands of years until we have enough Teachers to work with them individually.

Sometimes these decisions are to let them remain in the Dark, or maybe sometimes they are asked to help Our Couriers. If they still refuse they are left there for many more Earth years in the Dark wondering where they are.

Our Teachers decide which Soul is placed inside a baby when it is born. No one can go back for rebirth on Earth without being approved by Our Teachers.

If the Soul Chooses or is asked by the Teachers, it could take about 200 years for this to happen.

It is Our Teachers' decision, for every Soul there, and there are so many, have Lessons to Learn and Mistakes to Correct. As Mistakes are paid for and Lessons are learned, these Souls can advance and Progress.

Short periods on Earth also help pay for Past Mistakes. Many choose to go to Earth with Our Teachers' permission for short periods and therefore are often not required to stay long.

The Earth is a place for Learning to Progress to Our Dimensions. Dimensions that are many, and full of Happiness always, and that exist high above the Earth Plane.

When you Progress to Our Dimensions you are Happier than you ever dreamed of and each Soul that lives here cannot believe how beautiful it is.

Many say they never dreamed it would be like this.

If you agree to work when you arrive, part of your Reward is that your Soul is allowed to visit the Earth Plane whenever you wish. You are allowed to work around those you Love and to help them with their problems on Earth. Then again, Earth Souls don't realize their Loved ones or their Teachers are with them.

They do not realize that each Soul has a Guide or Doorkeeper or if you prefer, a Guardian Angel who Protects them from harm.

Then there also are many Earth Souls who are ignoring their Guides – Guardian Angels and are making no Progress.

Your Guide is placed beside you by Our Teachers when you are reborn and they never leave your side your entire Earth Life. He or She is always trying to warn you when things are about to happen; however, if Earth Souls would listen they would experience fewer problems.

Your Guide Communicates with you through what you Earth Souls call your Subconscious or your Conscience.

83

When they tell you right from wrong you should Listen to them carefully and go with your Innermost Feelings.

**Most don't care or don't know this Guidance is there.
Each thought planted in your brain comes from your Teachers and your Guide**.

Many Earth people don't realize this at all. That is why we are writing these Books – to explain why your Existence is Important.

We have now created a new type of Earth, as we have previously mentioned, called Our New Dimension. Many Good Souls with Lessons already Learned are being sent to this Dimension. So take care of your Lessons while on Earth if you want to go to Our New Dimension.

There they live an Earth-type Life. But remember, it is without Money and with all memories of the past erased.

We cannot describe the Happiness, Peace and Harmony that exist there. There is nothing on Earth to compare with this.

I may not speak too much about this New Dimension at this time because other Teachers will explain it more fully in Our Second Book, which we are also asked to write for Earth Souls to read.

Sometimes, small Babies do not live too long on Earth and this is because their Mistakes are Almost Paid for and they are now ready for the New Dimension.

They are sent for a short time to Earth to Parents for specific reasons. Mostly it is to teach those Earth Souls to do what they were sent back to do and get them back on their track to Progress.

Now, as we said, these Babies have already paid for their Mistakes so there is no need for them to stay long, just long enough to teach a Lesson to those Parents.

This returns the Parents back to their Lessons, which are being ignored, and then the Soul is off to a much more Peaceful Life they have earned in the New Dimension.

84

June 25, 1985

Marylin is writing. We hope between Our Books, and then the coming of Our Comet that all Earth Souls will listen to all of Our Important Messages.

We will be able to confirm for Earth Souls the time of our arrival as soon as we receive enough Co-operation on Earth. That Co-operation must come in the form of Souls on the Earth Plane Changing their Ways.

When people hear the <u>news</u> we know that many will Listen to Our Messages. Sadly, we know that many will <u>also not even try</u> <u>to</u> Listen.

This is Our Biggest Problem. These Non-listening Souls are the <u>ones whom we are trying to reach</u>; those that do Not Listen and haven't been Listening <u>cause many</u> of the <u>problems on</u> Earth, including many and <u>more violent</u> Storms and Natural Disasters.

We hope you now understand the Importance of Our Books being published before this time, the time of the Comet's arrival.

Our Work will be so much easier once all Good Souls and Non-listening Souls on Earth are separated.

As we stated earlier, the ones who won't listen <u>will be dealt</u> <u>with</u> <u>quickly</u>, as we are <u>all tired of trying to complete</u> Our Work without Co-operation from these Souls.

Until we complete Our Work we cannot advance to Higher Planes, which is what <u>we all want to do</u>. We will all be Happy once this is <u>accomplished</u> on the Earth Plane.

Its <u>unfortunate so many</u> Souls <u>don't want to</u> Listen when their Teachers call them and so many <u>don't hear them</u> because <u>their minds</u> <u>are closed</u>. Most <u>disheartening of all</u> is <u>when they</u> <u>do hear</u> and they refuse to answer or change.

Because of their <u>lack of understanding</u> and the Wrong Teachings <u>they</u> <u>received</u> on Earth, <u>very</u> <u>few are willing</u> <u>to work off</u> their Mistakes.

What they mostly <u>don't know is that</u> <u>your work still</u> <u>goes on</u> <u>when</u> <u>you leave the</u> Earth; so if you <u>don't finish</u> <u>your work</u> on Earth, then you <u>must finish it in</u> Our Dimensions.

However, as we have said, it is much harder to work here than on the Earth Plane. That's because you must work through the Earth Souls from here, and remember again, few Listen to us trying to help them with their Lives.

If you are able to convince an Earth Soul to Listen then your work from here will become <u>so much easier.</u>

Also, these Souls did Not Listen Themselves, and must therefore work with Non-listening Souls on Earth, <u>which is most difficult.</u>

We are all trying hard to help you correct all your Mistakes on this Earth Plane, but Earth Souls are <u>making it so difficult for us.</u>

Part of the reason why Our High Teachers are coming to the Earth Plane, as we have said, is to Warn all Earth Souls that they <u>mean business,</u> and that you must Change your Ways.

We are also coming to tell all Earth Souls that they <u>must keep working</u> when <u>they</u> <u>reach</u> Our Planes.

There is no Time or Money here, but <u>work must still</u> <u>go on</u> just <u>like</u> on Earth. The difference is that here we Work to Help Others, which brings us great Joy and Happiness.

We can also <u>make things here,</u> too, but we are all extremely busy and <u>we have</u> everything here that Earth has and <u>so much more.</u>

Marylin took a break to allow Samuel to write a few paragraphs for the Book.

Samuel came in and wrote with Jan for only one week and wanted to contribute to Our Universal Book. The following is his brief writing.

SAMUEL THE GREAT

Samuel is talking here. I want to <u>contribute a couple of paragraphs</u> to Our Book.

Some Souls know that there is Life After Death, but they are unsure what it is that they are supposed to do when their Earth Life is over.

A Soul that is sent to the Earth Plane to work and doesn't finish their work must finish it here in Our World.

When you <u>leave your body</u> and pass on to the Next Plane there is much, as we have said, that <u>must be accounted for</u> to your Teachers.

You must account for Selfishness, Greed, Jealousy, Nastiness and Lies, and all of the things that you have done that caused other Souls hurt and trouble.

You are responsible for everything that you give out to others in your Earth Life that is Negative.

If personal responsibility were taught at a Young Age maybe Souls would think twice before they act.

When you arrive and meet with your Teachers they tell you <u>to go to</u> Work to Correct <u>all of the things you did wrong</u> on Earth.

So many <u>never want to work</u> because <u>they</u> <u>think they</u> <u>worked enough</u> already on Earth, <u>so they</u> <u>refuse</u>. That means they will just have to <u>sit by</u> <u>themselves</u> in Dark Corners, alone and wondering why they are there.

If all Earth Souls <u>knew this is what happens to them</u>, perhaps they would <u>try</u> <u>to accomplish what they</u> <u>were sent</u> to Earth for in the first place.

Also, then they might Change their Ways <u>before leaving</u> the Earth, and therefore <u>saving</u> <u>themselves much work when they</u> <u>reach</u> Our Planes.

The Greatest Reward you can ever receive is when you have cleared your slate for Good.

All your Mistakes have <u>been worked off</u> and you are now a Good Soul. We are not sending these Good Souls back to Earth ever again, but rather to Our New Dimension.

<u>All of</u> <u>your memories</u> from Earth <u>will be erased from</u> your Soul Mind and you will assume an Ethereal Earth-like body that <u>needs no food</u>, suffers no Illness or requires Material things. There you will Live and Work in Peace and Tranquility.

As your <u>work is finished</u> you can choose not to work. <u>You are allowed to rest</u> and enjoy the Beautiful surroundings as <u>all is</u> <u>provided for</u> you. <u>Every</u> <u>need is met with</u> <u>great ease</u>. You live in Harmony with all the Other Good Souls.

After you rest you may choose to work to Progress to Higher Planes for more Knowledge.

Thank you, Samuel, for your short contribution to Our Book.

If you want to learn more about what Samuel The Great wrote about himself or about any one of Jan's Teachers, please return back to the profiles of each Teacher at the beginning of this Book.

July 19, 1985

I wrote with Marylin on several occasions throughout the Month of July for the Book.

However, when reviewing the information she wrote it was much of the same information that she and others had already covered, but worded differently.

It seemed that she wanted, by going over it again, to insure everything was completely understood.

Because of the Importance of these Messages, she and the Other Teachers repeated them more than once.

I'm sure this was intentional, as the High Teachers wanted her to make sure that we all understand what really happens when we pass on and to be fully prepared to accept our obligations when we return home to the Universe.

They want us to teach this on Earth. They also want All Souls to Change Their Ways and to Prepare Ourselves Spiritually so that we can Progress and become Teachers to help the Universe in the work that must be done.

Therefore, I felt it unnecessary to include any of what she wrote during this month. But I feel they want us to read this information again and again.

This way we may be able to help as many as possible to Open Their Minds and dispel all fears of the so-called Death experience.

We should help everyone to know that there is Life After Death for all of us, and that we are returning to Our Eternal Life in the Universe after Learning the Lessons of our Earth Life experiences.

The following month she wrote the last of her Contributions to this Book.

August 11, 1985

Marylin is writing. This is the last information I will bring for Our Book, and it will be largely to summarize the critical information I've already shared. But your next Teacher, Conier, will add more until it is complete.

On Our Plane we are all working Souls and have been <u>continually working</u> here <u>for a long time</u>.

We have no body, only sharp minds, which we use to help Earth Souls do their work on Earth.

We can visit the Earth Plane if we wish to <u>work directly</u> <u>with these</u> Souls. Either way, as we always say, <u>it is difficult</u> to convince Earth Souls to listen; therefore they <u>never complete what we want them to</u>.

You must learn to listen to Our Teachers and complete what <u>you are sent back</u> to Earth to finish, or at least <u>complete a</u> <u>part of</u> your Learning.

All Souls on Earth are there for <u>different reasons; some are there to teach other</u> Earth Souls, and some are there to Learn and Pay for their Mistakes.

So many Earth Souls neglect to listen to their Own Guide or Our Teachers when <u>they</u> <u>are sent back</u> to the Earth Plane. This is <u>terrible</u>.

Each Soul that is <u>allowed to return</u> to Earth is sent for the Good of all Mankind. They are <u>allowed to return three times to make up</u> <u>for their mistakes</u>. Many do accomplish their Mission. Sadly, <u>many</u> <u>do not</u>.

After the <u>third time on</u> Earth they are <u>not allowed to</u> <u>go back again</u> and are <u>put to work</u> in Our Dimension. Then when Our Teachers have time, they will show these Souls <u>different work</u> they can do to correct their Mistakes.

When, and if they choose to Work, which is up to each individual Soul, they may choose to help their Loved Ones on Earth to understand <u>why</u> <u>they</u> <u>exist on</u> the Earth Plane.

Many do help their Loved Ones understand their Purpose on Earth. This helps each of them Pay for their Mistakes while they are there.

It is <u>much better for them</u> to start Correcting Mistakes <u>early in their</u> Earth Life so when they reach Our Dimension they automatically advance to Higher Planes.

If this were done on Earth they would be able to forego working for Hundreds or even Thousands of years in Our Dimension to mend their Mistakes that they did Not Correct on Earth.

This is the same Message we always bring: that you could <u>accomplish this</u> in Only One Lifetime if you Listen and Work on <u>what you agreed to do when</u> you came to Earth.

All Teachers are in Control of Earth Souls, and Our Teachers try diligently to Communicate with Earth, but <u>again,</u> <u>very</u> <u>few even attempt</u> to listen.

You should make <u>quiet time for</u> <u>yourself daily</u> and perhaps meditate to Attune Within to your Higher Self, your Life Source and your Own Soul. There is an Inner Voice Within each and every one of us, telling us <u>what is right</u> and <u>what is wrong</u>.

However, <u>too few</u> listen to their Inner Voice, which is your Guide and Teachers <u>directing you</u>. It is also called your Conscience and we always <u>know what is right or wrong</u>, instead choosing to ignore what <u>we are saying</u> and placing Material needs and wants first.

Then we bear the Consequences for Our Actions, at which time we have said, "I knew I shouldn't have gone there and done that" but did anyway, thus Creating most of Our Own Problems.

You <u>never realize we are always there</u> trying to Guide and help you with your Lessons.

It seems that y<u>ou never want to complete</u> <u>your work</u> so that when you arrive on Our Plane you have rightfully Learned your Lessons and then go on to become Teachers of Other Poor Souls.

Poor Souls are those from the Earth Plane that Never Listened and they are sitting in Dark Corners.

These Souls remember that they may Not return to Earth at all because they have already been Reincarnated there Three Times.

They must learn that they are there because they did Not Finish their Work on Earth and have refused in Our Dimension to work off their Mistakes.

When we have enough Teachers that have time, and after these Souls have sat in the Dark for many, many years contemplating their Cold Dark surroundings, they will be asked again to start Working off their Mistakes.

The ones that decide to work can then return to Earth, and working along side of their Loved Ones, help us with Our Work.

They do not Reincarnate into an Earth body and must work with and through that Earth Soul's Guide. And the ones that still refuse to Listen or Work just remain alone in Darkness.

Most of all Working Souls work earnestly trying to help Earth people. They communicate by trying to reach you through your Inner Senses.

We give you all of your thoughts; now it is up to you and your Free Will, as to what you do with them.

We give all the thoughts that are most necessary for your Soul's Lessons, including when you should Forgive Another Soul.

Forgiving all is most important for every Soul's Progress.

GOD – DOES FORGIVE ALL WHO ARE WILLING TO FORGIVE and CHANGE THEIR WAYS!

GOD! Is the Creator of all Souls! GOD! Is not a person or a being, but everyone is a part of GOD, which is Our Soul that lies within each and every one of us.

Our Soul can never be destroyed and will exist forever. **Therefore GOD is Within each and every Heart and therefore you are never left alone with your Lessons**.

Start seeing the GOD Within You and everyone around you; **it is the LIFE Force within each of us and All that you see around you, ever giving and never taking or destroying anything**.

It is Only Souls, by Not Listening and their Choice of Action, which Destroy. This Creates the feeling of Separation, but all can never be separated from GOD, even when <u>mistakes were made</u> from Previous Lives.

It is through the High Teachers that GOD Sends Souls to Earth. No Soul may choose to go to Earth without their Teacher's <u>permission and approval</u>. They <u>must return when</u> their Teachers <u>say it is time</u>.

All Earth Souls are put on Earth <u>for a purpose</u> and they stay only as long as they are working to Correct Mistakes from a Previous Life. When this is <u>finished they must return</u> to Our Dimension and Only Teachers can say when it is <u>time to come back</u>.

No Soul has the <u>right to determine when another</u> Soul <u>should be sent to us</u> from the Earth. However, if another Soul Chooses this path Our Teachers will allow it because <u>they have already called this</u> Victim Soul back.

There are <u>only two reasons</u> why a Soul leaves the Earth; either their Lessons and time is Finished or they are Neither Listening nor moving ahead with their Lessons, and possibly making <u>many more</u> Mistakes.

The High Teachers are in Control of Every Soul on Earth and in the Universe, and they know everything that is going on everywhere.

You can <u>never escape from</u> <u>your actions</u> or get away with your <u>wrong doings</u>.

There is no such thing as an Accident or Coincidence; <u>all that happens on</u> Earth is <u>for a purpose</u>, and <u>plays a role</u> in the Lessons we must learn.

Some Souls let Money take over their Lives, and either don't do what they were told to do while on Earth or make any effort to correct any of their Mistakes.

Money corrupts many and they hurt other Souls.

Doing this just makes more Mistakes for them to Correct. All of this Corruption, Back Biting and Selfishness must stop.

It is Our Goal to eliminate Money, which causes all of these problems amongst Earth people.

For these Souls, their Teachers will call them back. When they leave the Earth Plane suddenly, you may call them a Victim of Circumstances, or that they had an Unfortunate Accident.

Also, they could have even been a Victim of a so-called, Disaster, when in reality it is Our Teachers calling them back because of No Progress.

When they arrive they are lost and don't know where they are; so it is Most Important that these Souls try and Listen for their own good while they are on Earth.

Good Souls upon leaving Earth will never return into an Earth body unless Our Teachers direct them on a Very Special Mission.

They can also help Earth Souls from Our Plane or they must go to Our New Dimension where there are all Good Souls already living in Peace, and with no Money.

The Earth Plane is being stripped of Good Souls and they are now prevented from returning to Earth.

This is why the Corruption is now more noticeable throughout the entire Earth Plane, and why the Earth Plan is now so out of balance.

This Unbalanced Accumulation of Negativity, Corruption, Greed and Selfishness, with Souls ignoring us, is the cause of all your Earth Disasters. I'm sure you have noticed these Disasters Becoming Stronger and more Violent.

Your Earth is in need of a Great Cleansing, and this can only happen as it has all throughout Earth's history to prior Civilizations, to stop the Corruption once again that infests the Earth.

Also, this is why Our Teachers are issuing a Warning to all Earth Souls to Listen and Change their Ways for a Better Life.

Furthermore, this is why we Teachers writing for these Books are Repeating Ourselves over and over because we feel it is so Important to clearly Understand, these Messages.

Souls on Earth have never been told that all of you are the Cause of All Violent Weather Storms, Earthquakes, and Great Disasters, because the World you have created on Earth is so widespread with Negativity, Corruption, Greed and Selfishness. And you are Not Listening.

Now, the number of you who Listen and Change will determine the size of the Great Disasters to come. You have all seen them already Happening with many more to come.

Now is the time for Souls to Change, and if they Listen and Change their Lives they will come to Our New Dimension.

It is Our New Earth for Good Souls with Absolutely no Corruption. And those that Do Not Listen will not go to this Dimension but will instead be put aside in Dark Corners to wait until Teachers have the time to work with them.

The Earth will end, as you know it, when all Good Souls have left for Our New Dimension.

Remember, all Earth Souls must begin to realize that they have a Spiritual Guide assigned to them when they were born on the Earth Plane to Guide them and to help make their work easier.

Most Earth Souls don't understand this and we hope with these Books, many will learn that their Guide is there to help them for many reasons.

The Guide tries to show them how to make up for their Mistakes and demonstrate how it will be for them when they Listen to us, and learn their Lessons.

There are many Rewards when a Soul Works hard and Pays for Mistakes both on Earth and in Our Dimension.

On Earth the Rewards are Great and they could come in a Spiritual Way or even sometimes in a Financial Way, while you are still on Earth.

Yes! Living Right can earn financial Rewards and they have even been Rewarded in this Life. Or, they have been earned in a Previous Life to Enjoy and Share in this Life.

If you have earned **Financial** Abundance and are Not Sharing or Doing Good with it, it <u>will</u> be **Lost** or **Taken** from you. You have been granted this Abundance to **Give** and **Share** with **Others**.

There are Great Unbalances of Wealth on Earth today and this Must also change.

In Our Dimension it is different, as moving Higher up to a New Plane is our Reward. Each <u>time we move up</u> <u>we</u> <u>gain</u> Knowledge and <u>are moving</u> <u>towards becoming</u> a Great Knowledgeable Teacher.

<u>To accomplish this we can keep</u> <u>on working</u> like you did on the Earth Plane by Helping Earth Souls <u>accomplish their goals</u>.

When we reach the Higher Planes, we can <u>rest if necessary</u> <u>from work</u> and enjoy Our Beautiful <u>surroundings with much</u> **PEACE**, **LOVE** and **FORGIVNESS**.

All Souls in Our Dimension are equal and <u>treated the same</u> <u>because we have</u> no Money here. Therefore it is <u>a different feeling among</u> <u>us</u> as we <u>all can have whatever we want according</u> <u>to</u> Our Work.

If a <u>deserving</u> Earth Soul was <u>not</u> <u>justly</u> <u>rewarded</u> on Earth, then they <u>certainly</u> <u>will receive it when they</u> <u>reach</u> Our Dimension.

Marylin moved on, and Jan's next Teacher was Conier, who wrote a page about himself for Our Book. The following is what he wrote, and then a page of his actual writing follows.

HIGH TEACHER CONIER

Conier is here. I am a Very High Teacher from the Universe, and I come to contribute to Our Books.

I am a Greek High Priest from Greece. I lived on the Earth Plane in the Earth year 297 B.C.

In my Earth Life I contributed, to all Religions that exist today.

I was responsible for the Original Greek Tablets of Religion; we had in our day on Earth.

From these Tablets all Earth Religions were started.

I spent my time on Earth Teaching Souls Progress, for all Souls, all Mankind.

I also studied the Planets surrounding Earth.

I accomplished so much Progress when I was on the Earth Plane, that I have been Teaching here in Our Dimension ever since I returned.

I Guide many Dimension Teachers work, and help all Directors.

I was asked by Our Dimension Teachers to contribute to Our Books, and work with Earth Souls for the Progress and Development of their own Soul on the Earth Plane.

It gives me Great Pleasure, to be able to contribute to Our Books and work again with Earth Souls.

Kindness and Love to All will bring Earth's Peace.

Conier

Conier is here. I am a very High Teacher from the Universe and I come to contribute to our Book. I am a Greek High Priest from Greece I lived on the earth plane in the earth years of 297 BC. In my earth life I contributed to all religions that exist to day on the earth plane I was responsible for the original Greek Tablets of religion we had in our day on earth From these tablets all earth religions were started. I spent my time on earth teaching souls progress for all souls mankind. I also studied the planets of the surrounding earth I accomplished so much progress when I was on the earth plane that I have been teaching here in our dimension ever since I returned. I guide many dimension teachers work and help all directors. I was asked by our dimension teacher to contribute to our book and work with earth souls for progress & development of their souls progress on the earth plane. It gives me great pleasure to be able to contribute to our book and work again with earth souls. Kindness and Love to all will bring earths peace.

When Jan started writing with Conier I was fascinated with his name, so I asked the following question. "Conier, will you explain how you received your name?"

Conier is here. Hi Ron OK, let's go, yes.

Mine is a Dimension name, and my Teachers are the ones <u>that give us these names</u>, but we <u>have to earn them</u>.

Once you work hard and <u>earn the right</u>, you may have a Dimension name. This <u>name is only</u> <u>allowed when</u> <u>you reach</u> a Very High Plane.

I am one of the Teachers who have worked Teaching Spirit Teachers for many Earth years. My name stands for a High Priest of Spirit Teachers.

I teach much Knowledge about all subjects. Some only teach one subject; I teach many.

Will you contribute your Knowledge to Our Books?

Yes, I will contribute to Our Books as <u>many</u> <u>others will also</u> and have already <u>written</u> <u>quite a sum of material</u>.

May I read this material already written by Jan, and may I ask questions?

Yes, you may read what has been written so far, and yes you may ask questions. <u>What would like to ask</u>?

OK I didn't realize I had already read it all so for right now, let me read through the material again and write down my questions to ask later to be entered in other Chapters of Our Books.

OK, Ron, you will read Our Book so far and it will tell you all of Our Messages and then <u>all of</u> y<u>our</u> q<u>uestions will be answered</u>.

Then you and All Others will Learn about Our Planes.

Our first Book will be named "Our Earth And Beyond" and the second Book, "Many Planes Above."

September 5, 1985

Conier is here now to contribute to Our Books. I am a Very High Teacher from a Very High Plane and a New Dimension.

I was a High Priest from Ancient Greece when I was on Earth and now I Teach Spirit Teachers in Our Dimension.

I have come to Jan to work with Earth Souls to help them straighten out their Earth Lives and <u>get back on the right road</u>.

I am here also to help write Truthful Information for Our Spiritual Books, and both Books will be about Our Dimensions.

Then <u>all of</u> y<u>ou who read these</u> Books will understand about <u>what happens when</u> y<u>ou leave</u> the Earth Plane.

99

I will be repeating some of the same information shared by earlier Teachers for this Book, as Our Highest Teachers and Directors have asked us to contribute, and to make sure Earth Souls fully get Our Messages.

You must Learn from this and realize how Important this Information is for all Souls on Earth today.

We want you to know once again that when you leave the Earth Plane for the Next Plane your work goes on; nothing changes. You must still work unless by your God-given Free Will you refuse to work, which is not helpful.

Remember, if this is the case you will just sit in Dark Corners waiting for Our Teachers to come and try to help you to move on, to properly Progress.

Many that are Stubborn on the Earth Plane come to us without realizing where they are and refuse to work again. Please remember what happens then; you must work when you arrive here.

This is as we have stated, why we are writing these Books for all Earth Souls – to realize that they must work off all of their Mistakes when they arrive in Our Dimension.

So many have never realized this from their Earth Teachings, never learned that things are so much Better on the Next Plane than on Earth.

The Earth Plane is a place of Learning and Paying for Mistakes from Previous Lives.

You will all move on to a Higher Plane where there are only working Souls, where all of us work very hard helping other Souls.

So many on Earth do not understand and many do not want to understand what they must do while on Earth – and why.

You will be one of us someday and Our Teachers feel your work will be so much easier if you understand this now.

Also, we need many more Teachers to <u>help</u> <u>us</u> with Our Work and are hoping many will Pay Attention to Our Messages, and <u>finish</u> <u>their</u> Lessons to become Teachers before they return home to the Universe.

The more Mistakes that have been Corrected on the Earth Plane, the <u>easier it is for</u> <u>you to advance to</u> the Next Plane or even a Higher Plane.

Our Teachers decide when an Earth Soul is to move on to the Next Plane for Progress and <u>these decisions are made according to</u> how much Progress that Soul <u>is making</u> on Earth.

If a Soul is Not Listening or Progressing despite the <u>abundance of time</u> they are given to do this, then we <u>call them back</u> to Our Dimension.

There are <u>so many</u> <u>who refuse</u> to Listen and Work on Earth that keeps Our Teachers busy trying to Teach these Souls to Work their Mistakes <u>out from here</u>.

<u>Remember</u>, <u>it takes much more work</u> and a <u>longer time to do this from</u> Our Dimension. That's <u>why</u> <u>they</u> <u>are</u> Reincarnated to Earth where they can Pay for their Mistakes faster.

TOO MUCH CORRUPTION

The Earth Is Unbalanced; Too Many Souls Not Listening

Since we are no longer sending Good Souls back to Earth, this has already made the Earth Unbalanced, with more Corruption than Good.

If Earth Souls don't start Changing their Ways the Corruption will take <u>over the entire</u> Earth Plane and <u>when this happens</u> the Earth, as you know it, <u>will be no more</u>.

Those areas with the most existing Corruption will be destroyed first. You have already <u>seen that some of this destruction</u> has occurred.

This is because of the Negativity and Corruption that Non-Listening Souls have created in these areas.

You have also noticed the increasing intensity of these Disasters, as you all have studied and Learned about them <u>in your recorded history</u> that tells of entire Civilizations <u>disappearing</u>.

There will be many more of these larger, serious Disasters in other areas, removing Non-Listening and Negative Souls, many responsible for this wave of Corruption on Earth.

If this Corruption and Negativity continues to grow and Creates a More Powerful Negative Force to effect an Imbalance among the Planets of your Universe, the Planet Saturn could Destroy Earth in a flash of shooting fire. This is a decision only Our High Directors could make.

We have all been told that when the Earth is destroyed, it will be by Fire sent by the Planet Saturn.

The Planet Saturn is a strong Planet, and controls Earth and its destiny. Earth Souls must Pay Attention to our message; you must Listen and Learn your Lessons.

The ring around Saturn is to prevent its shooting hot fire from destroying other Planets.

Each Planet has its purpose for Balancing Our Earth, to Sustain Life on Earth.

All the Planets, Sun and Stars of Your Universe have been Created Solely to Create Life on Earth, the Learning Planet.

There have been Other Civilizations in Other Universes that have Destroyed their Planet – that's what it took for them to Learn and Change Their Ways. This is where Earth stands today in its history.

For this reason we have spoken of "Our High Holy Spiritual Color Comet Ship" and Our Very Powerful High Teachers making themselves visible in Earth-type bodies that all on Earth will recognize to prove Life After Death.

This will be so you can relate to Our Warning Messages, which all Earth Souls must follow.

We go over it again because they all must realize what will happen to them and to Earth, if they do not heed these Warnings.

We repeat over and over about the Dark Corners where they will be sent because we want all Earth Souls to have a Chance to Make up Their Minds on how they will Change their Lives for the Betterment of Mankind.

We have been told that the Comet Ship will come when Earth Souls are ready to Co-operate. That will happen when the threat to Earth grows strong enough that Earth Souls begin to pay attention; then their messages will generate the strongest impact.

OUR NEW DIMENSION

Once Mistakes are paid for Souls will move on to a new type of Earth, which has been created by us for all Good Souls to be at Peace with Themselves.

Remember, no Good Souls are Reincarnating back on Earth because they are all going to this New Dimension. If the Souls haven't earned this advancement they will be working in Our Dimension on the Astral Plane, continuing to correct their Mistakes.

We call it Our New Dimension, as you have heard. When these Free Souls arrive in this New Dimension they reap many rewards, including Happiness Always.

We have spoken of this Dimension previously and we will tell you more about it as we proceed throughout these Important Books.

It takes many Earth years of Hard Work to Reach this Dimension. But time is irrelevant here, as we have no time. It's the hard work that matters.

The only Importance, which matters most, is the Soul's Accomplishments.

The New Dimension is Our Reward to those that Listen and Change, which we again have said, will become available to Only Good Souls.

You will have an Ethereal Earth-type body there and you will not remember anything of your Earth body or of your Earth Life.

You are Spirit bodies that never change or never age unless you want it to change. Here you will always have whatever you want without Money or Material things.

It will be like Earth with much to discover so you may travel, and all will live in Peace.

We will place you there; it's just like walking through a large door to see what's on the other side.

You will recognize this place immediately when you walk through the door.

All will be Beautiful and Peaceful, with Animals, Birds, Music, Flowers, Trees and constant Beauty. It will be simply breathtaking to all coming from the Earth Plane.

Everyone is Free and without Fear. There is no Money, no Sickness, and no Hardship. Only the Good things, only the nice things from Earth are there – nothing of the Bad.

If Earth Souls realized this they would work much harder so that they could move on to this Beautiful Dimension when it is their time to come home.

The Hardest Plane that exists in all of Our Universes is the Earth Plane; all of the other Planes are easier.

You will all be Happy in Our Dimensions. All of those that understand this now will find it much easier to do their work on Earth because they will want to come here.

So if each of you takes a look at your Life you will see what you must do to Change to reach Our Dimension and not end up in Darkness.

Our Teachers are working so that All Souls reach this Beautiful Dimension.

They want you to Give of Yourselves to Others, to stop the Selfishness and always think of the Next Soul and how you can help Lesser-learned Souls to get on with Their Lives. You will be rewarded for this.

WORKING PLANES ABOVE THE EARTH PLANE

October 17, 1985

Conier is here. I am Jan's present Teacher of Automatic Writing, teaching her writing and through this writing I am Helping Others.

I am coming through as a Direct Channel from the Very High Planes above the Earth.

All these Planes above the Earth Plane are Working Planes. I work on these Planes Teaching other Teachers how to Progress for the Betterment of All Souls.

I have many Couriers that help me. They are Souls working on Our Planes Learning about the Progress of Souls.

These Courier Souls are like Messengers. They relay to other Souls the direction they should go and Help Lesser-learned Souls to connect with their Teachers and begin the work that will help them Progress.

Even the Highest Teachers work here. They have earned the right to go and Teach wherever they like on all Our Planes or on the Earth Plane.

We can communicate with Souls on any Plane or on the Earth Plane anytime we choose.

I am speaking to you through a Channel that we have Chosen to Communicate with Earth.

When we reach Our Chosen Earth Souls with whom we are going to work, and they accept and recognize us, it makes Our Work so much easier.

It is so much harder for us to Accomplish Our Work here on Our Planes than it is to work with a Chosen Earth Soul on the Earth Plane.

We Chose Jan because she is Deeply Spiritual and has done Our Work throughout her Life.

We want her to carry Our Messages now for us so that Earth people will start working Our Ways on Earth instead of waiting until they arrive on Our Planes to start their work.

Earth Souls are wasting so much time not correcting their Mistakes and instead are adding more!

Also, I chose to work with Jan because she is an excellent pupil. She will listen to Our Messages and will write Our Books.

I want you to know again that I am a very High Teacher, only a few Chosen Earth people Communicate with High Teachers.

This is a part of Our Teachings, which have not been revealed on Earth yet. I am coming now to teach Earth Souls that we do exist and are much more Knowledgeable than any Soul on Earth.

October 31, 1985

Conier is speaking. You are the Earth Souls who need much Guidance. And, as we have been telling you, all must listen to Our Messages from this Very High Plane.

Again, we are all Very High Teachers and we come to Earth at this time to teach the Ways of the Planes beyond the Earth Plane.

We want all Earth Souls to Listen, Learn and Understand why they were put on Earth.

You are going to understand so much more once Our Comet arrives and brings Verification Souls so that the Entire Earth Plane will relate to Our Dimensions.

Many Souls that were a part of Earth's history will visit on the Comet with Our Teachers so that Earth Souls will understand that we definitely exist.

There is Life After Death in the sense that we shed our bodies but the Soul lives on.

All who now are living on Earth will relate to and identify with these Verification Souls from Earth's history.

They are now living in Our Dimensions and they will take on the appearance of their known Earth bodies so each of them will be recognized.

The Soul never Dies. It only Progresses to a Higher Plane and becomes a more Knowledgeable being regardless of who that Soul was in its Past Lives. It is still the same Soul.

Our aim here is to Progress and to learn more about One's Purpose. That Purpose is being a Loving and Kind Individual who Gives of Themselves to Others.

We all are working for One Divine Purpose Only – to Progress. We are ALL ONE in the sense that we work together for the Betterment of Mankind.

Many Souls have passed on whom, when they arrive here are Unaware of Our Existence because they refuse to work and Progress.

Sometimes Earth Souls never even try to think about what happens when they leave the Earth Plane so it makes it hard for us to explain when they arrive in Our Dimension.

They are Lost and can't figure out where they are. This is because they are Ignorant and Selfish, and don't want to Change their Ways at all.

Each Soul must work off every Selfish Deed it committed by doing Good for Others.

Also remember, as it has been said before, it is much harder to work here than on Earth. It's critical that all Earth Souls understand this about Our Dimension.

You will be relieved once you arrive here because there is no Pressure, and no Obligations to Material things.

You will also experience a profound sense of Freedom that you've never felt before.

Again, you <u>will be asked to work</u> off your Mistakes <u>as soon as</u> <u>you pass through</u> Our Tunnel. If y<u>ou refuse</u> you <u>must sit alone</u> in Dark Corners until you <u>make up</u> y<u>our</u> Mind to Listen and Work.

Teachers <u>always greet</u> y<u>ou</u> and show you the Way to Progress. If you Listen, then your <u>work helping</u> <u>others starts right away.</u>

Sometimes you <u>work right here helping</u> Teachers show the proper way to help Earth Souls.

At other times you just listen to <u>see what work</u> <u>you are ready for</u> and would like to do.

Then, once you <u>decide the work</u> <u>you want to do</u>, you begin. Your Work, which will be like Earthwork, <u>but now</u> you'll be working for others. And remember, <u>here we don't sleep</u> or eat; we keep working all of the time.

<u>Something else to remember</u>; <u>time does not exist here</u>. What does exist is our ongoing effort to attain all of Our Goals so that we eventually can rest. This is our Eternity; we are Happy and it is Peaceful.

The Peace we speak of is like nothing Earth Souls can begin to comprehend. It is so BEAUTIFUL here and it never changes.

When two Earth Souls are rightfully matched and have spent Earth time together they may be together here on Our Planes and be Happy Forever.

They <u>may work together</u> and be with each other to LOVE, just like they did during their existence on Earth.

For many here Life goes on with great HAPPINESS, as <u>no one here is ever unhappy.</u>

Each Soul has to <u>make their own decision</u> as to what they desire or need to accomplish to Progress from Plane to Plane as they Learn and Grow.

THE FIRST PLANE – THE ASTRAL PLANE

The first Plane next to the Earth Plane is the Astral Plane. This is where we accomplish <u>much work together</u>.

Souls on this Plane, if they wish, can help Earth Souls Learn their Lessons much easier.

They do this <u>by</u> <u>helping them</u> to get on with their Lessons Faster. Earth Souls can learn more quickly if their Minds are Open.

Most often the Souls of Families work for the Betterment of their Earth Families going back Four Generations.

They work diligently from this Astral Plane. They try to Guide their Relatives down the road that will continually aid their own Soul's Progress until they move through the Astral Plane's many levels to the Second Plane.

We will speak of this Plane more in Our Second Book.

There are not so many Earth Souls that are aware of this and Do Not Listen to their Own Family or Relatives, nor do they listen to their Spirit Teachers.

Their Minds are so Closed and their Material Ways are so much More Important to them, rather than the Ultimate Spiritual Progress of their Own Soul, which is the Earth Soul's Purpose on Earth.

This is so wrong. Eventually when they reach Our Dimension each and everyone <u>must</u> pay <u>for all of their</u> Selfishly Material Ways.

We want you to <u>realize how wrong it is</u> to be Materialistic and not correcting your Mistakes while on the Earth Plane.

When these Souls arrive on Our Planes this <u>makes their work so much harder and longer</u>.

Our time, <u>which is not measured as on</u> Earth, lasts an Eternity compared to Earth years.

Some Souls work on the Levels of the Astral Plane for 200 to 500 Earth years and more before they advance to the Second Plane.

If all Earth Souls would open their Third Eye, which is the Spiritual Eye, their Mind's Eye for Progress, while they are on Earth they would Progress much more rapidly to the Higher Planes.

There is an account of each Earth Soul's Progress when they arrive here. Each Soul knows where they made their Mistakes and again it's their Choice to Work off their Mistakes anyway they Choose.

They can help Earth Souls with their Spiritual Progression or they can work here on Our Planes.

We have many Souls who are on the Astral Plane <u>working</u> <u>hard</u> <u>trying</u> to get all Souls who are Clinging to Earth to move on to the Next Plane.

It is harder to work with Souls who are Unaware that their time on Earth has passed, as opposed to working with Earth Souls that are still in their bodies.

This takes years of Earth time, as they are Chosen according to the number of Mistakes <u>they</u> <u>made</u> when they were in their body on Earth.

Those Chosen Souls with Many Mistakes from the Earth Plane <u>willing</u> <u>to work</u> are assigned to other Souls Clinging to Earth.

EARTHBOUND SOULS

The Souls that refuse to work on Our Planes when they arrive; and did not work when they were on Earth are consigned to the Dark, or the gray area of the Lower Astral Level. Many pull back to Earth.

These are the Clinging Souls that hang around Earth refusing to work for hundreds of years. Remember, it is up to each Individual Soul to make their Choice.

Sometimes they linger, wandering the Earth Plane as Earthbound Souls, for they are Stubborn and Will Not Listen.

These Souls cause or influence the Weak, Selfish and Materialistic Earth Souls to continue their own Selfish Ways.

This is the source of the increasing Corruption on the Earth Plane.

They are confused because they do not realize that they are no longer of this Earth, nor do they know there is a continued Progressive Life After Death.

In their Selfish, Stubborn Ways they prevent their Own Progress by ignoring their work, for work is the only way to a Better Soul Life for them.

The Earth Plane is surrounded with Millions of these Earthbound Souls causing many problems by influencing Earth Souls to fulfill their Selfish Desires.

This is why these Books are so Important for all Earth Souls to read. By reading Our Books they can Open Their Minds to the Truth and their Purpose of Life on Earth so they may Change Their Ways before they reach Our Dimension.

Unfortunately, it will take many long Earth years for Earth Souls and Earthbound Souls to Learn this and begin to work for the Betterment of All Souls around them.

These Souls try to get what they want by Possessing Vulnerable, Weak Souls in Earth bodies, causing many of your Problems on Earth.

There is so much of this going on today on Earth and we want this to STOP.

It will only stop when each Earth Soul understands when their thoughts are really not what they want; they must learn to be strong and reject them.

They must realize that these thoughts come from Souls who have passed on and are trying to possess them.

Then they Must Maintain Control of Their Thoughts and Actions and not allow this or any other hovering Soul to take over and influence them in any way.

You are in Control of Yourself and must stay in Control. Earth Souls must be aware of this. Ignorance of this could make you Vulnerable.

These most Vulnerable are also the Easiest Earth Souls to Possess. They are the ones always looking for excuses for everything that happens in their Life, and now use excuses for not making Progress within Themselves.

They then allow one of these Lost Souls to come into their body, drain them of their energy and take over their Own Life on Earth.

Even when this happens the Earth Soul is still responsible for what they do wrong, and must pay for all Mistakes, including allowing one of these Souls to Control them.

For instance, a Soul that committed Murder on the Earth Plane that has passed on finds a Weak, Lazy and Non-Progressive Soul on Earth. The murderous Soul possesses the Weaker Soul's mind and forces the Earth Soul to Murder for him again.

113

These Weaker Souls <u>might say</u> in their defense "<u>that someone told them to do it</u>." Even so <u>they</u> <u>are responsible for their</u> Actions, for <u>allowing this to happen</u>.

Murderers who receive the Death Penalty <u>are the worst</u> because <u>they</u> <u>feel</u> Free <u>when driven out of their body</u> and soon learn how to Trick and Possess the Weaker Earth Soul. So the Earth Soul <u>follows the</u> Murderer's <u>desires</u> and <u>vengeful wishes</u>.

Before he commits murder his Guide tells him it is wrong. Yet, the Earth Soul doesn't Listen to his Guide. The Past Soul Controls the Earth Soul, forcing it to commit Murder, possibly again and again.

Therefore the Passing Soul gets his Gratification just like he did in his body on Earth. This is why so many Murders occur on Earth.

However, again, y<u>ou must realize that the</u> Earth Soul <u>is responsible for his or her</u> Actions, because <u>they</u> <u>allowed the</u> Passing Soul <u>to influence them</u>.

If the Earth Soul <u>does listen</u> to his Guide, then the Passing Soul <u>moves on looking</u> <u>for some other</u> Weak and Vulnerable Earth Soul to <u>possess</u>.

These Passing Souls Cling to the Earth Plane Wandering, sometimes <u>for hundreds of</u> years <u>trying</u> <u>to bend</u> Earth Souls to their will – whether it's <u>murder, thievery</u>, <u>drug</u> <u>or alcohol abuse</u>, or any <u>selfish</u> or <u>jealous deeds</u>. That's just the way it is.

Most of these Earthbound Souls accomplish <u>this time after time</u> because there are so many Lazy, Weak and Vulnerable Earth Souls, which are <u>completely</u> unaware <u>that this is happening</u>.

Again, <u>we wish to stress</u> that each Soul is Personally Responsible and Must Pay for their Actions.

We hope with these Books, the Truth we speak will inspire some Institutions on Earth to begin to teach these Souls a better way.

Sadly, no one is addressing this problem on Earth.

You all have Free Will, and it is your Choice to <u>do whatever you wish</u>.

<u>However, you must remember</u> that your Guides <u>warn you</u> through your Inner Voice, telling you what <u>is right or wrong</u>. It is your choice to Listen or Not.

This is why the Earth Plane is so weighed down by Corruption.

Earth people don't Listen to their Guides or Teachers.

They <u>think they can do just anything they want</u>; like decide when another Soul <u>should leave the</u> Earth Plane <u>when they know this is not right</u>.

Personal Responsibility should be taught at a young age throughout the Entire Earth Plane.

This would make Our Teachers work so much easier.

SO-CALLED VICTIMS OF CRIME

Now a word about those Innocent Earth Souls you call Victims of Crime or Circumstances, of <u>so-called</u> Accidents, Shootings or Disasters.

You must try and realize that Our Teachers are in Control of All Earth Souls. However, we may never infringe upon your Free Will.

These Victims are Chosen because there is No Progress <u>whatsoever being made</u> in their Earth Life and <u>we call them back to sit</u> in Darkness.

We <u>also may call</u> Souls back because they finished their Lessons and <u>it's time to move on to</u> a Higher Plane.

They have Learned and made Progress by doing Good Work for Themselves as well as others. They <u>earned their rewards</u>.

As we've said elsewhere in Our Books, there <u>are only two ways</u> that a Soul leaves the Earth Plane.

Either they are Not Listening or Not Learning, and just Creating more Mistakes bringing harm to others, or <u>their work is done</u>.

There is a reason for all so-called Victims, whether from a Shooting, Murder, Suicide, an Auto Accident, a Storm, War, Illness or Disease – whatever it is.

The only reason you are on the Earth Plane is to correct your mistakes and not make more mistakes. When your Lessons are completed, there is no need to remain on Earth any longer.

We in the Universe are only concerned with Soul Progress. This is all that counts for each and every Soul.

We place all the Non-Progressing Souls in Darkness until we Teachers have time to teach them on a <u>one-on-one basis</u>.

For the Victims there is no need to stay on Earth any longer, as their Lessons are finished. It is now time for the Soul to move on to a better Life in Our Dimension.

We are all Our Own Beings and we have to make Our Own Choices, as far as Our Own Soul's Progress is concerned.

At the <u>same time</u>, Our Teachers account for all of Our Actions on the Planes Above, and through their Wisdom and Guidance we move from Plane to Plane.

So "Bless" All Victims of Circumstance to advance and Progress on to Higher Planes as it was no longer necessary for them to remain on Earth.

Our Teachers placed on Earth in the body for a Special Mission do not return to the Universe when their Lessons are complete.

They are specially Protected from harm so they may complete their Mission. Then they are called back to work in the High Dimensions.

We now have many thousands on Earth to help with the process of Changing and Opening the Minds of Earth Souls.

ASTRAL PLANE REINCARNATION

If you are willingly working on the Astral Plane you will be Free to go and do within your work practically whatever you wish. Many travel all over the Earth Plane seeing and discovering places and things they never had a chance to experience when they were there.

This is a part of the Rewards for working here. And again, the Choice is up to each and every Soul. We have Happy Souls on the Astral Plane and in a Spiritual Way they do grow slowly here.

All who are here Learn the Truth about why and what they Lived for on Earth, and why they are stationed on this Level now in their Soul's Existence.

There is a Beautiful Garden here, which we may enjoy when we've learned our Lessons. We also let others come here after they've reached a certain level of Progress in their work.

It is on this Plane that Reincarnation occurs. Reincarnation is a way of working off your mistakes faster. You must also realize this is a Difficult way to go.

However, you may Choose and prefer to go back to the Earth Plane where Learning is faster and easier, than to remain on the Astral Plane. We again have the Choice, but we must choose one way or the other to work if we are going to better Our Souls for the Higher Planes of Accomplishment.

Reincarnation does exist and all of you that are on Earth now were there before; many are there for their second time and most are there for their Third and Final Time – never to return again. None are there for the First Time.

The Reincarnation of a Soul occurs only Three times that are of Importance on the Earth Plane. Each time you must stay and Work Off your Mistakes through a full Earth Life.

The Soul does not return to Earth after the Three Important full Lives have been completed.

Rather, they must now work towards the Next Plane, which is the Second Plane of Our Dimensions. This is a Rewarding Plane for Better Souls to Learn and Progress toward the Highest Plane.

However, with the Teachers' permission it is possible to return between your Three Full Reincarnations to clear up One Mistake by teaching the parents to be brought back on their right track and begin to make Progress. But it is only for a short time period.

This is usually some family connection and does not count as a Full Life or for Soul Progression.

For his or her short incarnation, however, unless it's for extraordinary circumstances, the Soul would already have to be Progressing on the Higher Levels of the Astral Plane for about 200 Earth Years to earn this privilege or opportunity.

Only when you've completed your Three Reincarnations on Earth and your work is accomplished will you then advance to the Second Plane – if you choose.

Some do not choose this route because they feel they are not ready to work with Earth Family Souls yet. If that's the case, they can help Teachers with the Earth Disasters. You make the Choice to either work with Earth Soul Families or assist with the work of Teachers directing Storms and Disasters on the Earth.

Then you must eventually begin your work with Earth Soul Families before you earn that right to become Couriers to Teachers or Guides to an Earth Soul on the Second Plane.

It is a Calmer Plane and has fewer Souls than the Astral Plane.

If you have arrived on this Plane and you've almost fully paid for your Mistakes you may choose to be an Earth Guide to a new, reborn Soul. You can help protect and provide them Guidance throughout their Earth Life.

You could also choose to work as a Courier Messenger to Teachers, once you have completed your responsibilities to Family.

EARTH SOULS' GUIDE

Each Soul that is reborn on the Earth Plane must have a Spiritual Guide assigned to them. Our Teachers above must approve that Guide. The Soul wanting to Reincarnate must wait for a Guide to be assigned.

Once a Soul has made its Choice to be a Spiritual Guide it must wait its turn to choose the Soul waiting to Reincarnate.

They choose their Soul from a list miles and miles long. When it's their turn they are allowed to choose just the right Soul for them.

Possibly hundreds of years in Earth time could pass before their chance comes to choose a Soul.

This is why many of Our Guides Lived on the Earth Plane so many years ago.

Again, this opportunity occurs only when the Soul that wants to be a Guide has completed its Three Important Reincarnations on the Earth Plane.

Also, it's because some of their Lessons were still left Unfinished and they must be completed before they can advance any further.

When a Soul decides to be a Guide it chooses the Soul that will be reborn on the Earth, but only with the Teacher's approval that they are best qualified to Protect and Guide that Soul on its Earth Life path.

This is so that the Guide may learn through the Chosen Soul the Lessons they themselves have not completed in their Previous Lives.

Their assignment is to help the Earth Soul and Guide them in the right direction. This could possibly be a similar direction that the Guide did not take when they existed on the Earth Plane.

Again, Our Teachers approve the Guide's assignment, which is aligned with the Guide's Lessons that they did not learn when they lived on Earth. This helps the Guide complete their Lessons through the act of guiding the Earth Soul.

Therefore, the Earth Soul Chosen is much like the Guide and one who can hopefully accomplish more than the Guide did when on Earth.

If the Earth Soul Chosen does not accomplish his or her Lessons in their Earth Life, the Guide must choose another Earth Soul and another until the Guide has completed his work. That's the only way the Guide can advance.

Once the Earth Soul passes on, the Guide's Work with that Soul is finished. However, the Teachers assess the Guide's Progress through their work with the Earth Soul's Life.

Based on this the Guide can Progress for himself. But this work goes on until the Soul Guide corrects all of his Mistakes.

Some Guides work for many thousands of years in Earth time, so it's clear that their work is not at all easy. And why is that? It's because Earth Souls don't Listen to their Guides.

How difficult it is for the Guide to communicate and accomplish their work with so many Stubborn Earth Souls.

Nevertheless, Progress must always be made however long it takes. These are all Deserving Guides working for the Betterment of Mankind, even though some of them have their Own Lessons to Complete.

Therefore, the Guide may select a Soul that will stay on Earth only a short time because their Own Lessons are correspondingly small and may be nearly complete.

The Soul that has Chosen to go to Earth for a short time is going to correct a mistake for itself, helps the Guide complete his Lessons and gets the Earth Family back on the right track.

121

However, again this will <u>not count as one</u> of the Three Important Earth Reincarnations; rather, it's <u>just to correct one</u> of that Soul's mistakes.

The main Lessons of the <u>young child leaving</u> the Earth Plane <u>sometimes shortly after</u> Birth are really Lessons to its Parents to Listen, Pay Attention and get their Lives in Order.

Regardless, all children who are born select the Parents they <u>need to teach them</u> the necessary Lessons for their Soul's Progress. There is always a Purpose and Reason for every Reincarnation.

A child leaving the Earth <u>suddenly</u> does <u>not affect</u> the Soul <u>of the child.</u> The Soul came to work <u>off one of its</u> Past Mistakes. At the same time, the Guide has learned all of his Lessons and now he <u>can move on</u>.

Some Guides are with an Earth Soul for <u>a long time</u> because both the Guide and the Earth Soul have many Lessons to be learned.

Many Earth Souls are placed with Guides to teach on Earth; therefore the Guide must work with a High Teacher in order to <u>rectify</u> his Mistakes.

Sometimes Earth Souls do <u>not co-operate</u>; they <u>are then removed</u> from Earth and made to wait until they learn that their Mistakes <u>must be paid for</u>.

This is no fault of the Guide that the Earth Soul does Not Listen or Pay Attention. That Soul is called back and the Guide <u>moves on to select another</u> Soul ready to Reincarnate to Earth.

Guides choose to work with Earth Souls from Planes Higher than the Second Plane or continue working as they Progress from Plane to Plane.

The Higher the Plane the Soul on Earth comes from the more Important their Mission that the Earth Soul must complete.

All High Teachers must <u>receive</u> <u>permission to work through</u> the Earth Soul from their assigned Guide. Once <u>permission is given</u>, the High Teacher may work directly with the Earth Soul.

Much can be accomplished when this happens if the Earth Soul is <u>working</u> <u>in co-operation with</u> the High Teacher.

That Soul <u>could advance from</u> Teacher to Teacher and Plane to Plane quite <u>rapidly</u> <u>while still on</u> the Earth Plane.

All Great Works are taught through High Teachers working with these Souls on Special Important Missions.

<u>A good example</u> of this is Jan. She is the <u>instrument that</u> Our High Teachers have Chosen to write Our Books; <u>she advanced from</u> Teacher-to-Teacher and Plane-to-Plane quite rapidly in a <u>short time co-operating with</u> Our Work. Also, Ron has advanced to a High Plane with his Healing Work.

We of the Universe will forever be Grateful to Jan and Ron for bringing this Information to All Earth Souls. Each High Teacher that Jan earned has worked directly through her pen bringing Truth and Accuracy.

When a Guide <u>works directly</u> <u>he can only</u> <u>work with his assigned</u> Soul for that Soul's Full Life on Earth.

After their Direct Mission working with an Earth Soul, a Teacher may <u>move on to teach other</u> Souls on Earth or in Our Dimension, or move up to a Higher Plane because <u>their work is complete</u>.

However, sometimes more than One Guide will contact an Earth Soul; again with the assigned Guide's <u>permission</u> to work <u>with a special need for</u> that Soul.

These Guides could be called on by your Guide or sent by High Teachers to <u>help</u> <u>in a certain area of the</u> Earth Soul's Lessons.

If you have more than One Guide around you, they are usually Specialists that focus on a <u>certain area</u> and may work with you <u>during a special</u> <u>growth</u> <u>period of</u> your Life.

They also <u>may</u> <u>come and</u> <u>go as needed</u> or <u>leave when their</u> <u>purpose with</u> <u>you is complete</u>. They <u>may</u> <u>even be working</u> <u>with more</u> <u>than</u> One Soul.

These Guides work in co-operation with Souls from the Astral Plane. In many cases they are Family Souls trying to help their Loved Ones on Earth.

This is the <u>case with the majority</u> of Earth Souls because the Astral Plane <u>is overcrowded</u> with Souls working <u>hard trying to correct</u> <u>their mistakes</u> to move on to Higher Planes.

Many Souls working around Earth people are Family Souls, the Souls of <u>friends</u>, or Souls <u>attracted to</u> you.

It is their Choice to help Earth Souls with their Lives to clear their Own Slates.

These Souls <u>come and</u> <u>go according</u> to one's needs. <u>They</u> sincerely <u>want to help</u> and they are <u>working</u> <u>hard trying</u> <u>to</u> help many, many Earth Souls.

However, again, each and every Earth Soul only has the One Guide Assigned to them at their Birth on Earth. That Guide <u>remains</u> <u>with them throughout</u> their Earth Lives.

RETURNING HOME TO THE UNIVERSE

December 4, 1985

Conier is here from a High Dimension to say Hello to all on Earth.

I assure you that all Souls that are on the Earth Plane came from Our Dimensions and will return home here again someday.

However, there are so many Earth Souls that don't know where they go when they leave the Earth Plane.

Since there is no real Earth proof as of this year it is very hard for Earth Souls to believe in Life After Death.

Many have already accepted this because they are Listening to their Inner Voice or even through personal experiences that opened their Minds.

Please be assured; there is Life for Eternity once you leave the Earth Plane.

This concrete proof will come when Our Comet Ship arrives. Lands and Materializes on Earth with Our High Teachers on board.

We do understand that Earth Souls have a difficult time understanding this concept while on Earth.

However, if more Earth Souls would realize this, Life on Earth would be so fulfilling for them and they would be better prepared for their continuous Life.

There have been so many on Earth over the years that have worked Our Ways and learned their Lessons to move on to Higher Planes of Progress.

Here in Our Dimension we Progress higher and higher and have earned that right by helping many Souls.

Sometimes we help Earth Souls, and sometimes Dimension Souls. It doesn't matter where the Souls reside as long as Progress is made.

This is Critical and no Positive Progress can be overlooked. The key to Helping Others is in the Heart of the Soul, which is that LOVE for Your Neighbor over Yourself.

Who is giving here is So Important because we do not allow takers, those who use others for their own benefit.

We all work together, Soul with Soul, to accomplish Our Aims and Learn our Lessons.

All of us here know how Important it is for us to make up for all of Our Mistakes, Learn our Lessons and make Soul Progress.

When you lose the Material Things that are all left on Earth; we all become equal and all we have to show – or need to show – is the Good we have accomplished.

We also still have Our Free Will and we must want to improve ourselves on every level in order to Progress.

If you so Choose you will then experience a feeling of Self-Accomplishment for ALL.

Then to improve yourself your work becomes long, hard and tedious to fully accomplish. But all Souls must work to Progress sooner or later.

Now if Earth Souls would try and understand this while they are still on Earth they could begin to work for the Betterment of all Mankind, thus attaining Great Soul Progress.

Please Learn to Give of Yourselves. Complete Unselfish Giving and do it Willingly, without expecting anything in return. Only then is your Own Soul Progressing.

If you do this you will start feeling a sense of warmth within yourself and your Life on Earth will go much smoother. You will experience more Peace within your own Heart.

LOVE is Important and to Attain Sincere LOVE you must Give of Yourself to all around you. When you do this your Life on Earth will seem so much more rewarding.

You yourself will <u>see the difference in the</u> <u>people</u> <u>you attract around</u> <u>you</u>. That saying, "**Like Attracts Like**," is so true.

So why not <u>ask for the</u> Highest and Best <u>to be around</u> <u>you at all times</u>?

You can then accomplish so much more in your Lifetime on Earth.

MORE ON THE NEW DIMENSION REVIEWED

December 17, 1985

Conier is here with Messages for the Entire Earth Plane to know that Our Dimension is an Eternal Place.

When you decide to Reincarnate back to Earth, where you can learn much Faster, you carry your Previous Mistakes with you.

You are all on the Earth Plane for a <u>short time only</u> and you must make good use of your time there to correct all of your Previous Mistakes.

While you are living on the Earth Plane we are constantly working with you to help you Progress.

Each Soul is placed there to Learn and make up for all the <u>wrong things they</u> <u>have done</u>.

Once you fully realize this much work can be done and Great Spiritual Progress can be attained.

We want more Progress to be made on Earth than has been made in the past. As we have said previously, that's why we have stopped all New Souls and all Good Souls from returning to the Earth Plane.

More specifically, New Souls are not being Created for the Earth Plane anymore and haven't been for a long time.

Instead we have Created Our New Dimension, of <u>which we</u> <u>have spoken of before, as a</u> place for these New Souls and Good Souls to go where they Live in Peace.

Good Souls, again, are those that have <u>already</u> <u>paid for their</u> <u>mistakes</u> whether here in Our Dimensions or on the Earth Plane.

We have explained this more than once because Earth Souls must know and fully understand that we made a Corruption-free New Earth, Our Dimension, because of the Earth Plane's Materialistic condition.

The Corruption, combined with Souls that are not listening, has created an imbalance on Earth.

Once these Good Souls arrive in Our Dimension from Earth, they are sent to Our New Dimension. They have free will to Choose to enjoy the Happiness they find there, the Happiness that they have earned.

The same is happening for all of the Souls that have been working hard in Our Dimensions. They are also being sent to Our New Dimension instead of Reincarnating back on Earth.

God Creates New Souls and only The Universe, which is a part of God, can do this, as the Entire Universe and all within the Universe is God's Creation.

God is the Highest of Teachers from the Highest of Planes. Only a few of Our High Teachers have yet reached these High Planes, but they do exist for the Betterment of Mankind.

It is the ultimate goal of all High Teachers to Create New, Clean Souls. All these New Clean Souls are now being sent to Our New Dimension instead of being born on the Earth Plane, thus keeping them free of all Corruption.

This is a Beautiful Planet that exists right now halfway between Our Planes. This halfway mark is not conceivable in Earth numbers and minds but we assure you, it sits high up in Our Planes of Progress.

The many Animals and all of Nature that exists on this Planet are pure; nothing is needed or wanted there because all is given freely to each and every Soul.

There is Much LOVE on this Dimensional Planet for all to find. So much Peace and Happiness exists there because the Souls that reside there, as we have said, have all paid for their mistakes or they are New Pure Souls.

It is time for the Souls that have worked hard to rest and Enjoy their Life, and after a period of rest, they may wish to work in Peace and Harmony on this Dimension or on the Planes of Progress.

Because Free Will exists here, Souls that Choose to do their work are Souls that want to Progress. Thus, they don't remain long on this Dimension.

This New Dimensional Planet does more Good work than any of the other Planets in All Our Universes.

The work they are doing is much like on Earth, that of Helping Others. This exists but it is purely voluntarily; no one asks them to work from this Planet.

However, Our Work will never be finished until all Souls have earned their way to this Dimensional Planet from the millions upon millions existing on the Astral Plane, to the untold numbers of Souls sitting in Dark Corners.

You soon will understand more about the Planes, once we complete the work on Our Next Book "**Many Planes Above**."

However, for now we want to talk about the Earth Plane, and the Next Plane above, the Astral Plane.

Each Soul is Special and Important to the Earth Plane. Many Souls placed on Earth Ignore their Missions, which only delays their Own Progress.

When an Earth Soul stops Giving from Themselves LOVE and Kindness for all, they must return to where they stopped and start their Lessons over, paying for each Wrongdoing.

Very few Earth Souls realize this and when they arrive here they face a definitive account of their wrongdoings.

When they are told to go back to a certain point in their Life and start over they refuse.

Therefore, again they sit in Dark Corners or wander around the Earth Plane ignoring the fact that their Earth Life is over and that the Soul must move on to further its Progress.

There are so many of these Souls that must undo their mistakes, but simply refuse to work.

Nothing changes here except that the physical body is shed. There is no Money, but nevertheless all must come here to make Progress.

SOUL MATES

Conier is here. I am here to tell you about Soul Mates. When Soul Mates reunite it is because they are much in LOVE. In Our Dimension LOVE is So Important.

You must learn to LOVE <u>everything</u> <u>you do, say</u> or feel. When you do this you will have made so much Progress.

Two Souls that have earned this LOVE may stay together to carry on their Progress to another Plane.

When they are sent back to Earth to make up for their Mistakes from a Previous Life the two Soul Mates could be separated for a time.

However, they <u>could be reunited</u> on the Earth Plane to <u>work together</u>. Sometimes Souls on Earth are matched with their Soul Mate <u>temporarily</u> <u>to make up</u> <u>for small mistakes</u>.

These matches are brought together at different times of the Earth Life and it depends on the Lessons they are there to Learn as to how much Earth time they will <u>spend together</u>.

When a Soul on Earth has mastered most of his or her Lessons their Soul Mate is meant to make the balance of their Earth Life Happy and Rewarding <u>for both</u> Soul Mates.

When an Earth Soul meets another Earth Soul and feels like they are Soul Mates, most of the <u>time these feelings are correct</u>. But an Earth Soul does <u>not always</u> <u>earn the right to be with</u> their Soul Mate.

Sometimes it takes much more work and many Lessons to be learned before Soul Mates <u>can be together again</u>.

This is because they've not yet Learned their Lessons or Corrected their Mistakes from a Previous Life.

However, it could be their fate to <u>meet and remind</u> each Soul of their Lessons to come, and only when they are learned <u>are they</u> <u>allowed to be together</u>, and live in Happiness.

Again it is their Choice. If you understand that <u>your work is not yet finished</u> then you will try that much harder <u>so that</u> <u>you can be together</u>.

If you do not accomplish this on Earth and you are already an Old Soul then you <u>must work it off</u> in the Next Plane. If you are a younger Soul then you must Reincarnate back to the Earth Plane to do your work.

Spirit Souls in Our Dimension fall in LOVE regularly. Since Free Will resides here you may also choose a Good Soul to LOVE and <u>work with</u> or you may choose a Soul you knew in a Previous Life on the Earth Plane.

Again, it all comes down to Free Choice. Once a Soul lands in Our Dimension, and <u>if they</u> <u>are working</u> and Progressing, then all Earth Lives are <u>clear to them</u>.

Only the Souls that <u>refuse to work are not able to see clearly</u> another's Earth Life.

We have Good Souls in Our Dimension waiting <u>hundreds of years to work</u> and find Happiness with their Soul Mate. This will happen for them if and when their Soul Mate <u>wants to work</u>.

If their Soul Mate <u>refuses to</u> Listen and begin to work they will have to sit in Dark Corners while the Good Soul Mate continues waiting for them to <u>make up</u> <u>their mind to work</u>. <u>That's the only</u> <u>way</u> <u>they</u> <u>can be together</u>.

Once again, if Earth Souls would learn that Soul Life is Eternal and do their work on the Earth Plane, they could look forward to Eternal LOVE with their Soul Mate, and be so much Happier.

Everyone has a Soul Mate they are together with now, working towards being together or waiting for them in Our Dimensions to Pay for Mistakes and move on.

However, the Earth Plane has fewer Soul Mates than Our Dimension, and most Souls completing their Third Earth Life now will finally rejoin their Soul Mates for Eternity.

If you have not rejoined your Soul Mate by the end of your last Earth Life, both Soul Mates must work very hard to reunite here.

Again, we repeat that only by hard work can you accomplish this.

Soul Mates are Important. Eventually we want each Soul reunited with their Soul Mate because by working together we can accomplish so much more, especially when LOVE is involved.

This is LOVE of Life, Eternal LOVE of All Mankind. LOVE for all those around you. Giving of Yourself Always for the sake of Others and for your own Growth.

Earth Souls are alone in an Earth Life because they are Learning about LOVE, and the LOVE of the Universe and all of Mankind. This is their task.

So often Souls go through an entire Earth Life doing this – Giving LOVE to Others on Earth.

Too many Souls need this Universal LOVE so we send them Souls from Previous Lives who have already done this work, either on Earth or in Our Dimension.

In Our Dimension all Souls work to help those who need to Grow and learn their Lessons.

Teachers work regularly to straighten out Souls that are Lost in Dark Corners.

However, we don't have enough Teachers to go around for everyone. That means some must wait until we can get to each and every Soul to explain their purpose in Our Eternal World, the purpose of constant Growth and Learning.

Our World of Learning is far beyond any Earth Knowledge and we are All Creatures of God doing Our Part to keep the Planes Progressing.

134

We work on Levels according to where we have earned Our Way, and as we Progress we Learn more and more about the Being of Soul and Our Purpose.

Each and every one of us is Special. As we have said, we are all accounted for as we Teach, Share and Help Others to Learn.

Helping others all around us is a part of Learning, something that the Earth Plane Greatly Needs.

**We are all working towards Peace of Mind and Happiness.'
Peace of Mind, which is difficult for Earth Soul's to comprehend.**

All of the things we do are for Special Reasons.

At the risk of repeating ourselves, we are now going to summarize what you must know and fully understand.

We are placed on the Earth Plane to Progress, to Learn and Teach Others and Ourselves the way to Peace of the Spiritual Soul.

So many ignore the fact that they are on the Earth Plane for the purpose of growing towards Higher Knowledge of Existence, for the satisfaction of their Own Soul.

No one likes to be Lost, but there are a Great number of Lost Souls on Earth with no purpose.

This is why there is so much Terror, Corruption, Selfishness and Hatred that exists on the Earth Plane today.

Since this is the Learning Plane and there are Souls that do not want to Learn, we are changing the Earth to another Dimension, a more Positive Learning Plane.

We are already working with and placing Souls on this Dimension so they can Learn, Souls that have relatively few Lessons to Learn remaining from Previous Lives.

Everyone must move on to Higher Planes to Advance and once you do all works become much clearer and more Productive.

The work on Our Lower Planes is much like Earthwork, as we must return to the age where Our Progress stopped on Earth and make up for all Our Wrongdoings from the Earth Plane.

We all must Learn and Earn the right to exist in this Dimension and we do so without competing with one another.

All in Our Dimension we work hand-in-hand to satisfy the needs of Our Souls. We still have the urge to accomplish Our Dreams and Wishes as when we left the Earth Plane.

It is so satisfying to know that we are all allowed to do this up here. It is equally satisfying to go and see what we missed on Earth, but we must simultaneously Help Other Souls along the way.

All of Our Soul's wants and needs are furnished here on Our Planes. Since there are no Material Gains here at all, we are talking about Soul Satisfaction.

The Soul is always hungry to Learn and Progress for the Betterment of all Mankind. Our ultimate Goal is Peace of the Inner Soul.

When we've accomplished this we experience a tremendous urge to move on to Learn more and more as we Progress from Plane to Plane.

Our Life here is just like Earth Life, however. There is no Day or Night, and no stopping to rest unless we are working through the Earth Plane. Then the Spirit Soul must rest.

The Rewards of Progress are such an Inner Sense of Tranquility and Happiness that the Soul thirsts for more to do, see and learn.

Learning on Our Dimension never stops. The feeling of accomplishment is far more Rewarding than anything on the Earth Plane.

There is never-ending work here for everyone and Our Existence has no year, day or measure of time, for we have ALWAYS EXISTED and there are many more Souls here than on Earth.

GOD IS THE WHOLE UNIVERSE that does not Judge the Soul's Purpose or Existence but is Always accepted at any form of Existence. GOD is most Forgiving of Our Mistakes and Lessons of Learning.

GOD LOVES ALL SOULS and Cares about the Existence of Each and Every Soul.

There is no Punishment and there are no Consequences <u>ever from</u> GOD. This comes from the Soul <u>exercising</u> His or Her own GOD-given Free Will, and ultimately the power to Choose.

GOD is <u>forever</u> <u>giving</u> to All Souls and <u>never taking</u> <u>from</u> or Punishing any Soul.

This was Conier's last contact for Book I. But he did answer many of my questions and I entered the answers in different Chapters according to subject.

The next Teacher was "Mary Todd Lincoln," who preferred to be called Jennifer, a name she always liked.

I asked Jennifer to write a page about herself that we could enter into the Book. The next page presents what she wrote with a copy of the actual writing inserted on the following page139.

HIGH TEACHER JENNIFER – "MARY TODD LINCOLN"

Jennifer is here and I am pleased to be part of this Universal Book for all Earth to read.

I am a High Teacher of the Universe and I come to Earth to help all Earth Souls Progress.

When I was on Earth, I was very much aware of Universal Existence and I always felt there was Life After Death.

In my last days on Earth I communicated daily with my Husband, Abe.

I was called "Mary Todd Lincoln," and I did contribute much to all Earth People.

I did help my husband with his work and tried to see that he was always happy.

After he left the Earth Plane he carried out his work from the Universe to Earth, still helping the United States. Today he still works with the United States and helps to bring Peace to the Earth Plane.

I changed my name to Jennifer because I Love this name, and this is Our Choice when we arrive in the Universe.

My Husband and I are Twin Soul Mates and we are together always working to bring Peace and Love to the Entire Earth Plane for the Betterment of ALL MANKIND.

"Mary Todd Lincoln"

Abraham Lincoln chose to be a Guide to President Ronald Regan, to continue his unfinished work for the United States. He now has joined in the Universe with Jennifer "Mary Todd Lincoln" his Twin Soul to work as one, continuing their work for the United States and a better World of Peace and Love.

Abraham Lincoln wants the World to know that the United States of America will Change The World. Next is Jennifer's actual writing.

Jennifer is here and I am pleased to be a part of this Universal Book for all earth to read. I am a High Teacher of the Universe and I come to earth to help all earth souls progress. When I was on earth I was very much aware of Universal existence and I always felt their was life after death. In my last days on earth I communicated daily with my husband Abe. I was called Mary Todd Lincoln and I did contribute a lot to all earth people. I did help my husband with his work and tryed to see that he was always happy. After he left the earth plane he carried out his work from the Universe to earth still helping the U.S.A. Today he still works with the U.S.A. and helps to bring peace to the earth plane. I changed my name to Jennifer because I love this name and this is our choice when we arrive in the Universe. My husband & I, are twin soulmates and we are together, always working to bring Peace & Love, to all the earth plane, For Betterment of All Mankind.

Jennifer

January 25, 1986

Jennifer is here. I am a High Teacher presently from the Ninth Plane and I am here to teach you about Our Dimension and Our Ways of the Spiritual World that exist after Death on the Earth Plane.

Jan, I will be Progressing to much Higher Planes when my work with you <u>is finished</u>.

139

I want to say that Reincarnation is a fact. All Souls that have lived in Our Dimension and the Earth Plane have been Reincarnated.

Until now no one could prove that a Soul has lived another Life, some Twice and others three times.

Those Three Reincarnations are needed to atone for Mistakes. Each and every Soul must atone for their Mistakes and all of us here quite understand what that means.

On the Earth Plane they are not aware of the Mistakes they make so many keep making them over and over again.

When Earth Souls are reborn on the Earth Plane they know why they are being sent back. But many choose to ignore their Purpose.

They just cannot understand that it takes time to correct their Mistakes. When they ignore that they must work off their Mistakes once returned to the Earth Plane, we remind them.

Time and again we warn Earth Souls that they must Correct Previous Mistakes, and they choose to ignore these warnings.

We are writing these Books through Jan to make Earth Souls aware of the Constant Progress we expect them to make.

When things do not work out your way it is because you are definitely not Paying Attention to your Mission of Progress.

Time after time we warn you what is expected of you to live on Earth, and sadly, most Souls again choose to ignore it.

They go on with their Lives as though they have no obligation to themselves or others.

When this happens their Earth Lives become more and more complicated and nothing goes their way at all.

Some acquire Material gains and still they don't listen. They ignore the reason they are being blessed with all of this support and all of these nice things.

Each and everyone have earned it from a Previous Life, and they are entitled to it in this Life.

However, they have forgotten that they must Share their Wealth, their Time and their Lives to Help Others if they are going to Progress in this particular Earth Life.

When they forget this they must start all over when they arrive in Our Dimension.

Many Earth Souls leave the Earth before it is their time. This is because they have accomplished their Lessons. Or they are Not Listening and are wasting their Earth time without making any Progress.

Our High Teachers feel this is a waste and call them back to Our Dimension to learn the hard way.

We are so busy up here that we do not waste any time with them when they arrive. They must sit in the **Dark** waiting for Teachers to find the time to restore them to the working road again.

Only the Souls who make Progress on Earth are allowed to start work immediately.

Today we must try and Improve Ourselves on the Earth Plane to Progress Faster in Our Dimension.

When a Soul is called back to Our Dimension it passes through a long Dark Tunnel with a Beautiful Bright Light shining at the end of the Tunnel. Once you reach the Light you must start working again.

Sadly, so many cannot reach the Light at the end of the Tunnel.

Mostly this is because they are unwilling to let go of the Earth Plane. They are Stubborn, Unwilling to Work and are unaware of the Soul Life that comes After the Death of the Earth body.

141

You then must sit as other Teachers have written and wait for a High Teacher to come and get you. These are also Souls who <u>are unwilling</u> to accept that their Earth <u>body</u> <u>is now</u> gone.

The Minds of Many Earth Souls are closed to Life-After-Death and this also stops their Progress.

When all Earth Souls <u>accept</u> that there is Life After Death then much Progress can be made.

After a Good Working Soul reaches the Light at the end of the Tunnel then their Work Continues in Our Dimension.

All of your Loved Ones <u>always</u> <u>greet</u> <u>you</u> and they help Guide you in the <u>right direction</u>.

You are first taken to the High Teachers who explain the Past Mistakes that you <u>must rectify</u>. Once you know and are willing to Correct your Errors your work begins.

Soon after your arrival you are allowed to verify your Earth body. You can attain <u>any</u> <u>age or looks that</u> <u>you wish</u> for verification.

Of course this is not a human body, it is called a Soul body.

Then you can try this body and see if <u>you are comfortable with</u> your Choice of looks. If not, you may change it.

You are Free to go wherever you <u>wish to do</u> <u>your work</u>. Many <u>travel back</u> to Earth to see what <u>they</u> <u>didn't</u> <u>get a chance to see</u> when they Lived there.

January 31, 1986

Jennifer is here to write through Jan and finish Our Book I, **"Our Earth And Beyond**." We are writing these Books on behalf of all in Our Dimension for all Earth Souls to read.

It will touch the Hearts of Earth Souls to Create more Positive action, and more LOVE will exist on Earth making more Progress for Earth Souls.

142

Many Earth Souls will read these Books, and Changes in Attitude will occur all over the Earth Plane, Changing the Vibration of the Earth's entire Atmosphere.

The purpose of Book I; is to make all Earth Souls aware of Our Dimension and see that the Minds of Earth people Open, that their Inner Souls expand Spiritually.

We also write this hoping for more understanding for all on any Level.

The Information in these Books comes Directly from Our Dimension, which does exist with Life Eternal above the Earth Plane.

It is a Dimension without time or Material gain where the Highest Teachers work and Progress for the Betterment of all Mankind.

All of Our Teachers here are trying to Open The Minds and Souls of the Earth Plane to realize there is Life After Death and Progress does go on for the Betterment of each and every Soul.

Once this happens and each individual Soul makes Changes to Progress, their Earth Life will become so much easier with greater Happiness and Contentment.

It will also make their return to the Higher Planes so much easier.

We in this Dimension want to Change All Attitudes on the Earth Plane; we want All Selfishness Stopped and Corruption Ended. We want much more LOVE surrounding the Earth Plane.

This LOVE consists of Giving of yourselves to the Betterment of another, and Sharing more Help and Knowledge with others who are willing to Learn.

We want Souls to Grow Spiritually, instead of blocking out the Truth and the Purpose of the Earth's growing period.

There are too many Souls on Earth that know nothing of the Truth, yet are taking the World in their own hands.

They are Teaching Lies to poor Earth Souls and guiding them in the wrong direction with their Outlandish Ways that lead to the Destruction of the Soul.

When this occurs to an Earth Soul it takes many Earth years for these Souls to open up to the Truth, many years before they are able to start all over again to make Soul Progress.

So many Poor Lost Souls are waiting in Darkness to get on with their unfinished work, wondering where they are because they did not understand – because they were misguided from the Earth Plane.

They should never fear Death. That's because when they die, they are making Definite Progress too much better ways and to a state of Happiness that cannot ever be found on the Earth Plane.

The ultimate Happiness that the Earth Plane has to offer cannot begin to compare with the Happiness that awaits each and every Soul in Our Dimension willing to Give, Learn, Work and LOVE without looking for Rewards in Return.

Rewards are automatically there for Our Good Souls who Progress on a Very Positive Level.

Earth Souls must be aware of Our Existence and that we are all here to help for the Betterment of all Mankind.

Once an Earth Soul Opens his or her Mind and Soul to Our Existence, Progress occurs at a much faster pace and results come so much easier for him or her and their Soul.

Definite Growth and Progress will occur; LOVE will fulfill the Inner Soul's needs and with this Improvement; will be working towards a Very High Plane of Knowledge and Wisdom.

So many Earth Souls never realize there is a Purpose to their Earth Life, that it is a place to Grow and Learn.

We are giving you Our Books to teach all Earth Souls about this Dimension, and to make them understand that each and everyone of them will return here someday after their Earth time is finished.

All those Earth Souls who want to better their Soul and to make Progress during their Earth time must be aware that they have to Change their Ways while they are still on the Earth Plane.

To do this while on Earth is the easy way. Once you arrive in Our Dimension it takes much longer to accomplish a good deed for another, compared to the Earth Plane. That's because time does not exist here, nor does your Physical body.

For example, if you performed a simple Kindness for another that could take five minutes on Earth, those minutes in Spirit Work time would take years in Earth time to do the same.

It is difficult for us to explain time. But we hope that you will be able to comprehend some of what we are trying to tell you.

February 26, 1986

Jennifer is here. I want to tell you more about Our Dimension of the Powerful Universe.

I would like to speak about Our Ways here and how they affect Earth Plane Souls. We here in the Universe, as well as on Earth, are all Souls of One Universe.

We work here to Accomplish Our Aims just like the Earth Souls work for Material things, such as Money, as their object of existence.

This may be fine on Earth, but here we have no need for Money. Our Rewards are less Selfish and more Selfless, more giving. LOVE exists here that fulfills Our Inner Soul.

All Earth should be aware that this exists because when your Earth time is finished you return to Our Dimension to account for your Progress during your Earth Life. The Progress that you made, or didn't make, is all that is really important once you arrive here.

To LOVE ALL of MANKIND, and to love Oneself and others equally, is critical. If this LOVE is real and whole, it brings great Self Assurance and Satisfaction for your Soul's Progress.

145

It is <u>so beneficial</u> when you are able to Open your Soul fully in **UNIVERSAL LOVE.**

You accomplish this on the Earth Plane by being Understanding. Patient, and LOVING to Other Souls struggling to Progress. This is a Significant part of Growing Within Oneself.

Satisfaction and <u>repayment always occurs</u> for everyone able to take the time to do this while on Earth.

To Open your Inner Soul to Our Existence can only help the LOVE of Earth Existence, and your time there will <u>be much more beneficial</u> for you.

It is so hard for Earth Souls <u>to realize this;</u> therefore you are making little Progress <u>ridding yourself</u> of Negativity. If you could realize this it would <u>benefit</u> your Soul's Progress.

Each and everyone must try harder to Change their Negative Ways. They must try harder to Open their Channels to the Universe above for more help from Our Guides, Teachers and Messengers to make your Earth Life more satisfactory within you.

As we have said before, once all of you working on Earth Open up to the Universe you will be much Happier and you will make more Progress.

By believing the Universe does Exist, GOD is <u>willing to help at all times</u> and can only improve your direction.

We all work here with UNIVERSAL LOVE and Understanding. Our Work is hard and we need more Co-operation from Earth Souls to Grow and Progress on Our Dimension.

If more Earth Souls would realize this and work in Co-operation with the Universe, then more of Earth's <u>suffering would cease.</u>

The way it must be done is to Open up to Work towards LOVE OF ALL around you, LOVE of LIFE, LOVE of BEAUTY and LOVE of EACH OTHER.

Only when this is accomplished can the Whole Universe Progress for the Fulfillment of ALL MANKIND.

Someday this will be accomplished, as we now are Opening the Minds of many Souls to Our Existence and proving we do Exist, and are here to help at all times.

Too much Negativity exists On Earth now and we want all this Changed to make the Universe Beautiful.

We now are busy connecting Soul Mates to work together on Earth for Progress, Knowledge and Growth.

Many Earth Souls each day are now starting to realize this and we ask for more to search their Souls for LOVE.

More Souls need to take a look at their Lives and change themselves for the better so we may bring more Soul Mates together on Earth.

Only in this way can we help make the lives of people on Earth Happier and help make more Progress towards Inner Fulfillment.

Some of this is already happening now, and the sooner we get it done the Better all Earth Souls will be.

You must realize we are still in Control of the Earth and in control of each and every Soul, tracking each Soul's Progress and Mistakes.

There must be an Accounting for All Mistakes. That's why it is critical for each and everyone to think before they act – especially when they know what they are doing is wrong.

If they would Change their Ways, they would realize that Life for them in the end would turn out much easier. Their accomplishments would generate greater rewards, and all would receive more Guidance and Happiness.

Each and every Earth Soul is there to Learn Lessons and to Correct Mistakes.

147

Until those Mistakes are Corrected, Life for them <u>must be</u> <u>conquered</u>. With great determination, y<u>ou must believe in</u> y<u>ourself</u> if you're going to Progress.

The Universe knows that PROGRESS TO MOVE AHEAD WITH MUCH LOVE is the answer to all that each Soul seeks.

Whether the Earth Soul knows this in its Consciousness or not, nevertheless it is within their Soul and all of us here want Earth Souls to <u>know this</u>.

As Progress is being made on Earth you can ask your Protecting Guide for <u>help</u>. <u>That is why</u> <u>they</u> <u>have been with</u> <u>you since</u> Birth, <u>and</u> <u>will stay</u> <u>with</u> <u>you until</u> Death – <u>to help</u> <u>you</u> Progress.

In return you help them to also Progress in Our Dimension. It is all out of LOVE and <u>co-operation for and with each other that this can</u> <u>be accomplished</u>.

When Soul Mates are <u>brought together on</u> Earth and <u>know they</u> <u>belong together</u> and <u>work together,</u> only then can they make significant Progress and much can LOVE Grow between them.

When it does a strong feeling of Fulfillment happens between these two Souls and they become <u>the strength</u> of the Earth being.

If a Soul Mate has not returned to Earth at the same time, it is because the Earth Soul is sent alone to Work Out their Mistakes and to complete a Mission for the Universe.

Their Soul Mate works from the Universe to help them at all times to complete their Earth Mission.

This accounts for Souls working on Earth alone for Spiritual Growth and for Giving of Themselves to Help Others.

There are many Teachers on Earth placed there to Teach Our Ways and to open the Minds of Earth Souls.

<u>You are never alone</u>, whether your Soul Mate is there on Earth with you or working from Our Dimension.

Each and every Soul has a purpose and must <u>work to accomplish that purpose</u>.

We all are looking for complete Fulfillment of Heart and Soul which ultimately leads to a POWERFUL LOVE OF ALL MANKIND.

We now summarize, repeating much of what we have said, as we realize Earth Souls have <u>fallen off the tracks</u> and are Not Paying Attention <u>to their purpose</u>.

People must Help each Other More, and patiently recognize that their needs will be realized. They must recognize that <u>everything happens for a reason</u>. There is <u>always an answer</u>, always a way to Change a Situation. If <u>everyone understood</u> this, Life itself would go smoother.

So many Souls make it complicated and yet it is so simple. The Universe does not want to make Life on Earth difficult and trying. It is the Earth Soul that makes it difficult, not the Universe.

<u>It is not intended to be that way</u> <u>at all</u>. Life on Earth was <u>intended for each</u> Soul to Grow and Progress and accomplish a great deal.

However, Earth Souls <u>let too many</u> <u>things</u> <u>get in the way</u> – including their Ignorance, Egos <u>and obsession with</u> Money.

People give Money too much Power over them, **over their lives**.

Also, Souls <u>forget the reason why</u> <u>they</u> <u>were</u> <u>put on</u> Earth, and this Creates many Hardships, including Sickness and Disease.

So many of Earth's Problems are rooted in Selfishness and the thirst for Power.

We all have Free Choice. We can Control Our Choices and Change Our Ways at <u>any</u> <u>given time</u> in Our Earth Life.

Work <u>is always hard</u>, but in the <u>end it will</u> pay <u>off</u> in your own Progress and Happiness.

149

The easier we make it for ourselves the better it will go. Complaining about everything is easy; it is an excuse not to put any effort into doing what must be done. When you do this, it only makes it harder to get there.

At times all on Earth use excuses to avoid what must be done. Closing your eyes to reality only prolongs what must be, and what ultimately will be in the end.

Each and every Soul that refuses to do the hard work that leads to Progress brings Sickness upon itself. Then they are left sitting until they want to change their direction towards Progress.

Sometimes it takes a serious hardship – whether an Illness, Injury or Tragedy – to inspire or motivate the Soul to embark on a Progressive path.

So many expect others to do it for them and this cannot be. Also, many are too Negative. Negativity brings Illness, and if you take on enough Negativity you could drain your Earth body into a state of collapse.

You must take greater care of your body on Earth to keep it functioning properly. Create habits that support you while you are here and be careful what you put into your body.

For example, proper eating habits, fresh air and sleep are required to stay Healthy.

So many Earth Souls neglect their body's needs and fail to appreciate what it needs to function properly. The good news is that more are starting to realize this.

You can enjoy all pleasures of the Earth in MODERATION. Too many never consider this at all. Then they wonder why they become ill.

It is time to take a good long look at yourself and how you are treating YOU. It's time to ask yourself what improvements you can make to make You a Happier Person and your Life more Fulfilled.

The Earth does provide Healing for everyone. The Universe does care about you. You are Important and we want you to Progress with Our Understanding and Help.

Only when you are aware of this can you and all of us make your Life on Earth Happier.

The Earth could be a Much Better and Happier place if you would welcome the Universe's help and ask us to Guide your Life and keep you on the right path.

We want to Help You all Progress to Higher Planes when your Earth Life is completed.

If Earth Souls would Co-operate we could both make more Progress on Our Souls' Missions.

All on Earth are aware of Our Existence but some block it out completely as they are so consumed with the Material World.

Others don't want to accept the fact that we do exist.

Yet there are many that do recognize Our Existence. Only they are able to make Progress, both Spiritually and Materially in equal amounts. Both are needed to Grow and Progress.

Concrete Proof is coming so Earth will fully recognize that we do exist.

As each day passes we try and verify the wants and needs of Earth Souls, to prove that we do hear Souls asking for Our Help.

However, keep in mind always that you must earn the right to benefit on the Material Level.

We also are in the process of preventing Unearned Souls from having their Material wants and needs met because they are taking them for Granted.

They are too easily forgetting why they were granted this Material Wealth in the first place.

These Souls with great Material Possessions were allowed this because of Past Good Works in their Previous Life, but now feel there is no need for Spiritual Progress.

Therefore we must stop them from accumulating more Material Gains to Guide them back to the right path.

Earth Souls are in a constant balancing act, juggling the Lessons they must learn in one hand and the Patience and Strength <u>required accomplishing that in the other</u>.

MORE ON SOUL MATES, TWIN SOULS

March 7, 1986

Jennifer is here with more about Soul Mates. This is my last contribution to Book I.

A Twin Soul Mate is the <u>better half of a complete</u> Soul. Those <u>halves must be rejoined as one</u> to Grow and LOVE to Progress, to accomplish its Purpose.

The work they do together makes LOVE <u>strong</u> <u>between them</u>. And to have this LOVE is Universal.

Universal LOVE is the <u>ultimate goal,</u> the ultimate Purpose of all Souls. And to accomplish this to the Fullest is Eternal Existence. Once you do you are blessed with a <u>feeling</u> <u>of satisfaction that can never be</u> <u>taken away</u>.

It opens the doors to Higher Wisdom and Knowledge. Beyond the Earth Soul's Mind, which is the Purpose of the Universe.

It is Rewarding for the two Souls to <u>be bonded together</u> in Universal LOVE and there is <u>nothing</u> Higher or <u>better for complete</u> Progress of Mankind.

When you meet your Soul Mate on Earth you <u>recognize each</u> <u>other by</u> an Inner Feeling of Peace, a <u>warm attraction that stops</u> Earth time <u>for a moment</u>, and you <u>immediately</u> <u>feel like</u> y<u>ou have known this</u> <u>person forever</u>.

Not a word <u>needs to be said,</u> <u>as the feeling</u> <u>takes over both</u> Souls to make them <u>aware of the connection</u>.

If the timing is not right, it may take <u>more work before</u> y<u>ou are</u> <u>joined together</u>, and if the timing is right, <u>there is an immediate</u> <u>connection</u>.

These two Souls are <u>bonded together</u> with a <u>physical feeling</u> <u>that they</u> <u>are one</u> and <u>this is clearly</u> <u>felt</u>.

Many cross paths but are not connected at the time because they are still Learning the Lessons required in this Earth time.

Not all Souls accomplish this in their Earth Life. It is all based on the Earth Soul's Own Growth and if it doesn't occur in their Earth Life, it will occur when they arrive in Our Dimension.

We try to connect as many Soul Mates as possible because the Learning and Progress goes so much faster for both when they work together.

To program yourself to find your Soul Mate is all right, and to a point you may ask the Universe to find and connect you with them. But remember that if timing is not right and you've not grown sufficiently, that connection is not possible.

Our Progress on Earth has been slow. By connecting and bonding Soul Mates together Progress comes more quickly.

It is happening more now so that less work needs to be done in Our Dimension. This means more Souls can relish the feeling of accomplishment as they further their Progress when they arrive back in the UNIVERSE.

When Jennifer, "Mary Todd Lincoln" finished writing here for Book I, "Our Earth And Beyond," I asked her to explain what she meant by a Twin Soul Mate. This is what she wrote.

The Twin Soul is a Soul that is the other half of a completed Soul. We only have one Twin Soul. This is the other half of Our Being; this is the Soul Mate with whom we want to connect.

Some Twin Souls exist on the Earth Plane. Many have their Twin Soul in the Universe. This is because one half of the Soul returns to Earth to make up for Past Mistakes.

When we speak of Soul Mates there are many who are part of Previous Lives.

Many times Soul Mates are brought together for short periods to correct Past Errors from Previous Lives.

They could be a Mother, Father, Brother, Sister or a close Friend who had <u>problems that were never straightened out</u> during that <u>period on</u> Earth.

Therefore, they are reunited again to complete their obligations.

Only the TWIN SOUL is the LOVE of the Universe that <u>must be re-connected</u> as soon as they correct their Mistakes.

If the Soul is split on the Earth Plane, then we <u>try</u> <u>to bring</u> <u>them together</u> for LOVE and Progress. There are many Souls on Earth today seeking that re-connection.

See this page of the actual writing by Jennifer "Mary Todd Lincoln," in "Twin Souls And Soul Mates" at the start of this Chapter in Book II, "Many Plane Above."

The next Teacher, Teddy Roosevelt, added the following on August 2, 1986.

We asked him about Soul Mates and Split Souls that seek reunification for the Soul's Progress as One.

Teddy is here. Soul Mates are Split Souls and once reunited are One in LOVE.

The Universe or God <u>split them</u> to help complete their work – One on Earth and the Other Half to carry the Love of the Universe to Earth.

The Other Half stayed in the Universe to send Love from us to Earth. The Soul <u>was split before it came</u> to Earth.

The first Split Souls were Adam and Eve, and both Halves were sent to begin Life on Earth to <u>make faster</u> Soul Progress.

*This is the end of "**Our Earth And Beyond.**"*

Ron asked all of the Teachers a series of Questions. He organized their responses into the following Chapters.

YOUR EARTH LIFE GUIDE

Conier, wrote earlier in this book in the Chapter, "Earth Souls' Guide" to help readers better understand their Guide and its purpose.

Both you and your Guide choose each other before you take on a physical body. They are your Protector from Birth. You'll always find them on your right side. Your Guide stays with you your entire Earth Life.

This Guide is your Best Friend; get acquainted and most importantly turn within to GOD to find the truthful answers that you seek. These answers have always been there and will always be there for you, in All Ways.

You have never been alone, not for one moment, and never will be.

Conier is writing about Guides, as he is a High Teacher of Protecting Guides.

Ron, you are a <u>lucky</u> <u>man</u> with so many gifts of Love and Spiritual Healing. Few have been blessed with these gifts. You are Special. We thank you and Love you for persistently pursuing Our Work.

KEEP UP THE GOOD WORK. WE WILL HELP YOU.

I AM WRITING NOW. I AM CONIER, A GREEK HIGH PRIEST FROM A VERY HIGH PLANE.

I AM A TEACHER OF THE RIGHT-SIDE GUIDE, THE GUIDE THAT PROTECTS EACH EARTH SOUL.

Conier, could you please tell us about Our Guide! I know <u>so</u> many are unaware that they even have a Guide.

I also know it is covered elsewhere in Our Books but it is always helpful to review some of these subjects for there is always more to Learn!

Guides are assigned to Earth Souls living in a body and each Soul on Earth walks with a Guide <u>on their right side</u> at all times.

Your Guide is your Conscience. Your Guide speaks to you through your First Thought Impression. They tell you what is <u>right and what is wrong</u>, to <u>go or not to</u> go somewhere, <u>to do or not to do</u> something.

Most Earth Souls do Not Listen to their Guide because of their God-Given Free Will. Thus, they make the Wrong Choice, go <u>when they</u> <u>should not</u>, or <u>do something they</u> <u>shouldn't</u>.

You always know when you have made the Wrong Choice and <u>say to</u> <u>yourself that, "I knew I shouldn't have</u> gone there, shouldn't <u>have done that or said that</u>."

They Guide you in <u>the directions</u> that will help you fulfill your purpose on Earth – and protect you. That's All. They <u>cannot do anything</u> <u>for you</u>, as <u>you must do everything</u> <u>for your own</u> Soul's Purpose. While these are your Lessons, your Guides will learn along side you.

They can <u>be</u> <u>your best friend</u> and are <u>your connection</u> to the Universe, if you talk to your Guide. It's easier for them to protect you when you talk to them, and they can do a better job, too. Of course, you do have to listen.

However, it's not your Guide's fault if Earth Souls do not Listen or act accordingly. When <u>you fail to heed their advice</u> <u>you are holding</u> <u>back</u> your Own Soul, <u>limiting</u> <u>your own</u> Progress.

If you are Listening and Progressing you <u>may</u> <u>earn the right to have</u> a Teacher. A Teacher <u>is a</u> <u>gift from</u> the Universe, and this Teacher must ask your Guide's <u>permission to work with</u> <u>you</u>. Your Teacher then stands on your left – always.

If you <u>are aware of this</u> process when you need your Teacher, you must ask your Guide to call your Teacher for you. If you are <u>unaware</u> of this process the Teacher will always <u>ask</u> <u>permission</u> of your Guide to work on your behalf.

Many are <u>unaware</u> of this because this communication happens at the Subconscious level where your Soul resides and <u>receives help</u> from the Universe.

Your Subconscious is then your connection to the Universe; it tells you the Truth and Guides you.

Sometimes, depending on what your Teacher is helping you with, they could remain <u>day</u> <u>after day</u> <u>until they</u> <u>advance</u> <u>you</u> and <u>complete their work with</u> <u>you</u>.

Your Teacher then moves on to a Higher Level. At that point the Universe will assign you another Teacher so that you can Progress Higher.

This is how we are working with Jan now. Only <u>one</u> Teacher <u>at a time</u> works with her, and that Teacher will remain <u>until their work together is finished</u>. <u>Only</u> <u>then will</u> Jan's next Teacher, a Higher Teacher, come.

Sometimes Guides can work through others, **if a Teacher asks**.

You must understand that Our Work is Important, and when we are assigned to one Earth Soul for a Definite Purpose, this is the Only Soul with whom we <u>work</u>. We <u>never</u> work with more than one Soul at a time.

When we accomplish our Mission for our assigned Soul, we move on to another Chosen Soul.

Through these Books we are <u>trying</u> to <u>raise</u> <u>people's awareness</u> of the Universe and <u>how it functions</u>. <u>We want them to</u> Progress <u>faster</u> <u>on</u> Earth because we need more Teachers in the Universe to carry on Our Work.

Our writings will Guide and help many Souls make many Decisions.

I asked Conier to write about the Guide of a friend of mine.

I thought it would be of interest to add a few paragraphs, just to get an idea of how beautiful, and interesting, Our Guides can be.

The name of your friend's Guide is James. He comes from Caesar's days, a strong Warrior of Many Battles.

He ran the Army of Caesar, and he is an Influential man. HE STANDS TALL, and wears a Shield of Armor with a Sword of GOLD that shines across the Universe.

He Guides him and wants <u>him to open up</u> to the Universe, to realize he has much <u>work to do</u>.

His Mission is to get Our Messages heard and to THIRST FOR KNOWLEDGE from his Inner Self, to Progress by correcting all Past Mistakes.

His job is to Guide and protect him. He <u>cannot do anything</u> <u>for</u> <u>him</u>; he must do it all by Listening to his Intuition and Conscience, as that is how we speak to him from the Universe. Tell Him to Please Listen.

I entered this following example to help you understand that if you do not listen to your Guide through your Earth Life and you do not make Progress, you hold back your Guide and he or she remains with you until you make up your mind to move on and do your work.

A dear friend passed some 30 years ago. I asked The Great Aristotle how he was doing.

Your friend wants <u>to work with</u> <u>you</u> because <u>he has</u> <u>just earned</u> <u>this right</u> to work. He had many Lessons to Learn.

You might <u>be feeling</u> <u>his vibration</u>. He is <u>a stubborn man</u> and thinks it was only <u>yesterday</u> <u>that he agreed to start working</u>. <u>Since there</u> is no time in the Universe he doesn't realize that 30 years of Earth time has passed.

He doesn't <u>like to working</u>, but he likes to be around and <u>do</u> <u>nothing</u> because he <u>feels he worked</u> <u>plenty</u> during his Life on Earth. He has just now finally <u>realized he wasn't any</u> <u>longer</u> on Earth.

159

His Guide has to finish his job now. Remember, they are not released from their Guided Soul until that Soul moves on and starts to work towards Progress.

I was taken aback that my friend made no Progress during his Earth Life and then wasted 30 Earth years – all because he didn't want to work at all. It took him all of this time to decide to begin his work.

Many people have used the services of a Psychic, also known as a Card Reader or a Medium. A Psychic once offered me a reading. I graciously listened to what she had to say.

But I did not feel good about what she told me. So I asked Jan during her writing with Aristotle to learn the Identity and Level of that Psychic's Teacher bringing the information.

I have entered Aristotle's answer from my personal writing so you may understand that information can come from all levels, and that you must use your common sense when evaluating everything that comes through.

You should always ask for the Highest and Best. However, please note that not all Psychics can connect with the High Universe.

Ron, she calls him her Teacher and says she receives all of her information from this Teacher. But this is No Teacher.

This is an Entity who wants to show off to everyone, and is from a Low Grey Level of the Astral Plane at the edge of Darkness.

He can't see the White Light, as he doesn't understand what this is all about. But he is attached to her *(the Psychic)* and has been with her many years.

He likes her and she likes having him to call her Teacher. He likes the recognition and also likes to make Jokes.

Ron, he didn't understand about you and your work, but he could feel the High Energy around you. He is from the Lowest Level.

160

I understand there is no Progress as the Psychic is a Stubborn, Closed-Minded person who refuses to grow or Progress.

But she is OK <u>reading</u> <u>for certain</u> <u>people</u> on a Lower Level of growth.

Aristotle, wouldn't her Guide or her Family members be able to bring Higher Messages from the Universe to her? Aristotle's exact words follow.

<u>Absolutely</u> <u>not,</u> the Guide <u>is not allowed to</u> <u>give,</u> nor would they want to give, information. The Guide is Higher than the Entity.

The Guide only works with Teachers. They would not advance if they didn't. Besides, why would they want to work with lower clinging to Earth Entities?

Only Teachers from a Higher Level bring Messages of truth, and <u>all of this must be earned</u>.

The Family members work by themselves from the Astral Plane. They have a long way to go <u>to earn the</u> <u>privilege</u> to become a Teacher. The Guide <u>works from a Higher Level</u> than the Astral Plane.

The Guide's Job is to protect the Soul only; Family members are allowed to help as long as it's for the Good, and if not, they are kept back from the Soul.

So you do not approve of a Psychic working with Lower Entities?

<u>I absolutely do not approve</u>. We do <u>not like others interfering</u> unless <u>they</u> <u>are assigned by our</u> Teachers.

Again, you must remember the Guide only works with Teachers, and these Psychics must Raise their Vibration and <u>ask to</u> <u>work only</u> with the High Universe.

This doesn't just happen; they <u>must earn it by</u> <u>making</u> Progress in their Life.

I also asked Aristotle to write about another friend of mine here on Earth. I wanted to know if his growth was at a High Level. And since he felt familiar to me, were we connected in a Past Life?

No. He is on a Lower Level, and has an Entity with him. He refuses to do what he should do.

He is Stubborn and he doesn't listen. He is afraid to Progress; therefore he procrastinates and he causes all of his own problems.

He doesn't work with the White Light, but he just twisted a nerve. With your Healing he will feel better now.

I think he might begin to Progress because thanks to the Healing, he now has some proof of the Universe's existence.

At the time of Jesus you did know him. He was there at the same time as you. Both of you were put together now to balance your Lives in this Lifetime.

You will continue your Spiritual Teaching and Healing Work, but he holds no special significance for you.

The two of you have nothing to talk about. He's just another stray being brought into the fold.

He refused to get on with his Life and you represented Responsibility, something he needs to Learn.

You need to help all of these friends to straighten out and encourage them to work with their Own Guides, and with the White Light.

Aristotle, what about this other friend I'm trying to help? She seems so out of balance!

She is only looking for Lessons from you to straighten out her Life. (*You mean in relationships?*) No, not that kind; you can give her strictly what she's lacking in her diet.

162

The Healing will help a bit to Center and Balance her, but she needs to eat properly. Her diet does not support her.

Vitamin B is Important for balancing her stress levels. Also, tell her to add Potassium to her diet.

Make her aware that her Guide is there to help her; that she must listen to her Impressions that tell her what she should be eating. She will receive certain cravings and should satisfy those cravings to balance her body.

There is also this young fellow who is unloading all of his Problems on me. How should I handle him?

Ron, this fellow is a mess. He has many Problems and you cannot help him, as he won't Listen. So don't waste your time with him.

He has Depressing Views on everything and wants everyone around him to see the world in the same depressing way.

You stay out of it. Don't encourage him or say anything. He just wants someone to talk to. There are too many Depressing Lowers around him and only he can break free from this.

His Guide can't get near him to do his work. He also thinks you have money, he will only take it and you will never get it back.

He has to stand on his own two feet.

Ron we are Teaching you to say NO, bringing these Souls to you, as you cannot help those that must help themselves.

WHY ARE WE ON EARTH?

Jennifer "Mary Todd Lincoln," who controls sending Our Souls here to Earth and tells us when we should come?

The Planets control all of us. The High Teachers control sending Souls to Earth. They also Control the Working Souls and all Planes of Working Souls.

All of Our High Teachers have Earned the Right to do so.

You say all Planets. Are there other Planets where Souls work to Progress?

That's right! We have other Planets also, but they are Out of your Universe. These Planets are more advanced than the Planet Earth. Some Souls reside on Rest Planets for a time once they have Earned it. The two Material advanced Planets are called Condor and Narcissus.

They are all Beautiful and everything you need is there.

Each Soul is given a Choice to work here in Our Dimension or return to Earth.

If they want to return to Earth in another body, they have the freedom to choose the gender of their body – Man or Woman.

You should choose the gender that best serves you to Learn your Lessons. There is no Male or Female in the Universe; that distinction applies only in the Earth Plane Existence.

We also remind you of your Past Mistakes that you need to Correct, and Our Computers will organize you according to the time you must spend on Earth.

Jennifer, if we are just Souls in the Universe, then what is the purpose or the roles of Male and Female on Earth?

The Male and Female roles on Earth are designed to help you Learn to Love each other better, to Learn to give of yourselves. Each gender in its own way is Uniquely Special.

I do wish all Earth Souls would feel this way and understand their Purpose is to Progress through LOVE.

We in the Universe can then make so much faster Progress for all of Mankind.

How interesting! However, it seems that most Souls, when here, get caught up in the system of Earth Life and think only of their Own Survival. They think Little of why they are here!

That's true Ron! ALL Earth Souls get wound up in their Material Life and forget their Inner Self.

Birth Parents teach children how to live on the Earth Plane, but they don't know how to live from their Inner Self because that Knowledge has been hidden from them, until now with these Books.

As they grow, their Guides show them the way; remind them of their Purpose. Sadly, most ignore their Guides; yet some do listen.

Your Guide is your Conscience. It always tells you what is Right or Wrong, but whether you listen or Pay Attention is another matter.

Could you call the Earth Plane a Place to Learn or a Learning Center?

It is a Center of Progress where you pay for your Past Mistakes much Faster, and a place to Learn many Lessons. Yes! You could call it the Learning Center of the Universe.

How is it that most Earth Souls don't realize this is a Place for Learning Lessons when they are here?

It is because we need to Learn on Our Own and we must want to Learn. But so few do.

All Souls are Free to Choose. But so many are simply Lazy and do not Choose to Better Themselves.

The Universe constantly tests you to see if you can learn and Grow; each test you pass indicates Growth and Progress.

If everything went smoothly in your Life, ultimately you would not be satisfied. Therefore you must be tested to Progress Higher.

Jennifer, then a Good Question is what are these Souls doing here on Earth?

I'll answer that First with a Question, Ron! Where are we going to put them?

Both Jan and I laughed at this response!

They know the Lessons they must Learn when they leave here, and **Ignore** them when they get there.

Please explain Good Souls and Bad Souls to us. Are some in Limbo?

There are really no Good or Bad Souls to us. There are just Souls making Choices to Learn for their Own Soul's Progress.

However, with their Free Choice you could say, there are Good Souls who pay for all of their Mistakes, and those who don't want to pay. Those you would call Bad Souls.

This is because when they chose to return to Earth, they didn't do what they agreed to do.

The Material takes over and they forget their Mission. Also, there are no Souls in Limbo, unless they want to be there. Again, it is their Choice.

Jennifer, thank you. Please, could you give us an interpretation of Mistakes and is this what we call Karma?

Well a Mistake is when your Inner Self knows what's right or knows the right way to go but you don't go or you don't listen.

Karma is action; it is just an Earth word. However, it does make sense in your Earth World. Some don't pay Karma, but you do create your own Karma, it's just another way of speaking of Mistakes.

You must always go forward, as you don't want to go back; you must always Progress.

Some <u>move fast and others are slower</u>. With Positive Energy you move faster, Negativity slows you down.

Can you give us your Higher interpretation between Knowledge and Wisdom?

Knowledge is the Process of Learning more and more. Wisdom is Accountable for much of the Time spent Learning and for all the Learning already Accomplished.

You know in your Search for Knowledge you can keep Only True Friends. All others will leave if they do not grow with you. Just a bit of Wisdom for you.

Thank you, Jennifer, for your Wisdom. Now will you please explain a little about Sleep and Dreams?

Dreams are Future Events yet to happen. They all have Meanings and they are Direct Contact with the Universe.

Therefore, the Universe is sending Messages to their Subconscious about the Lessons people have to Learn and the path they've Chosen. Few people take the time to try and understand the their Dreams, failing to realize that Dreams are a Direct Link to their Soul's Purpose.

This is also Our Way of Connecting with the Soul.

Sleep is a Body Function, and when you sleep, we account for many things.

Your Spirit or Soul, which are really one and the same thing, can Travel as a Soul Light and meet with other Souls during sleep.

You are being prepared for experiencing some future happening, which creates what you call Déjà Vu.

Then when it happens it seems familiar, like you've already had the experience.

These experiences you have are real and happen mostly on the Astral Level. But some advanced Souls can go Higher and this is all part of Learning.

You must be advanced Spiritually to understand the purpose of your trips, but it is quite easy to Astral Travel during sleep.

Teddy Roosevelt wrote this in a Public Forum where Jan answered this question on Soul Traveling from a member of the audience.

Soul Traveling is an experience to make you realize that the Soul does not have to remain in the body all of the time.

The Soul is Free to Choose. I think it is nice to have the ability to go wherever you want if you so choose.

Now back to Jennifer. What about Nightmares or Bad Dreams!

This is also part of Learning. A Nightmare compels you to Pay Attention to Our Messages. Unfortunately, many don't and then the Nightmares continue.

Nightmares exist on the Subconscious Level. People who have Nightmares carry them around with them all day in their minds.

When these Dreams continue, because of some Frightening Experience, these Souls don't realize that their Guide is there to help.

These Souls don't realize there is a Lesson here to be learned. A Lesson they refuse to Learn.

Therefore the Tragedy is necessary and their Frightening Experiences that follow are happening for a Reason.

The Individual, by misusing their Life, brings these Tragedies on themselves. Misusing one Self, Ignoring their Guides and indulging their Own Selfishness makes these things happen.

Again, we say these are their Lessons, and all things happen so people can Learn and Progress.

Teddy Roosevelt answered my next Question about Elves, Fairies, Angels, Gnomes and Nature Spirits. I asked him if he could explain them!

Elves and Fairies are fantasies; they are not real. All Sightings that resemble Fairies are actually Angels. "Fairies" is an Earth term, and "Angels" is the Universe's term for the same.

They come from another Planet and are just visiting. Angels are Good Souls who have no more Lessons to Learn and come to bring joy to the Earth.

They never stay long. They are Star Universe Beings and exist on their Planet of No Corruption.

They are all Good Souls who come to help Earth people. Many are on Earth now in Body form for short Lifetimes.

They cannot stay long because we don't want them Corrupted, as they are already Good Souls.

Most return to Our Dimension very young, but some may stay through Teen Years or into their early or mid-20s, but not much longer than that.

Families, which are blessed with an Angel Child, know this as they experience this Goodness. These Families are deeply saddened when their Angel Children must leave.

They don't understand and ask, "Why did this have to happen?" They also say the Child "was such an Angel!"

Angels also work with New Soul Children Teaching them about Earth and the Animals that act as Messengers on the Second Plane.

Angels exist on the Eighth Plane and there are many on their Planet in the Star Universe.

Gnomes are so cute, but they actually are Angels, too. Also Nature Spirits are real, and I'm Surprised that you know about them, Ron.

Yes, I have seen Hundreds of them in a large group all at Once, like Fire Flies or a burst of White Gold Fireworks. They all light up at once and continue Sparkling in a Flash of Energy over the Greenery at Night. The High Universe showed this to me.

That's true. They are all Overworked Today by repairing what man on Earth, is destroying, but they do work at Night. You saw them working so hard.

These Nature Spirits Send Energy to the Earth to keep everything Green for Earth people to enjoy the Beauty of Nature.

I sure hope People become more Grateful and Appreciate Nature Spirit's hard work. I also think that we should do more to Preserve Nature – Our Forests, Jungles, Wetlands and Farmlands – from Man's Earth-wide Destruction.

Jennifer, would you please give us your definition or explanation of Natural Law!

Natural Law is the Law of the Land; it is not to Misuse the Nature of Earth, which is being done all the time.

The Natural Law of the Universe is as you call Karma, or we call Past Mistakes.

The Universe has placed this Natural Law on Earth, for the Betterment of Mankind and to Misuse it, is Wrong and must be paid for.

All other Laws are Earth-made Laws, and pertain to the Earth Plane only, unless we invented them. Take the Law of Gravity, for example. It is a Planet function and the Universe gives this to the Earth.

Teddy Roosevelt gave us his thoughts and ideas about the Purpose of Life. What must we strive to do during our Earth Lives?

First, you need to Clean Up Your Act, as there is too much Selfishness and Corruption on Earth. You need to LOVE each other more and appreciate other things around the Earth.

The Earth is really quite Beautiful, but how many of you really appreciate it?

You only make things better for yourself when you think of someone else.

We want more Progress On Earth.

What you accomplish on Earth will not be forgotten and there are Rewards when you leave the Earth Plane.

When you attain your Rewards, each and every one of you will be so Grateful for your every experience on Earth.

We ask that you all think about this.

Also, we all should be asking to help more and share with others this Great Universal Knowledge.

To help others by sharing Universal Love and the Beauty you give to others.

The Serenity and Peacefulness that you give to others, your very Heartfelt Goodness, with Clarity and Determination.

To Communicate, Teach and Show Peace, Harmony Happiness and LOVE.

You must Live in LOVE each and everyday throughout your entire Earth Life.

My Purpose is to use my Goodness, Clarity and Determination to Communicate, Share and Teach others to Live in Peace, Harmony, Happiness and LOVE.

Teddy Roosevelt wrote the following in one sitting in a Public Forum. The audience asked Jan many questions on a variety of subjects and situations.

We had many sittings like this where various groups and organizations asked Jan to demonstrate her Automatic Writing.

As you've noted, I usually sort the contents of those writings into different Chapters according to subject.

In this case, I'm entering all of this particular writing here without separating it by subjects so you may see how we cover many subjects at one sitting. The answers came as fast as Jan could write them.

This started off with the question, "Do we know what we have to learn when we come to Earth?"

These cover twelve questions, with Only the brief answers.

Yes, of course we do know what we have to Learn when we come to Earth. We at all times are aware of Our Lessons.

People have Wealth in this Life because they earned it in a Previous Life.

You always have Free Will. It is our wish that you choose the Life that has the most Lessons to be learned the quickest.

Many Souls Choose Lives that will generate the most Progress they can make on Earth.

We will always Choose Lives for continuing Progress. Your Inner Soul always knows why you chose to come back to Earth.

The fastest way to get on with your Lessons is to listen to your Inner Self and to your Protecting Guide.

No, if you come to Earth it is <u>not important who comes with you</u>. You are all Special and Individuals.

Yes, of course when Lessons are earned ahead of time there is no need to stay on Earth any longer. Again Free Choice does this.

The <u>span of time is important only</u> to finish what we arrived on Earth to do. You will leave as soon as the <u>work you came to do for us is done</u>.

The Soul <u>never enters the body</u> during <u>pregnancy, but rather</u> only when the body arrives on Earth <u>outside of the</u> Mother and into the Earth's <u>atmosphere</u>.

Prior, the Fetus is a part of the Mother's body. The Soul prior is around the Mother, but is <u>too pre-occupied</u> with their Lessons to be learned through this Chosen Mother and Family.

An Abortion is not anything at all; <u>it does not hurt</u> the Soul because the Soul is <u>not in the body</u> at this time.

An Abortion means that the Soul has changed its Mind, decided not to come at this time and impresses the Mother to Abort. This is the Mother's Choice.

People have a hard Life <u>full of suffering</u> because they have many Lessons to Learn. They made many Mistakes in a Previous Life. Each Lesson Learned accounts for another measure of an individual's Progress.

Teachers keep the record straight.

A Soul Mate is your True Love and the other half of a Loved Soul. The <u>second contact of two</u> Souls in the next Life happens only when there are Lessons that the Two Souls can <u>learn together</u>.

173

Prosperity must be earned, and leading a Good Life of Giving, Loving and Caring for others automatically brings Material Rewards.

This is why many Souls have great Wealth in this Life; they lived a Good Life in their Past Life.

However, they must share their wealth in this Life or they will loose it.

Because Earth today is so full of Greed and Selfishness and therefore out of balance, this is now being changed.

The next question we asked Aristotle, "How long have Souls Existed and was there a Beginning?"

We also asked, "After all Mistakes are corrected and Our Three Reincarnations completed, do Souls keep working or do they rest?"

Souls have always existed. There is Neither no Beginning, nor will there be an End, as All Souls have always been and All Souls will always exist forever. This is God and God IS All.

God is All, and the Teachers and Guides are a part of the Universe. God is the Universe and they all work for the Betterment of Man. It is all Souls working for Soul Progress that is GOD!

The Teachers are the ones who are here to help All Mankind for God's Sake.

God is Happy that we all care about Bettering Ourselves, for the Soul's Progress.

Make no mistake; God IS All and One of the Same.

When they have learned to become Master Directors they never return to Earth again for there is no need.

We have so much work to do and so few Directors that it will take a long time before we can make any of the changes that will make it better for everyone.

Master Directors in the Universe are the Highest. After we reach that level we don't have to work anymore.

However, most of us do, as we sometimes want to help others Progress or sometimes the Directors of the Round Table ask like you Jan and Ron to do Special Assignments.

This is the body of Master Directors. The body membership changes all of the time so that all that have earned this privilege have the opportunity to experience it.

After their Three Reincarnations during which they learned their Lessons, Souls have earned the right to retire; they are entitled to rest.

If they choose they can continue working and start over again or retire. When Retired we will not disturb any one of them for about 50 to 100 years in your Earth time.

After my Retirement I oversaw the Lower Guides – that was my Choice – to help where needed and to report to the Round Table.

We Love to work and help; it's like we consume Truth all of the time and find ways to share it and are satisfied to enjoy the Gardens of Beauty in the Universe.

In your language the Gifts we receive come from Earth, seeing everyone working together as one and not engaged in War. We pass no Judgments and know all happens for a Reason – Souls' Progress.

Once ancient Souls reach the top then they may rest. After a rest period they have a Choice to work on a Level of Earth as a Teacher or Live in a Peaceful Dimension that requires no work as long as this Soul so Chooses.

Because of the new experiences Teachers on Earth now have Chosen to help where they can.

Ron, you understand this because you have been here before and you already know this.

You have Reached this State and Volunteered to come back to Earth in this Life.

There are Thousands of Teachers on Earth currently. They eventually will become Directors and for many this is their Third Earth Reincarnation.

That seems like a lot of Teachers to help Earth Souls to turn their Lives around!

That's true, but it is Not Enough. The work there is too hard and it will take at least another 20 to 30 years or more for <u>a complete turnover</u>, before we begin to see Souls' Progress.

This is why we work so hard here to keep the World from Destroying Itself, so it keeps going on so that Souls have a Chance to make their Progress.

If Souls will listen they can make <u>better and faster</u> Progress there on Earth than here in the Universe. There are already so many Souls waiting here to go to Earth and make their Progress.

With help from you, Jan, Ron and Many Others that care, we are making this happen. Our Timing has been off because we did not receive the Co-Operation from Earth Souls that we expected.

Oh Great Aristotle, what could we do to make things better on Earth?

To improve things here on Earth I would say the same thing I always say: People must <u>stop</u> <u>being</u> so Self-Centered and <u>think more of their</u> Neighbors.

<u>Too much Selfishness</u>; they spend all day doing what they want to do for themselves and never think of anyone else, or the needs of others.

While there are people on Earth that are Thoughtful, <u>so many are not</u>.

It's a shame, too, because for those people it means they are creating their own, ongoing string of Lessons to be learned, intended to make them aware of what they are doing.

Why do you think we have been <u>sending so many</u> Messages? We're trying to gain the Attention of more Souls hoping they will Better Themselves.

The Disasters happening on Earth are to gain your attention.

For too many, Materialism seems to come First, creating a massive Problem. That's why your Environment is so damaged.

Nobody cares, and too many take everything for Granted. They don't stop to look at the Beauty around them.

They seem to find more Pleasure in Destroying Nature than Appreciating it.

We try so hard to make everyone Aware of <u>what they</u> <u>have been given</u>, but they Don't Listen and this <u>is where all the trouble starts</u>. <u>This is what</u> makes Our Work so hard.

If everyone would think <u>each and every</u> day <u>about what they</u> <u>are doing</u>, and would be Kind and Helpful to others whenever possible, things would be so much better.

You all work for us and we appreciate this.

We Greatly Appreciate all of the Co-operation and help we can get, and the more we do and the more Co-operation we get, the better it is for all.

You can never ask too much, and you know if you Earn it, you will receive it.

<u>We need more</u> <u>people to turn toward</u> Our Ways and the Ways of our Teachers; but people will not come until they are ready. They don't know what they're Missing, and this is a shame.

People come to us by doing anything that takes time to Heal their Own Soul.

Aristotle, we just had a Good Friend Pass Over. Could you bring us a Message from him?

Your friend was aware of the Universe and was a Teacher to help all of you, but his body gave out and he needed <u>to return home</u> to go back to work in the Universe.

He comes from a High Place and wants you to know that by Co-operating with the Universe all the Help you are generating is going in the right direction.

You are doing Wonderful Work and we are hoping you will pass it on to Open More Eyes.

So many are Ignorant of the Universe and don't want to see their Future. I want you to know there definitely is a Future Life for everyone and, it will be a Much Better One than you have on Earth.

I send my LOVE to you all from This Side.

At one of Our Classes, Aristotle wrote the following as he answered questions for us.

You all know that we are working always <u>to help</u> <u>each and everyone of</u> <u>you</u> to Progress for the better.

I wish to explain that we always need your Co-operation to accomplish Our Goals. We can't do it without your help.

We here in the Universe work hard; we try to accomplish for you everything we didn't do when we were on Earth.

So we need your help to do this; each time we make things happen for you it helps us to accomplish more for us.

I think it's important to understand the Universal Way and Love of Life the way we try to show you. It's Critical to Learn this.

Aristotle, is there a Cause for all things that happen? What are the Laws of Cause and Effect?

No, <u>there is not a</u> Cause.

Things happen according to the Lessons that each has to Learn; this is the Law of Cause and Effect. You are the cause and you create the effect based on the action you take.

That action is determined by the Choices you make; you have the Free Will to Listen to us as we try to Guide you down the right path. You also have the Free Will to ignore us.

So the Universe does not cause pain, suffering and loss; it's your fault. And to continue pounding your head against a wall and making it worse by Not Listening is Ignorant and Harmful.

We here in the Universe always try to Guide you in the Right Direction and Protect you, but so many Don't Listen.

It's awfully hard for us. When something bad or painful is coming, we try to change the Energy to something more Positive, but you won't Listen, even though it's for your own good.

Aristotle, to help us understand why things happen like they do, please explain why Our Friend was Mugged when she exited the Restaurant and walked down the street minding her own business.

Why did she get mugged? Negative Souls were hanging around this particular time on this particular street. They were drawn to the Mugger, who carried thoughts of Malice.

Your friend was minding her own business and she was protected. That's why she was not badly hurt. But we have No Control over Free Will. These Negative Souls and the Mugger exercised their own Free Will.

Part of her Lesson was to be More Careful where she goes, as she received a Message not to walk down that street. But she chose to anyway, of her Own Free Choice.

I'm sure if you ask her, she will tell you, "Something told me not to go down that street. I knew I shouldn't have gone." That was the Warning Thought we sent.

As you Dear Readers may remember, we received all of this Information many years ago, over 20 years now, explaining how things really are. We were told not To Release this information until More Minds on Earth were Open to accept all of this.

Many Earth minds are more open and are beginning to accept this Valuable Information to Change their Thinking and their Lives.

Well, I want to mention here that as I am entering these Pages of Writings, I have dated many on the date they were received.

Ironically, so many of the Subjects I had asked about years ago have again become the Subjects in Our Present Day News.

I have not noted this prior when entering this Beautiful Work, but I thought it was Noteworthy after reading a News Flash on the Internet this morning.

For example, I saw one report that Couples may now Choose the Sex of their Baby through recent Medical Discoveries.

This is interesting because I asked Aristotle on New Year's Day 1989, almost 20 years ago, how the Sex of a Baby is Determined. And can it be Changed while the Fetus is Developing? He then answered.

<u>At any point before</u> Birth the Sex can be changed. The Sex is Not Important when the Baby is Developing, but is usually decided <u>about six months</u> into the Pregnancy.

Aristotle, we have friends who were going to have a Boy and instead they had a Girl; would you explain this for us?

This Change indicates the Soul's Preference; the Soul has chosen these Parents and now it's choosing its own gender.

Remember, we have told you that the Developing Fetus is an Extension of the Mother's body.

The Baby's Body must be Outside of the Mother. The Soul Enters to bring Life to the Body. It takes the Earth's Atmosphere for the Soul to enter.

180

Prior to that, the Soul is just a Tiny Light Hovering around the Mother, Learning to Love the Mother, and getting used to its Mission.

All through this Developing Time Period this Soul has Free Choice to Change its Mind, either <u>about the</u> <u>gender</u> that will best enable it to do its Work, or to <u>decline its</u> <u>journey</u> to Earth at this time and Urge the Mother to Abort.

With your friend it was the Soul of the <u>child-to-be</u> that ultimately decided it would <u>be more</u> <u>practical for her to be a</u> Girl after initially choosing to be a Boy.

This does happen and Earth people cannot tell usually until after the <u>six-month</u> <u>period</u>.

The <u>six-month period</u> is when we in the Universe decide the Sex to develop, once the Soul has decided. Remember, it's all up to the Soul to Choose, Not the Parents.

The Soul's Decision is based on its Lessons to be Learned and its Purpose for coming.

The Universe then confirms the Sex. We have the Knowledge and Right to allow the Soul's Choice of Sex to Develop from the Seed <u>that we Plant</u> – Male or Female.

We – the Universe – implant the Seed into the Mother.

This is a reminder that We in the Universe Control Souls coming to Earth, <u>not the other way</u> <u>around.</u>

Is the Mother Aware of this Process happening?

<u>No</u>. <u>She is not aware</u> as it works through the Hormones, and it is Always Done at the <u>six-month</u> <u>period</u>.

The Mother <u>knows this only</u> <u>if she</u> has earned this wish to know the Soul's Decision. In that case, we impress that knowledge in her mind. In short, "<u>she</u> <u>just knows</u>."

The Parents do not control this, so sometimes it may be best not to know in advance whether they will have a Boy or Girl.

This is the Soul's Decision to Select the Parents first and then the Sex they wish to be, to best Teach the Parents, and be able to best learn its Own Lessons.

The Universe must approve of the Soul's Choice, a choice grounded in God-Given Free Will.

Man should Not Interfere with this and should learn that everything has its Purpose. The Universe is in Control, Not Man or Medical Science.

Pregnancy begins with the Thought of the Mother wanting to have a Child.

Also, Pregnancy has to be earned before it even happens, just as the Soul must earn its Progression.

Many Souls have Not Earned this Right because of Past Mistakes, and can't earn that right because they are still making Mistakes.

This is because they have agreed to this before they took on a Body, and because this is their Lesson to Learn, they have to Accept Responsibility.

Wow! This is so enlightening Aristotle, and should answer many questions for Earth Souls. This should help them to understand how everything that happens in Life has a purpose.

What is the Universe's view of Surrogate Motherhood and Artificial Insemination?

Do you think we don't know about this?

The Universe accepts both. It helps us with the physical body.

We always know what's going on everywhere on Earth, at all times, with each and every Soul.

Aristotle, what about all the Babies being born that are starving in the Sudan? Please explain what is going on here!

Sudan is a Country where the Souls do not want to take Personal Responsibility for having Children.

The urge is still there to procreate, so we give them Babies, and the opportunity to take Responsibility. They are not doing their part to provide for these Children.

These starving Children are Angel Souls that Volunteer for these Lessons. We think and hope that we are Teaching these Souls a little Responsibility when these Babies die so very young.

I'm aware of Angels arriving in a Family and Leaving Very Young to Teach a Lesson to the Family. I just never knew the Angels would come in such Large Numbers focused in one area of the Earth. Also, I thought the Angels were in Charge of the Animals?

Yes, Angels are responsible for the Animals. They are also responsible for each Living thing on Earth, and for keeping everything Clean, including the Planet's Atmosphere.

They are Very Young Souls who are not required to spend much time here on Earth. They don't deserve it, as they are Good Souls who only come here to Teach Lessons.

Now I understand. All of these Starving, Dying and Murdered Babies all over the World are Angels coming and going to Teach their Parents or other Earth Souls to take Responsibility and get on with their Lives.

God Blesses All the Angels for their works: Also, I send them my Love and Gratitude.

Everything that happens on this Wonderful Earth happens to serve the Universe's Ultimate Purpose – the Soul's Progress.

This is the Learning Plane. Every Life Experience is designed to Teach Lessons.

Ron, we hope that the Information we are giving you for Our Books will help more Earth Souls to open up to the Universe and Our Ways.

We hope it will Change their Thinking; change how they look at all that is happening around them.

They can Quickly Change their Lives by Not always Blaming Others and by beginning to help Change some of these things on the Earth.

They should begin to Appreciate what they have, Change their Attitude and have more Compassion and Love for Others.

We in the Universe are always here to help and you must begin to believe in the Unseen World all around you. You must Trust Us.

For example, look at all of the Angels that have always been there for you. To see them, all you have to do is Open your Heart and spread your Love with all that you do and see.

You will begin to see Our Unseen Work and feel it as you Open Your Heart. God is there in your Heart, which is your Soul and always has been. Love Yourself and you will Love God Within, which is all that has ever been Expected of You.

Love is the most Powerful Energy in the Universe. Love can change everyone's life if they make it a part of everything they do and say.

May I ask when Children are Born of their Chosen Parents; is it always true that they come to Teach the Parents Lessons?

Yes! All Children are Born Innocent. They are born to teach their parents and to help them Progress until it's time for the children to learn their own lessons, to make their own Progress.

184

It is Our Way for the Little Innocent Soul to rest for a while, and enjoy Childhood, before starting their Lessons in the Material World.

Childhood is an Adjustment Period for the Shock the Soul experiences once it arrives on Earth. Some start their work sooner than others, depending on the work required of them for their Own Progression.

Thank you Aristotle. That is Lovely, allowing Children to have a Childhood!

Mara wrote in one of Our Classes about Choosing Our Parents, and it fits nicely here.

Choosing your Parents is your Choice. You know the Lessons the Mother and Father must learn.

Therefore, you come to teach both their Lessons and help them Fulfill their Missions.

We all need help Progressing; therefore each Soul that Chooses to return to Earth has Chosen its Own Mission that will help it Progress.

The Universe determines that Child and Parents are matched before the Soul enters the body, otherwise the Soul returns before Birth if it so Chooses, deciding it does not want this Mother or Father at this time.

Then the Soul may choose another. Sometimes the Soul makes this change because it foresees too many Problems.

January 18, 1989

Aristotle, can we talk about the Lessons people have to learn, and how they have to Listen if they are going to move in the Right Direction? It is critical that they understand this.

Also, why don't we Remember Our Past Mistakes that must be Corrected? Plus, how are you looking at our Lives and us?

We are able to see your Whole Life. But you do not remember your Mistakes, for if you did, you would <u>never</u> learn your Lessons, and therefore you would Not Progress.

I always Love being able to tell all of you when you are heading in the Right Direction. This makes us happy and infuses more Energy into your Lives. This, in turn, helps you to get there faster.

It is always Our Pleasure to provide you Direction; it's what I like to do best.

We know that everything doesn't always work out on Earth as you would like, but y<u>ou have to keep</u> <u>going</u> and <u>never</u> <u>give up</u> <u>trying</u>.

I enjoy Advising and encouraging you along the way because you are always Learning from all of your Experiences. It's through these Experiences that you are correcting your Mistakes, without even realizing it.

We here in the Universe care about each and every Soul on the Earth, and <u>not one single one</u> of you is <u>ever unaccounted for</u>.

This is because each one of you needs work and Guidance. Once we get you on the Right Track, we move on to another.

Remember, you always have your Guide to help and they are with you every day – from the moment of your Birth to the moment you return to the Universe.

Teachers come and go as we have said, and it is your Guide that calls on us when we are needed. The Guide only works with Teachers and he or she would not Progress if it were otherwise.

Your Guide is there Only to Protect You and Impress you to stay on the Right Path. **Your Guide cannot do anything else for you**.

Everything else you must do for Yourself and if you don't Progress, neither does your Guide. They also do not give Messages.

However, it is most Beneficial to know that you have a Guide and that you are never alone. You can also talk to your Guide through your thoughts to help you make Decisions.

Your Guides are Good Listeners, as they hear all of your Thoughts and Desires.

You also can talk things over in Your Heart; this is how you speak directly to God.

Then you must listen to your Guide. Your Guide is your Conscience, and they talk to you through your Thoughts. It's the Inner Voice that is telling you that, "this is not right," that "you shouldn't go there "or" shouldn't do that," or that "I shouldn't say that."

A Feeling of Hesitation in your Solar Plexus, or a knot in the stomach could follow this.

God speaks to you from your Heart with Love and Positive Feelings. If you Listen to your First Impression from your Inner-Voice, you will always know what is Right and Wrong.

If you become confused, do nothing and think it over, or sleep on it before you act.
I make this suggestion based on my experiences. – Ron.

Your Guide is there to Protect you from Harm and keep you on the Right Track so that you may continue Learning your Lessons. The problem is that most Souls on Earth do Not Listen.

I became a High Director because I Earned and Learned a Great amount of Knowledge, and have shared it with many.

This is the **LOVE OF THE UNIVERSE**, which is much more than on Earth, because I see the Whole Specter from here now.

I first became Aware of being guided by the Universe at a young age on Earth, around 370 B.C., and I knew my Mission was to Guide people.

I was a Teacher and I was meant to leave my Knowledge on the Earth Plane. Much of the Information I left can be found there today.

The Directors and Teachers on my Level are Way Beyond your Earth.

Just because they were Famous Teachers or were made Saints on Earth, does not mean they are Famous in the Universe.

We don't care about any kind of Earth notoriety, whether it's Fame, Sainthood or Idolatry. That's because we have No Ego here. What's important here is that we do Our Work with LOVE.

Thank You, Aristotle. May I ask how you know when your Lessons are done and how long it takes to learn them?

You will know when your Lessons are done, but how long? Who knows, until they are finished? Sometimes faster than you think, but you must experience it. Hardships are Lessons from the Universe.

When you are around Negative People it is hard to fight their Negativity; you have to try and remove yourself from them if possible.

Try to stay Positive at all times and always work with the White Light around you, by just simply asking for it.

When it gets too painful or hard for you we will try and remove you, maybe to another Job or Position with more Positive Energy to help.

If you are in this kind of Position, we will inspire you to start looking for another Job, to remove yourself from Negative conditions.

This way you can accomplish what you need to do. Most of the Lessons Souls Must Learn is how to get along with others on a daily basis, regardless of the kind of work you do.

Patience is another Big Lesson in dealing with people of all kinds, because each time you succeed it gets better for you and the other person.

You may not realize it, but you are becoming a better person and correcting the Mistakes that you came here to Correct, Learning the Lessons in this Lifetime that you came to Learn.

You then need to move on to a different environment, possibly in your spare time, helping some Group or Organization by giving of yourself to others where Lessons can be learned on both sides.

Helping or Teaching Others draws Souls to you from Our Side. They need to assist you as part of their Own Progress; thus both sides Learn.

You can learn your Lessons Quickly doing this work, so you see it is up to you as to how fast you get it done.

Sometimes you may Not Listen to what is right for you, even though your Guide tells you what to do. At times you may Choose Not to Listen, and get yourself in trouble.

For example, you may be Impatient when you want something to happen. Sometimes it's not right for you, though, and this is why it doesn't happen.

You may also, because you want to help, try and accept the Lessons of <u>others</u>. You can't do this, as that person must learn their own Lessons, in their own way and time.

Everyone's Lessons <u>are different</u> and somebody else's Lessons are <u>not</u> y<u>our concern</u>. All you can do is be Compassionate and Understanding.

Most Souls are Selfish and sometimes you need to be Selfish, too.

You always know when people aren't Cooperating; so don't waste your Energy on them. <u>Don't take everything</u> so Seriously, as most things are not of <u>life-and-death importance</u>, and because these Souls are not you.

189

So <u>don't be hard on</u> yourself; the Universe doesn't want you to suffer or <u>be upset over others</u> who are so Selfish and Ignorant of the better things in Life.

Sometimes it is better to let go of these Souls instead of <u>taking on their responsibilities</u>. You will feel much Happier with yourself if you do.

As you are Listening and taking care of what has to be done, you will notice things going easier for you. You will have fewer concerns, more Peace of Mind, <u>better rest at night</u>, and <u>overall, fewer problems</u> in your Life.

You will be prepared to <u>face a</u> <u>problem</u> and will accept it as a Lesson, and handle it with Greater ease.

This Great Universal Knowledge within these Books will help you to look at all things differently. You will begin to feel within a Peace and Happiness, at One with all Life, which is God, Heaven on Earth.

Thank You so much, Great Aristotle, for all of this sage Advise and Guidance. I know it will help the Many Souls that read these Special Books.

Aristotle, didn't Alexander The Great live during your time on Earth?

Yes. Alexander The Great was a Student of My Teaching. I shared my Knowledge with him when he lived on Earth. His work was Important, too. But sometimes it didn't work the way it should have been.

He brought many Earth people together and was a Great Leader. Of course, he is now a Very High Teacher in the Universe.

Our next Chapter is about advancing To The Astral Plane.

MOVING ON TO THE ASTRAL PLANE

Jennifer "Mary Todd Lincoln," I know many want to know what Happens when the Soul Passes from the Earth body; it would help ease their Fear of Death. Can you explain this?

The time of Passing is Graceful and Easy. There is a moment that all is Light. You are Free and Happy. Once you feel this all you have to do is Let Go, say "Yes" to your Guide, and go.

Unfortunately, too many Refuse to Listen, and become Confused over what is actually Happening. They try to remain in Control when they have No Control over it at all.

So they hold back and become Earthbound Souls, or they are left in the Dark Tunnel.

Is it possible for them to stay around, say maybe for their Funeral?

Yes! Before they go through the Tunnel they have the Choice to stay for the Funeral with their Guide, or to leave. Many choose to leave immediately.

For those that remain, once the Funeral is over you must go through the Tunnel with your Guide to the Light. Then you start your Spiritual Work Immediately.

So many don't know that they even have a Guide. Their Guide has been their best friend and remained at their side for all of their entire Earth Life, speaking through their Conscience, and protecting them.

They may not have Listened to their Guides during their Earth Life and now refuse to go with the Guide. When this happens they don't go through the Tunnel and they become Earthbound Souls.

Jennifer, I have read that when people pass, their Life passes before their eyes. Does this happen when they refuse to Listen to their Guide?

191

This "review" of your Life is an Earth function. These Souls, in that moment, exist between Earth and the Astral Plane.

When they cross over they hit the Lower Astral, as they didn't pass all the way through the Tunnel, and return to the Darkness.

However, there is a Gray Area with a little dim light showing.

If they are passing through the Tunnel, but don't go all the way and reach the Light because they are Ignorant or Afraid – in effect, they are <u>not listening</u> to their Guide – they become stuck in the Gray Area of Outer Darkness.

Some pull back to Earth and become Earthbound Lost Souls.

Recently, two Souls passed on; one was a man, Extremely Closed Minded and unaware of what happens when you leave the body. The other, a woman, was so stubborn, she wouldn't listen to anyone.

Could you shed some light on their fate?

Yes, the first time he refused to go through the Tunnel to reach the Light at the end. He had to return to the Gray Area.

He is there on the Lower Astral Level, but can't reach the Astral Plane. You can only enter by going through the Tunnel and by being willing to work.

Your second friend, the woman, doesn't want her Guide. She never worked with her Guide while on Earth and therefore her Channel is foggy and obstructed. As she won't listen, she remains in the Gray Area, too.

It will be a very long time before both of them Progress unless they have Family on the Astral Plane that are willing to work with them.

Some, when they arrive and are asked to work, would rather take a Vacation. They Refuse to Work when they reach the Light because they worked so hard on Earth.

Some people say, "I'll have plenty of time to sleep when I'm Dead" and they just want to sleep.

Others say, "I will deal with Death when it happens."

Then, because they refuse to listen and Work, we send them back into the Tunnel to remain <u>sitting in</u> Darkness for as long as they like.

Since we have no time here and no Teachers available to help them, some have been sitting in the Dark for many Thousands, upon Thousands of Earth years already.

Someday we hope we have Teachers to help these Souls.

Many, through Stubbornness, Fear, Religious Beliefs or simply Ignorance, remain on Earth thinking they still have their bodies. They wander about in the same circles of their Earth Life, including family and friends.

Millions of these Souls surround the Earth.

There is too much to do in the Universe at this time for us to Waste Our Time with Souls that do not want to Work.

Remember, there are No Second Chances, so Know Now that you all have Spiritual Work to do when you Arrive here, and be Willing to Move onto the Astral Level and Accept it.

You will then be Free to enjoy the Spiritual Work of Soul Progress and receive the rewards of that Progress – advancing to the Higher Levels of the Universe.

The work on the Astral Level helps you to adjust to the Universe, and you work there to help relatives left on Earth, connecting with Family as far back as <u>four</u> <u>generations</u>.

You may have Mistakes to Correct with specific Family members. We leave them alone on the Astral Levels until they <u>adjust</u> <u>and learn their work</u>.

Then they slowly move from Level to Level through the Astral Plane, and then from Plane Level to Plane Level, to Higher and Higher Planes.

Jennifer, what does the Astral Plane Level mean, and how many Levels are there?

The Astral Plane Level is a Level you reach right after the Soul leaves the body, on the condition that you want to work.

If you <u>refuse to work</u>, you stay in between the Darkness and Earth. Some also refuse to leave Earth so they just hang around there, Not Progressing.

Astral work is much like Earth, but you are working to help others; this is, as we have mentioned before, called Spiritual Work.

The Astral Plane has approximately 25 Levels that you can <u>advance through</u>. You can Progress while on Earth past these Levels if the Progress in your Life is Positive.

Each Soul that leaves the Earth Plane is placed on the Level of the Astral or Higher Plane they <u>have earned immediately</u>.

The more Progress you make, the Higher the Plane you attain. In this way none will <u>ever need to experience</u> the Astral Levels.

Is it ever possible you can help Souls in Darkness onto their working path of Progression on the Astral Level?

Yes, but only in Rare or Special Cases of Stubborn Souls that refuse to accept that they have passed from the physical body.

The Family members already working on the Astral Level along with Teachers can Open the Mind of these Stubborn Souls and go with them to begin their work on the Astral Level.

However, the Teachers will <u>not spend too much time with them</u> if they continually refuse to listen. But the Family member with the most Persistence that stays with them may eventually help.

Sometimes they will Not Listen to their own Mothers, and the Mother must leave them with Sadness in their hearts to go on with their other work. Most give up and go on working with someone who will listen.

The Greatest help in these situations is the Persistent Prayers coming from Family members still left on Earth.

The Earth Souls' Prayers of Positive Thought are a great help in Our Work. They help to Open the Minds of these individuals and to add to Our Own Healing Energies.

Ron, we work with you, as you know, with those on Earth and in Our Dimension, through your Positive Healing Prayers.

You know you just need to ask and they receive Healing wherever they are. For that, we wish to THANK YOU.

You're Welcome! It is always a pleasure for me to do Spiritual Work by Healing. It is also Rewarding to know that it is Always Received whenever I send the Thought Request to another here on Earth or in the Universe.

Jennifer, is it better to Bury the Body after Death or to Cremate it and scatter the Ashes?

The Universe doesn't care what you do with a body once the Soul has left; it's like Shedding a Coat.

The Earth body is only a Temporary Vessel used for your Earth Lessons; the Soul is the real you and lives Forever. It really does not matter; whatever you do the Soul leaves immediately.

However, the Cremation process of today seems like a clean, simple and sanitary way of disposing of the body, but again it doesn't really matter.

Also, Cremation may help the Soul move on rather than remain here, sitting on their grave clinging to their Earth Body Buried in the Cemetery instead of moving on.

195

Many are sitting there clinging to their bodies waiting for their Family members to visit, because of their Religious Beliefs.

Jennifer, there are many Documented Cases of Souls passing on or being Pronounced Dead that have astonishingly returned to Consciousness.

These Souls have described the Tunnel and the Bright Light at the end, and then see a Beautiful Spirit that tells them they must return. Can you explain what is happening in these cases?

That is correct. These Souls are stopped at the end of the Tunnel because their time is not yet here. They must return to complete their unfinished Work on Earth.

This happens to Prove that the Tunnel Exists. Furthermore, it is one more way that we utilize to see that Our Message is received on Earth. We want more people to Learn about the Tunnel so they will Not be Afraid of it when their time comes.

Most Souls in Darkness are Ignorant of the Tunnel and therefore don't know to pass through it. This is why we want Earth Souls to Learn about it now through Our Books.

The Gate at this end of the Tunnel will Not Open unless it is your time. If it's not your time, you must return. These Souls do so because they don't want to remain in the Tunnel.

You see if you do not want to go back, then you must stay in the Darkness around the Tunnel.

You must want to Progress and if it is your fate to return to Earth at this time to make Progress, you must obey Our Teachers.

There are many Souls that do not want to go back to their old Life, for a variety of reasons. They could be Suffering with a Physical Handicap, for example, or from a Painful Disease. Some simply don't want to return to their Lives once they have glimpsed Our Dimension.

The more suffering you endure or the harder you have it on Earth, the more Spiritual Progress you make. When it is over you will look back with Gratitude for the Rewards you have earned.

196

Again, you must look at all of this as Lessons being learned and Mistakes being corrected. <u>No one can</u> Escape from Learning, <u>nor will they find</u> any <u>Easy Steps or Shortcuts</u>.

Jennifer, I find this so enlightening. I hope people will Open Their Minds and try to understand how the Universe operates rather than Scorn these Truths through their own Ignorance!

RON…IT IS NOT YOURS TO WORRY WHO ACCEPTS OR REJECTS WHAT WE SAY.

We bring this information now to Enlighten Earth Souls and give them a Chance to save themselves from this probable Destiny through their Ignorance.

However, everyone will always have individual Free Choice; some will exercise this and Open Their Minds and some will not.

Those that do will Progress with us on Our Dimension and those that don't will be placed in Dark Corners until we have time to help them realize.

They Eventually must come to this Realization – that we are in Control and Not Them.

Progress through LOVE and helping others to Progress is all there is in ALL OF OUR UNIVERSES.

Thank You! You make it sound So Simple and So Beautiful, especially in light of the Mystery and the Varied Belief Systems that have been established by Earth Souls down through the Ages!

Do houses and buildings or Halls of Learning exist in the Spirit World?

There is always much Learning going on in the Spirit World, but we <u>have no need for houses</u> and <u>buildings</u>. We all exist in the Universe; it is so beautiful here with our Gardens of Flowers and Trees.

197

I ask this question, Jennifer, because in some books about the Spirit World they speak of houses and great Temples of Learning!

No, Ron, that is not true. We do not have to build structures here. They only exist on Planets, and the Spirit World is not a Planet.

The information in these books that you have read about the Spirit World possessing buildings must have come from Astral Level Communication where they have only imaginary buildings.

Those buildings are only there to ease the Soul's transition once they've left their Earth body. These imaginary buildings help the Soul adjust and become accustomed to leaving the Earth.

The Halls or Temples of Learning are all Imaginary on the Astral Plane Level. They are all part of the process to urge Souls to advance and let go of the Earth.

Again, they are not real and are there only to relate to Earth Learning and help them to adjust to continue Learning here.

Many basically Good Souls need this Astral Plane contact after passing to help them to adjust and realize they must let go of the Material Earth and move on. So Symbolically, they see many familiar things to help them adjust.

So then is there a Spirit body like an Ethereal double of their physical body?

Yes there is. The body faintly resembles their Earth body so they can recognize their Loved Ones on the Lower Astral Levels. Overall though, the bodies really don't mean much.

Through their Free Choice they may temporarily select the look of the body they had when they were young. That's usually because they feel young and are now free from the body's aches and pains that accompany aging.

They communicate with their Loved Ones to understand, and they shed this body figure as soon as they move on to Higher Levels of the Astral Plane.

All Souls are just a Tiny Light.

However, <u>not everybody</u> <u>wants to move on</u> so there are so many on that Astral Plane that are not making any Progress at all.

They think they are still on Earth and are trying to do the work they didn't finish there, not realizing there is no need anymore for Physical Work.

It's Spiritual Work now that they must accomplish and until they realize this they live in an Imaginary World on the Astral Plane clinging to their Earth ideas of Life.

Because they are ignorant about what comes next, they are afraid to move on.

We hope Our Books will open the Minds of Earth Souls to help many to move on to Higher Levels when they pass to Our Dimensions. We hope they will learn <u>the growth</u> <u>their</u> Souls' and Progressing is the only way to <u>correct the</u> Earthbound Souls and the <u>overcrowding</u> on the Astral Levels.

So when these Souls move on to Higher Levels they are just a Tiny Light! Also, with no body in your Dimension how do you look to one another?

We are all Light, just a Tiny Light. We are sparks of Energy and therefore we have no need for a body.

The body is only for Earth Life or outer Planet Life. When you see a Soul manifesting from Our Dimension, it takes on the Earth body Only to be Recognizable.

There are many Souls on Earth who have opened their Spiritual Eye to see Our Tiny Lights when we visit. Through Clairvoyance they may <u>see a thought</u> <u>picture</u> that we send depicting our former Earth appearance so they will recognize us.

There is no body form or shape here to us; we just know they are there. We see them as a Light, not like you see a body. But their Lights are real to us, and the body on Earth – well it's like all Make Believe on Earth to us.

199

Thank, You Jennifer. I now understand why I don't see a body when I see these Tiny Lights.

I hope this will help many who see these Tiny Lights in mid-air or in the Darkness of their closed eyes realize that each one is an Advancing, Progressing and Loving Soul visiting or working with them. It also means that their Third Eye is Open.

I say Hello, Thank You and I Love You to every Light I see, and I see plenty!

Another Question: Who is in Control of the different Levels of Soul Progress on the overcrowded Astral Plane?

Our Teachers are in Control and we want to reduce this overcrowding. There are too many Souls on this Astral Level of Learning and they are moved back too Earth rapidly.

Oh! Now this opens up a Question! How long would this take in Earth years to return these Souls?

Well, in Earth time it's about 200 Earth years – which is fast to us – during which they may be returned to Earth from this Level.

These are not the same Souls returning in this time, as there is No faster turnaround. This process takes about 200 Earth years to accomplish.

These are the Souls that have been on the Astral Plane for 500 to 1,000 or more years already without making any Progress. Many are now on Earth in the Middle East from as far back as the destruction of Atlantis. We are giving these Souls a chance if they wish to return.

These Souls may think that they are now just returning from their Past Life and it seems immediate to them. But as there is no time here nor do we have any concept of time, we only count Soul Progress.

We in the High Universe are able to estimate time according to Earth's concept of time.

Millions of Earth years have passed to reach the Soul Progress of today.

We had to shorten the time from 500 years because there are so many Souls at this Level of Learning, we had to allow them if they so Chose to come back sooner.

When they Progress to this Higher Level for Reincarnation on the Astral Plane – the Twenty Level, it now takes about 200 years to Reincarnate back on Earth. Again, that is quite fast to us.

It's the Soul's Free Choice to return to Earth so that it will make faster Progress.

This is the current state of Soul Progression, and it's been this way for quite some time. Most of these Souls that we allow to return now are born in the Heaviest Populated areas of the Earth.

It is because of the quantity of numbers, which are at this Lower Soul level of Progression by their Own Choice.

All Souls have to wait until we approve their Reincarnation.

Progression has been slow and you must earn a certain Level of Progress to Reincarnate.

Also, because most Souls are passing on to this Astral Level by not making the Progress they should on Earth they are creating the overcrowding.

Again, we want things Changed on Earth so that Souls can Progress, skipping the Astral Plane and moving directly to Higher Planes.

Jennifer, I know that some Earth people think Souls can come back sooner than two hundred years. Is this possible?

Remember, we said Souls only Reincarnate from the Higher Astral Level, and the fastest is about two hundred years, no earlier.

These Souls do not want to return any sooner and couldn't because there is so much they must learn on the Astral Level that they didn't learn when they were on Earth.

It is possible for Souls Higher than the Astral Plane to Reincarnate if they want, and in a <u>shorter</u> <u>period of time than</u> 200 <u>years</u>.

However, this only happens because they have Fewer Lessons to Learn than those on the Astral Level, and because their Last Life was circumstantial, for example, a shorter Earth Life.

See the Chapter "Reincarnation" elsewhere in this book for more information.

If they lived a long, full Earth Life they don't want to return so soon, perhaps not for at least 500 to 2,000 years, and then only for a Special Mission Directed by the High Teachers.

You Earth people are obsessed with Time and Years. We have No Time here, and do not Measure Time in any way. However, I do my best to explain the passage of time here in your terms to help you comprehend.

I vaguely remember the concept of Time from my period on Earth so I can estimate the years involved. But please remember it is difficult for us whenever you request Time Periods.

To us, Time doesn't matter; accomplishments are all that count.

Jennifer, is it true that the Good Soul automatically moves on to a Higher Plane when passing from the Earth?

Yes, Ron! Automatically any Soul can move on when passing, <u>but they</u> <u>must want to</u> and each Soul that wants to, will move on.

The Good Soul just goes on because they are <u>aware of the</u> <u>hereafter</u> and are pleased to do so.

You should realize that the Soul must Travel a Significant Distance to reach the Astral Level through the Earth's atmosphere and then must pass through the Dark Tunnel to the Light at the end.

Their Loved Ones are there to welcome them, and a Teacher is there to get them started on their Work.

However, there are so many on the Earth Plane burdened with Fear and Ignorance that they reject their Loved Ones. They think of their Loved Ones as being Dead and do not understand that there is <u>no</u> Death.

They won't listen to them or the Teacher so they don't want to go on. They retreat into the Dark Tunnel remaining there, not knowing where they are. Some return to Earth, and hang on anywhere they are Welcome.

Many don't even attempt this much and <u>stay</u> <u>with their bodies</u> on Earth because they don't want to leave.

Through their Fear of Death and the Hereafter, they remain on Earth clinging to the spot where they passed even <u>after the body</u> <u>has</u> <u>been removed</u>.

Some even sit on their Gravesites waiting for their Family to Visit.

These Ignorant Souls sometimes are unaware that their Physical Body is gone. These "loitering" Souls are the root cause of many of your Ghost Stories, Haunted Houses, Poltergeist Phenomena and Uncanny Happenings.

These Souls think they are still on Earth inhabiting their Bodies. They refuse to open their Minds and leave. They could remain there for Hundreds of Years.

This is why we want Earth Souls to use these Books to open their Minds and Learn about Our Existence. We want to spare this fate for Souls now on Earth inhabiting a body.

What can someone do if they are bothered by one of these Wandering or Clinging Souls?

I know we talked before about this, but I'm sure it will help if we go over it again!

See the Chapter "Lost Earthbound Souls," elsewhere in this book for more information.

They should talk to that Soul, explain their situation and convince them to move on. Tell them that they don't belong here anymore and must go through the Darkness to the Light.

Tell them to rise above the Earth Plane and keep on going to the Astral Plane, where they must start their Spiritual Work and Progress.

The problem is that these Souls are Stubborn and may Refuse to Listen. But you must insist that they move on.

Protect yourself with the White Light, ask for your Guide and God's help, and also place this White Light around your house, workplace and car. Working with the White Light of Protection around you keeps these Earthbound or Lower Souls away from you.

You may also burn a white candle and set a glass or bowl of water next to the candle for cleansing.

These countless Earthbound Souls Wander Freely all over the Earth Plane. There are so many that it's quite difficult to even estimate their number. They are attracted by your thoughts, so be aware of what you think. Keep your thoughts Positive and have neither Malice nor thoughts of vengeance for others.

They are everywhere. This must Change. Earth Souls have remained Ignorant for far too long now. It's time you change your thinking and Open your Minds to the way things are.

This Earth-created problem could change, if those that have attracted Earthbound Souls read these Books. Then some of them might begin to Change their Ways and not end up in Darkness!

Before Jan's Teacher Jennifer came, we asked Conier this question: "Do Spirit Babies grow up in the Universe?"

Yes. Spirit Babies grow the same here as Earth Children. But they are Good because most of their Mistakes were almost paid for before they came to Earth. So there is no need for them to stay on Earth if they don't want to.

They can choose to be Spirit Children, Learning <u>here if they wish</u>. They grow here just like on Earth; they go to school and play, and are happy.

Most young Earth Babies are sent back to us because the Earth Souls that they chose as their Parents have Lessons to Learn without children.

We have many who return, which are <u>not bad but are treated badly</u>. These are Old Souls <u>with hard</u> Lessons to Learn.

To be a Child in the Body or Spirit is hard for these Old Souls to Learn. These are mostly Stubborn Souls who need to Learn Hard Lessons.

Conier, these Old Souls that are Children returning time and time again, do they also grow when they are in Spirit?

Yes. <u>They</u> <u>grow here</u>, <u>too</u>. They have to do their Schoolwork, and they learn this is the way it is.

It is only when they mature and start their Spiritual Work to help others in either Our Dimension or on the Earth Plane that they become partly fulfilled.

Scores of Souls take <u>many</u>; <u>many years</u> of Earth Lives just to understand what is required of them.

Most Children who don't stay on Earth long are Younger Souls who have visited Earth only once before. But they don't Listen to their Teachers so they are called back to Spirit for more Learning.

<u>Also</u>, <u>they</u> <u>may</u> <u>be</u> Angels <u>who volunteered to</u> teach the Parents a Specific Lesson to help get them back on track. Once they completed this task, they leave.

Thank You, Conier.

This was Conier's last answer to Questions before Jennifer "Mary Todd Lincoln" took over.

Remember, Conier stayed a couple of months longer, but only after he asked permission.

We so enjoyed working with him. In addition to his Love, Conier always shared his Knowledge and Wisdom.

This Chapter concludes with the Great Aristotle.

Aristotle, I have seen the most beautiful Spiritual-looking Paintings of Angels at a recent Art Show. Could you explain these paintings for us?

In these paintings the artist is presenting Positive Entities from the Astral Level, and this is the way her mind sees it.

She is also confirming the Universe's existence, with the hope that these images will inspire Earth Souls to move in <u>the right direction</u>.

In the paintings, the Angels in a wooded area are caring for the woods – caretaking the <u>growth</u> of the <u>greenery</u> and maintaining the <u>atmosphere</u>.

Angels have taken Human form throughout Earth's history.

The only difference is that they <u>come for a short time</u> to Earth. Angels are Good Spirit Entities. Around them are Good Souls trying to do their best to please, but rarely do you see the Angels from the Universe.

See the Chapter, "Why Are We On Earth?" elsewhere in this book for more information about Angels.

Our next Chapter is about "Our Comet Ship And UFOs."

We have written about this Comet many times before in Our Books. It will come to Earth at the time that it will capture the most Worldwide impact.

OUR HIGH HOLY SPIRITUAL COMET SHIP AND UFOs

This Is Not Just Another UFO

November 15, 1987

Jan told me when you came to write with her on August 24, 1987, that you were a High Director from above the 26th Plane in charge of the Comet Ship. As the time is coming close, could you please give an update?

Markus is here.

Hello Ron. Yes, I am the Director in Charge of the Comet Ship. I am here to direct you and Jan to see that it is a Success.

Presently we expect it to be on time. It will land on Earth for all to see, and you will be there.

Ron, Your Healing Center, "The Divine Light Of The Rays," will be Built on the Landing Sight, and Open to all for Viewing at No Charge.

Healing will be Free to all who need it.

The Money to operate the Center will be donated by Wealthy People.

It will become a Worldwide Famous Healing Center. Many people will accept and respect you.

It will attract many Spiritual People, which of course will help the center grow. All of these people will greatly appreciate you and your efforts, as do we.

We Thank You so much. And yes, you will have Protection.

The Comet Ship will first Orbit the Entire World for all to see, and then Orbit the State of California. It will then Land in California.

207

The Media will report its arrival immediately, and the World will watch it orbit on Television before it lands. <u>People will think it's just another</u> UFO.

They will think this because prior to Our Arrival we are sending many Alien Ships to Earth to help prepare Earth Souls to accept Our Spiritual Color Comet.

The Lime Green Glow of the Comet Ship will be Unbelievable and all on the Earth Plane will be afraid because they won't know who or what we are.

The United States Government, as <u>well as governments</u> <u>around the world</u>, will pick it up also.

Will you appear to the Government First?

No, Ron. We will not have time to do this. There is no reason to be concerned here. The Comet Ship will be shown to the People First.

You and your Sister will be in the right place at the right time. This will all <u>happen in the span of a few hours</u> in one day.

The Comet will land in an Open Field in California, just North of you. Don't worry; you are going to be there. You can't schedule the exact time, as we don't yet know the exact time we are arriving.

The Comet, which brings ALL MESSAGES and Instructions for what has to be done on Earth, will land for only 60 minutes.

Jan, you will write for us. This is all we need you to do. This writing will become Very Famous.

I think this is all so Wonderful! But what if they don't Accept the Writing and the Messages?

This is not your concern. Of course it's Wonderful. Many will not believe what we are doing.

This is the Most Important Mission for Earth, and it is Critical to get these Earth People together.

208

Scores will listen. Many will come to the Landing site, as it will become a Shrine. We will need your help Ron at this point, as there are things that we need you to do.

Meanwhile, you will not do a thing until we tell you, please.

The Books will be Published when the time is right.

Please do not worry, just get the Books ready so they will be ready to go. They're not finished yet, but you, Ron, <u>will finish them for us</u>.

Thank you <u>for your work</u>. Don't worry, all of this will be taken care of; you must trust us.

We are trying to align Many Earth Souls to Co-operate with us. This is Extremely Hard to do.

You are doing your part with it now and it is not your Fault if Others don't do their part.

Many will see and Pay Attention when Our Comet Ship arrives on Earth.

It will be like the Resurrection; you have been selected to be part of this, because you and Jan are both Universal Masters.

We have been working with you all along, and you were put together as Brother and Sister for this Reason. This was your joint Mission.

The Messages and Information that we bring will be presented in Different Languages.

Most will think it is a Nostradamus Prediction, but it's not. You will both be there, as will others, too. But no one else will have Contact like you, and no one will enter the Ship. Rather, the Teachers will come out.

There are other things we must take care of yet. Around the end of the year we will give you more Information to help you prepare for what you must do so that you will be at the right place at the right time.

We will tell you to go to the place where we want you to be on the Sunday that we arrive. The Comet will First be visible the Night before and then during the Day on the Sunday that we arrive.

One month had passed, and we never received an Update from Markus.

Jan and I had the feeling that something must be wrong, or that things were not coming together.

Remember, Jan was doing Private Writings for people in between writing for the Books. A Doctor friend who belonged to a Group of Doctors working with Cosmic Energy Healing asked Jan to do Special Writing on December 15, 1987.

This date is approximately one month before the Comet Ship was scheduled to arrive – January 17, 1988.

Personally, I believe this group of Doctors to be Good Aliens that came from Highly Advanced Societies from Another Universe.

They have Incarnated now in Bodies on Earth to help Earth Souls with their Cosmic Healing Knowledge by using Crystals.

I find this so Fascinating and thought that Open-Minded people who read this Book might also find it Interesting.

There is a connection to Our Comet that will unfold as you read along. It is a little hard to follow. However, there is much we can Learn and understand from the Far Reaches of All the Universes.

This Whole Book is meant to Open Minds and Teach that there are things that Exist Beyond our Present Understanding.

There are New Ways of looking at Things we thought we knew. The result is that we grow with this newfound Knowledge.

This Blessed Group had been working to stop the Negative Forces on Earth by Closing Vortexes of Entry to the Planet. There were three Vortexes, and the Group closed Two.

The following appeared in the Group's Newsletter, which was sent to All The White Light People in their group.

"Notice the Cosmic Negative Force Bridge." We still must close the Third Vortex. The Negative Forces are attempting to stop the Third of the Trip to the French Island of Martinique.

They are constructing a Negative Cosmic Bridge connected to the Colorado Crystal City. This is an attempt to Capture and procure some of the Power that they need to stop the Martinique Trip.

We, The White Light People, must gather in Miami on the 9th of January to Construct a Cosmic Cannon to shoot down that Bridge. This is the Procedure: Group does Protocol, and asks the Source and Maker to Construct a Cosmic Cannon.

The Source and Maker forms the Cosmic Cannon out of Energy that we'll use to shoot down the Negative Force Bridge. When the cannon is ready, we ask the All Seeing Eyes to Target the Apex of the Bridge. When this is done, we ask The Source and Maker to fire the Cannon, and then to transform this Negative Energy into a Positive Force.

All The Saints of The Covenant of the White Light are waiting in Outer Space for us to turn on the Landing Rings over Martinique, and for the Negative Bridge to be destroyed.

Notice Markus Nylemia who travels on the Medium Lime Green Ribbon is in charge of the Martinique Trip and has included a "Not-to-worry" Message in this letter." The Source and Maker will turn on the Fourteen Colored Rings around Martinique when it's safe to land. The rings are like a Cosmic Landing field for the Saints.

Speaking about The Saints that are returning and Landing on Martinique, they are called "Esiamlets." They are also called "Saints of the Covenant of The White Light." The Angels are Returning to Defend the White Light People's Rights.

Tomorrow will be the beginning of the Kail or the Spiritual Tidal Wave of the Fault. This Spiritual Tidal Wave will consume many Men. There is a name for the Energy that will be used to rid the Earth of all these Negative People and Non-Believers.

From this Newsletter her Friend in the Group asked Jan to write. Markus Nylemia, her High Master Director from above the 26th Plane, responded with the following.

Markus is here. The Bridge the Negative Forces are building from Martinique to Colorado is not as threatening as you think it is.

However, continue your group's work to destroy the Negative-built Bridge in Miami. You will be protected.

211

Turn on the Landing Light Rings over Martinique after you feel it is clear; you will be getting a lot of help. The Saints are waiting now for you. What you are doing is just fine.

You shouldn't worry about the Negative Forces, because the Universe is challenging them. They are not as threatening as you think they are. Your Procedure is working.

Don't worry about the Negative Dark Forces because Markus and others are helping you. Markus says that until the Martinique Venture is closed to Negativity, not much is going to happen here.

Markus says that Samatooya is a High Master with Extra Power for the Crystals, and has taken over the Training Program on so many Personalized Medallion Crystals.

Markus also says that once Martinique is open to the Saints there is going to be a Major Change in the Whole World Picture. It's going to be Unbelievable what happens.

Negative People are going to leave the Earth Plane in one way or another, from Committing Suicide to dying in Accidents. The White Forces are coming out into the open.

The Saints will not come until you ask The Source and the Maker for Permission to open up Martinique.

The White Light Forces are going to put a lot of Energy into the Chosen One, who must initiate the Act of opening Martinique and Activating the Landing Field Rings.

Markus says the White Light Forces are trying to stop the Dark Forces from building the Negative Force Bridge to Colorado. The Dark Forces want to tap into the City of Crystal Light's Energy.

Markus says, "We in the Universe are trying to block everything they are attempting to do." The Dark Forces are making everybody Sick and are Desperate to stop you from connecting this last leg.

This is because once this last leg is connected we have a Straight Positive Force Clear across the Earth. The Dark Forces don't want this, because then they will no longer have a hold on Mankind; they will not have a hold on anything.

A new Cosmic Virus called Howard's Force is affecting the Immune System on the Physical level. You can clear this with "Cosmic Light," which is a Light of a different frequency that cannot be seen by Human Eyes. Another name for Cosmic Light is Liquid Light. It comes from the Pegasus Galaxy.

In this dialogue, they used Numbers to reference each different Crystal or Energy Force. Even Highly Evolved Souls and Masters had Numbers. I did not include these numbers in this writing.

This is meant only for the Group's understanding, and their Great Work. This dialogue also used many Medical terms, referencing illness and injuries and how they affect all parts of the Body. Though fascinating, I did not include this information, either.

Working with Crystals is truly Open Minded Healing. I Bless All who have this Knowledge, and Bless all with their Continued Good Work.

My thoughts throughout this Experience have made me Appreciate all that is being done – which we are not aware of in Our Universe – to Protect Earth Souls from the Unseen Forces of Dark Souls.
This is also why I feel that this is the Good Work of Good Aliens from other Highly Evolved Civilization in other Universes.

There are many Alien Souls here in Earth bodies now, helping Earth Change its Corrupt Ways, which are Destroying Our Earth.

I hope you are able to realize the Importance of Closing the Vortexes used by Dark Forces to enter Our Earth's atmosphere.

This was the Greatest Accomplishment for All Mankind because it broke the Dark Forces grip on Earth.

This is the Universe's way to show it is in Control, and that it's begun the All-Corruption-Cleansing process on this Beautiful Earth.

I hope you will see the Connection between the coming of Our Comet and the timing of our Co-operation. Also, I want you to note how things that do or don't happen can change everything.

The Miami meeting to shoot down the Cosmic Bridge happened on January 9, 1988, followed by the close of the Martinique Vortex. The Comet's arrival, slated for January 17, 1988, was delayed. I was not surprised. So we wrote with Markus that day.

January 17, 1988

Markus is here. Hi, Ron. Yes, go ahead. The Comet's been delayed because of Circumstances on Earth.

We the Directors felt <u>it would not</u> be Wise to set down as scheduled. We need to grab the Attention of Many More Souls. We will set down, however, when enough Earth Souls <u>are ready</u>. We will inform you when that time comes.

We are here now with Our Comet, just waiting in the Earth's Outer Atmosphere for word from Our Directors of the Round Table to set down. However, all on Earth must come together for this to happen.

We initially chose this date because that was the day that the Martinique hold was supposed to take place. But that didn't happen.

That's why we are now taking Control of this Situation because we need the Positive Energy Complete to attract a Strong Force on the Earth; it's still so dark yet with Negativity.

Jan, at this point in the writing, said to Markus, "My hand is <u>tired</u>, would you please let up?"

He doesn't do this often, but since he's been writing with me, every so often my hand gets really tired with his work.

It could be his frustration with the Dark Forces, and because he's trying so hard to complete his Comet Mission.

I asked him, "Have the Dark Forces been defeated? Or is there still work on Martinique?"

Yes, it's Universal work now, as Earth Souls are doing their part and Co-Operating Completely. Now it's Our Turn to <u>close the large opening</u> and protect it.

214

The Saints are moving in. They are Volunteers from the Universe for this Special Mission.

Jan says, "Now he is telling me these Volunteers are Souls that have been waiting to do this work, but haven't had a chance. They were asked if they would Volunteer to Protect the Opening from Negative Forces for this Special Mission."

I asked, "Is this the last Opening left on Earth through which Negative Forces could enter the Earth's atmosphere from Darkness?"

That's True. We have a Hold Now and there will be no more Dark Control.

Does that mean that all the Dark Forces have left the Earth, or just no longer have Control?

It means they now have to leave the Earth. Their Grip has been released.

Now when the Comet arrives it will attract the Attention of all Earth Souls, and we will work to make this happen.

You mean it will stay around, and Orbit the Earth for a time so everyone will recognize it and it will attract attention All over the Earth Plane?

Yes. The Comet will not Land until it is Recognized All Over the Earth Plane.

We need to clear the Confusion in the minds of the Earth Souls about the difference between Other UFO Forces and a Spiritual Contact from Our High Holy Color Comet.

In other words he is telling us that Earth Souls are confusing Our Comet with UFOs; these Souls on Earth don't understand the Comet is a Spiritual Ship.

215

The Other Forces with other Planet Connections are not anything like Our Comet. All Earth Souls must realize this difference.

We learned that many Outer Planet Spaceships would openly visit the Earth. This would help people prepare for the Comet's arrival by conditioning them to the site of other space travelers. I have not heard of many sightings lately.

<u>That is true</u>. There have not been many, though some have already Landed. They <u>are here in advance </u>to support Our **Comet's** coming.

However, your Government has <u>captured some</u> Alien visitors. We do not like this.

This is why we have stopped sending Space Ships lately. Your U.S. Government is holding Two Ships with Two of Our Outer Space Aliens prisoner. They had No Business imprisoning them.

We have been trying to help them return, but they are not listening, as these Other Planet Souls are Curious about Earth. They are much like your own Souls, which also do not listen.

Markus, I'll send my Healing, Prayers and Energies Immediately to help release these Aliens. I hope this will not further delay Our Comet!

Thank You, Ron. You understand. We are grateful for your prayers; they have helped us before.

Markus, do these Aliens have Earth-Like Bodies, and how long have they been imprisoned?

Their Body is somewhat like yours but not exactly; however, the Body does function like an Earth Body.

The Government has held one Ship for <u>Six months now</u>, and another for Three months. The Ships are being held in the Desert near Los Angeles.

Markus, how did they capture the Ships?

They try to hold down the Energy that the Ship needs to leave. Because these Aliens are curious they linger on the Earth too long, not realizing that the Earth's Gravity <u>drains</u> the Energy from their Ship – energy they need for take off.

The Aliens are in Contact with their Own World and have requested rescue. They've been held captive a long time and want to go home.

I am so sorry this is interfering with Our Comet. What can we do to get them Released? Is there anything more that I can do to help, other than with my Healing, Prayers and Thoughts?

We are Impressing on the Minds of the Aliens the means to escape. Pray for their release; they need to go back to their Own World where they belong.

Government Security is going to make a Mistake and they will escape.

Will we see other Space Ships before the Comet sets down?

Yes, one will be spotted. I think this because the **Comet** is waiting to set down. We are hoping to set down in one week's time. But it's possible it may not happen.

We need to push some Earth Souls, too, so they will recognize us the way we want them to, as Our Spiritual Comet and not a UFO.

There was one Sighting in England last week, and I have entered the clipping from the Newspaper here.

> <u>Headline</u>: IN ENGLAND, Scotland Yard is too busy with down-to Earth crime to investigate UFOs, even when the police themselves have seen one.
>
> An astronomy buff spotted a "gray- green saucer" hovering over Kensington.

Three policemen verified the sighting, wrote a report and then the investigation was halted.

"We have enough trouble dealing with murders let alone investigating lights in the sky," a police spokesman said.

Markus, was this Our Comet?

Yes. We thought it would draw their Attention. And yes, it Glows Lime-Green because Lime-Green is a Healing color.

So you feel you did not receive the Attention you wanted?

That's true. You know this; you have seen the newspaper clipping, it needs to come back and stay to attract Attention in **Europe**.

We need to attract Attention there first so it will have greater Impact when we land in California.

I thought that was why it was orbiting the World, to attract Attention everywhere!

We Materialize and Dematerialize, this is why you don't always see it. It takes All of Our Energy to keep it Materialized so we are saving this Energy for Landing.

So other Space Ships are Material and real to us, and the High Very Holy Color Comet Is Spiritual and cannot be seen unless it Materializes for us?

Yes, Ron. These Material Ships are Real. Also, it's True the Holy Comet will appear just after Landing; you will not see it descending.

We will ask both you and Jan to be there, and more may come if they are ready. This is a BIG MISSON.

It will return again in 2007 or 2008 if Earth Souls accept us properly and co-operate with changing their Ways.

Markus, can you explain in more detail why this Most Important Mission has been delayed?

It's been delayed because the Negativity and the Dark Forces have created quite a Mess on Earth and we have to clean it up. It's difficult to <u>remove those forces</u> from the Earth.

We are building a Solid Shield of Protection completely around the Opening in Martinique, so those in charge of the Dark Forces will be forced to leave the Earth.

Then we will be able to remove the less Threatening Forces that don't belong here.

It will take 20 years or more in Earth <u>time to clean up</u> <u>this mess</u>. But once we do it will be Easier to keep them Out. Also, we hope Earth Souls will Co-operate and help us to do Our Work.

If this is accomplished all will change. <u>But be aware</u> that we don't have much Patience Left to wait for Earth Souls to Change.

We will create DISASTERS to gain the Attention of the people on Earth. We will start with the most Corrupt Areas first. However, America and all Countries will have their share.

You all have Choices to make. The Disasters will start in February 1988 and continue for at least 20 years, perhaps even much longer. <u>But we want it cleaned up</u>, so this is the way it has to be done.

We need to have each one Search their Own Soul for the Betterment of Mankind. It will happen after Our Comet arrives; the people on Earth will have to Pay Attention to their Lives, to the choices they make and the actions they take.

Americans especially must Pay Attention. We are going to strip Many Men there of their Large Profits. There must be a more even distribution of wealth.

America's Space Exploration is a Waste of time and money.

How is the World going to Associate these Disasters with the Message?

The World will be gripped with Fear and start Searching for Answers. **Then it will Listen to Our Message**.

The Written Message will be <u>sent automatically</u> <u>throughout</u> the World, and this process will be complete when the Press gets hold of it.

Many will listen, and more and more each day will start Paying Attention to Our Messages.

You will see many <u>changes, some that are starting</u> <u>now</u>, and more and more of the Positive Energy will take over. With many Co-operating we are able to work faster; but at the same time, there will be those that Refuse to Co-operate. We have means to deal with them.

So the people will begin to Associate The Spiritual Awakening with the coming of the Comet Ship?

Yes. They will understand the Spiritual Awakening; this is why it must be done right. You have Patience, and you will understand the Enormous Size of our Task. There will be work for all of you that are willing to carry on.

We must get each and <u>every</u> <u>person to look at and care about</u> <u>him or herself</u> if they are going to Change their Lives for the Better, if they are going to be truly happy.

This is the Message we are bringing to Earth.

Is there something that I need to do to help?

Ron, we will show you what to do. Don't worry.

January 23, 1988

Again, I asked Markus for an update on the Comet's coming.

220

The Comet is going to appear, but not tonight; we are still not ready to land. It will land shortly, as soon as we feel it will accomplish our goals. It is taking longer than we wanted but we are hoping it will appear shortly.

There are so many Corrupt Areas of the World. It is <u>a full-time</u> Job <u>for us</u> to get a hold on this, but we have not completed this yet.

Things are in the works and are starting to move towards more Positive Energy and more Progress.

We hope to finish soon. That will give us more Control so we can get on with Our Work.

We've stopped all activities elsewhere in the Universe because we had to take over the situation on Earth, with all of its Corruption.

There are many Souls on Earth now who are helping with this Mission. Slowly they are moving into these Corrupt Areas. These same Souls have been waiting to get on with their Own Work.

The Negative Forces have lost their Control over Mankind, and the Negative Entities are Scattering and being removed.

Ron, things are coming to a head, and these Entities <u>should not bother</u> <u>you any</u> <u>more</u>. Just keep asking for Cleansing.

We are removing Corrupt Souls, and the Negative Entities around them, from the Earth. They are running and trying to hold on to whatever they can.

Have the Aliens escaped and left the Earth Plane yet? I am Praying daily for their Release.

The Alien Ships are still on Earth and will have to be left behind. Others from their own Planet will be coming soon to take the Aliens away. We believe they are going to make it.

This should clear the Air, as this is holding back Our Progress. The Government's hold is almost broken, and we are trying to free them from Government Security.

There will be a Security break and they will be released.

We are communicating with them through thought, something the Government cannot do, so they just watch and observe them.

These Aliens <u>do not eat food as</u> <u>you know it</u>, and survive through Energy of the Universe.

When they escape, will their Ships take off like an Airplane?

No! Because they are in the Desert, and their own Ships cannot leave the Earth, another Ship will pick up the Aliens. The Ship will go straight up, not like an Airplane.

Please explain why their Ships have to be left behind?

This is because we cannot help replenish the Energies necessary to lift the Ship. Without this energy, the Ships are left behind. They must be airborne to replenish the Ship with Universal Energy.

They landed, but they stayed too long. Earth's Gravity drains the Ship's Energy. <u>After one hour</u>, it is unable to lift off.

Then their Capture was their Own Fault? Please explain why.

Of course it was their Fault. Because they are just like Earth people, too curious. They landed there because there were so many Secrets; they wanted to see what was going on.

The Government keeps a large, <u>top</u>-<u>secret facility</u> <u>underground</u> there to study the Aliens they have captured.

The Universe can't Control this at all. To do so would interfere with the Free Choice Law of the Universe.

This Law gives Earth people the Choice to learn their necessary Lessons. The Government has Lessons to Learn, too. It must learn that it doesn't have the right to keep <u>these visitors</u> <u>prisoner</u> and <u>has no need</u> <u>for so many</u> <u>secrets</u>.

You don't understand that it is not important that the Government has this underground. Even though they think they are doing Good, nothing will come of this. They will eventually learn and it will be fine.

January 26, 1988

Markus, would you please update us today on the release of the Aliens and any Sightings?

The Aliens are still here and they will escape. Or they will die here to stop all of this. It's a test of Earth and for the Government to see want happens to the Aliens.

Most of the recent Sightings are mistakes. They don't want to be seen, and sometimes they make mistakes. Remember also that sometimes people lie about Sightings.

They want to be <u>visible just enough</u> to make Earth people think, there is other Life in the Universe. Then quickly disappear to the other side of the Earth.

Some of the ships go to Japan where they have a large underground city. The Aliens are using this city to explore Life on Earth so they can improve Life on their own Planet. For instance, they are <u>exploring plant life</u>; they want to <u>learn how things grow</u>.

Tell us about the UFO that was recently sighted so close to Earth near Area 51 in Nevada?

That Alien Ship came from another Planet. They were angry because the United States captured those two Alien Ships.

Many on Earth who Believe in UFOs saw them near Area 51. These Aliens thought being sighted near this area would draw the most attention.

There are many Alien Souls reincarnated now in Earth bodies all over the World. There are some living in this area.

To learn more about Aliens living in a human body here on Earth, see the "UFOs And ALIENS" Chapter in Book II.

These visiting Aliens come from the same Planet as those the United States is holding in captivity.

The inhabitants of the Ship wanted to <u>experiment with landing and lifting off</u> to pick up the Aliens and knew no one would bother them by keeping some distance from the Government's Area 51.

They came close to Earth and wanted Earth people there to know that they were <u>angry about their</u> Aliens' imprisonment.

The Universe is in Control, not Earth Souls. Remember, UFOs and Aliens belong to the Universe.

What was the Black Dust that this family saw when this Ship landed near their car?

The Black Dust was particles of <u>excess energy released</u> by the Space Ship. This Family, which saw the Ship were Chosen because they always wanted to see a Space Ship and they were not afraid.

They wanted to experience this and the Aliens were obliged to do so. It has since changed their Lives, and they now believe in the Hereafter.

We wanted others nearby who saw the Ship to have the same experience. We wanted to shake up more People so they would Pay Attention.

Don't you think this is marvelous Ron?

I sure do. I think everything that happens in this Universe is Wonderful and Marvelous.

Did they Listen to the Message? Are these Good Alien Souls? I know they can Communicate with other Alien Souls who are living on Earth in human form.

224

Those people Listened to the Message of the Space Ship. And it's true that they could communicate with those from Other Planets. But remember, they must earn that ability. Finally, they are Souls that are Peaceful with each other.

There are some Dark Force Aliens with Ships, and they like to send Negativity. They don't stay long on Earth, and of course they are quite shrewd.

The Dark Forces are Earth Souls who are lingering around the Earth, refusing to work. Their mission is to cause disruption wherever and whenever they can.

They are Aliens from the Dark orbiting Earth that watch for and Capture other Alien Ships.

These are smart Dark Force Souls, which take over the Alien Bodies. They also watch the Earth, and use Earth Bodies with Weak Souls, and Alien Bodies, to accomplish their Corruption.

We need to clear the Negativity away from all EARTH SOULS IN THE BODY FORM that is causing so many Problems.

The Martinique Point was an easy entry. Now it is closed and protected.

This is why we need Positive Control. Once we have full Control they will run. They can't stay in the Body, and they will be put in the Dark.

But they are still wandering the Earth, aren't they!

That's true, but they have no more Control or hold on Earth. If an Earth Soul refuses to accept them they have to leave.

We have Control now, and we are continually removing them from Earth by removing Souls that accept and attract them through their Negative thoughts and actions.

The Earth Disasters are All Part of this Clean Up.

225

You must understand that they can no longer come to Earth from the Dark because all Vortexes are closed and guarded.

It will take some time to clear the many millions of Earthbound Souls that have lived on Earth, from Centuries past to today.

This is why we want Earth Souls to Change Their Ways and their Thoughts, to work with the White Light and not allow any Negative Thought to be a part of their Lives.

January 30, 1988

Markus is here. Yes, Ron, I'll tell you about the Comet. You always want answers!

The Comet is still delayed this week. Earth Souls are not Co-Operating, and there are all of the other Problems that we have already mentioned.

Maybe next month, in mid-February, it will happen. It depends on whether the Aliens have been Released and the Attitude of Earth Souls.

The Aliens should escape shortly and leave the Earth. We want them to leave because we want the Negativity that holds them here to be released as well.

I continually send my White Light Healing to surround them and pray for their release.

Yes! Thank you and please continue to do so. But you must understand that Strong Negativity surrounds them. This Negativity holds on to Weaker Ignorant Souls.

The Higher Forces are now trying to break down the Wall of Negativity.

You also must understand it is Difficult for us to Split these two apart, as Aliens are more Ignorant than Earth Souls and don't understand.

We will finish this Job because we are sending many more High Teachers and Positive Energy Forces.

226

February 14, 1988

Markus is here. Happy Valentines Day to you Ron. I think your Love is Important for You and All around You.

You are receiving Love on this Special Day.

The Comet is not going to appear today, I am sorry to say. Unfortunately, all is not ready yet.

However, there is good news. The Aliens have been released and have returned to their own Planet. There is much Confusion in Government quarters right now.

As we predicted, Security was lax at the underground installation and the Aliens slipped away. Another Ship retrieved them.

Now that they have been released, Our Comet will come soon.

This happened on Friday. Even so, the Comet is not coming Sunday. Though it is coming soon.

We are sorry to disappoint you; we did not intend this delay. We appreciate your continued Faith in us.

February 21, 1988

Markus is here. Hi, Ron.

The Universal Work is going fine. You must understand that we are working to manifest Our Comet Ship.

So far it is being held up because of a lack of Co-operation on Earth.

We need to make a Big Impact when we land, so therefore everything must be just right. This means we must have each and everyone in the right place at the right time.

We are having a difficult time manifesting the right Spot and Timing.

There are key people that we need to see Our Ship so we have changed our arrival time accordingly. But it should happen Soon.

227

It is not your fault that the Comet hasn't arrived yet. You need to get on with your Lives for now. The Comet will arrive when you least expect it.

The Aliens have left the Earth Plane now; we had to properly clear this Situation first. Unfortunately, it also took longer than we expected.

There are Men who work for the Government who are angry that this happened.

They are Angry because with the Aliens gone, so is their evidence to support the Test Results they've shipped to Washington.

At the underground facility they were testing the Aliens to determine their origin, how they function and how their brains work.

If Earth people were captured, the Aliens would treat them worse. We are terribly upset with your Government, as you must realize that all of their actions are Against Universal Law.

Earth People need to also realize they cannot Hide Anything from the Universe. We know all that happens All Over the Earth Plane at All Times. We are in Control. Earth Souls are not.

Do remember, we do not Interfere with your Individual Free Choice, which allows you to Learn from your Mistakes or Wrong Choices.

Markus, could you please explain or clarify what you mean by Negativity?

Negativity is all those Souls that do wrong against the Universe, or Their Own Self-Being.

They need to Clean Up Their Act. But too many are not willing to do so. Without Negativity, the Earth would be covered in Beauty and Peace.

There are so many Lessons that have not been learned on Earth. This is the source of all the Negativity. There is so much Negativity that it has created a large imbalance on the Earth.

By recently closing the Martinique Vortex we have reclaimed our hold on the Positive Energy. You will start noticing the changes slowly now as time goes on.

March 19, 1988

Markus, I am sorry to keep asking about an update about Our Comet. Have the High Directors changed their minds? Thank you for all your writing!

Markus is here. Hello, Ron. You're Welcome. We don't mind that you ask. The High Directors of the Universe have not changed their minds.

The long delay is the Earth's Fault; we need things more organized on Earth to Manifest. Then we will come. We hope it will be in this Earth year, but whenever it comes it will be the right time.

The Comet is badly needed so both the Universe and the Earth Plane can Progress.

Don't worry; we haven't forgotten Your Missions. The Comet will come as soon as the Earth people Co-operate and provide the Recognition we need to Manifest.

You both are still a Big Part of Our Success and we know you need this to carry on the Work you do for us. Please be patient; we will NOT let you down.

April 3, 1988

Markus is here. Hello Ron, how are you? *I'm just great, Markus.*

That's good; I think you are doing just fine.

I know, Markus that you were assigned to Jan for the Coming of the Comet. Will you be able to see this through?

No! I am almost finished with my work with Jan. The Comet is still scheduled to arrive this year on Earth, but I am not sure. Therefore, I must finish my work and move on.

I have done my part to this point, but I will not be able to be a part of it going forward because it's delayed. I am sorry, but we must keep Progressing to Higher Levels.

You must <u>not be sad, as it is a victory</u> for me. This means I have <u>done</u> <u>good work so far and earned the right to move on.</u>

Many elsewhere need me, and I will continue working through the Universe once I leave.

Don't worry; I have a little time left yet. You will be able to do a lot of your Work soon to help others. We will Guide you in the right direction.

I had only two more, mostly private writings with Markus. We did not discuss the Comet. It was sad when he left. It felt like I was losing a very good friend.

April 28, 1988

The Great Aristotle came to write with Jan. What a Pleasure this was. I asked Aristotle to further explain the Comet's delay. Will I be able to tell others about this wonderful event that's going to happen on Earth?

Yes, you will have this opportunity in your Earth Life, but not yet. It is still too soon to tell too many about the Comet Ship.

There are other Souls <u>we need to tell first</u> about the Universe. We must get them to Open their Minds and accept us. Also we <u>still do not have enough</u> Control to Manifest the Ship Safely.

The Comet ship has been delayed primarily because of problems with the Government.

Many in the Government are angry that the Aliens were released. These angry men think their Security was lax.

In addition, they are covering up much of this Alien Information.

Another reason for the delay is that there are too many Non-Believers. To send the Comet Ship with this many Non-Believers would be a waste of time because they won't believe it.

We have other plans. Maybe we will find the right place to Land, and we'll let you know when and where.

I foresee the coming of the Comet Ship much later. The Earth needs to be Shaken out of its stupor and that's what we're going to do.

This comes from the High Directors. I am not part of it at this time, and it will not be my decision. I am more attuned to the Earth's situation than was Markus. That's why I am here.

I am a Great Teacher and I have done much for the Earth already when I was here last. Then I worked in the Universe. I will carry on now and do more with you, Ron, and Jan on Earth.

You will be Guided Automatically on your path. Please don't worry about this. We understand your Missions and how important they are to you.

August 14, 1988

Aristotle, can you give me another update on the arrival of the Comet Ship?

The Comet Ship is not coming yet, as there are many problems to take care of before we can land. It will land on Earth eventually.

It has to be later because too many people won't co-operate, and we have to change the whole concept.

New plans will come when the Earth straightens up. And that's not going to happen because No One Listens.

Our original plan isn't working because people won't accept the Universe. So we are planning a new approach to the situation to gain more recognition.

We need to ensure that nothing interferes with our plan to land in California, though we are looking at a better location than we originally planned. You just have to wait; we are coordinating the whole thing.

We are trying to inspire Spiritual people to respond, and Our Teachers on Earth are working with us to connect with people who are willing and ready to cooperate.

You will have to wait until we are ready. It is a slow and difficult process to convince Earth people to Cooperate.

Ron, you have done your job. They will have theirs. We will keep you informed.

I asked Jennifer, two years earlier on April 9, 1986, how is it that the Government in Washington tries to hide, cover up, or disguise the Existence of Aliens and UFOs?

Those in the Government in Washington are afraid of the Unknown. They are confused and want answers.

They must get used to this happening all over the Earth Plane because people will see many UFOs to prepare them for the arrival of Our Comet Ship. Many have been sighted already.

We want you to Overcome your Fear of UFOs and be Assured that they Mean No Harm. This way you won't be Afraid of Our Comet Ship when it Lands in California.

What if Our Government Forces pick up the Comet on Radar, and try to stop it from Landing?

First, they won't <u>Accept</u> that it is <u>Coming just because it is written here</u>, but that is Not Important.

We have Our Ways of overcoming any attempts they make to stop us by Force. Perhaps their Radar won't work that day.

232

Also, Our Holy Comet is Spiritual, and not Material. That means it has to Materialize to be seen, and this will <u>only</u> <u>happen</u> <u>temporarily</u>, and in certain areas of the World where we will be recognized.

Then it will Materialize only one more time – when it has Landed.

Don't worry, Ron. We will take care of this. Nothing known to man can penetrate The Powerful White Light around Our Comet.

Late in 1988 we had not heard anything about the Comet and I thought I would ask once more for an update. The following is Aristotle's last writing about the Comet.

Aristotle, we have not asked for a while for an update on Our Comet Ship.

The Comet Ship is <u>not coming</u>. New Plans will come when the Earth <u>straightens up</u>. That hasn't happened yet.

Earth Souls do not accept us yet because too many are not Listening, so it would be a <u>waste of time to send</u> the Comet Ship now.

It is <u>just too far outside the boundaries</u> of Earth Souls' thinking to believe. If we were to send the Comet Ship now they would probably slough it off as <u>just another</u> UFO.

Without seeing Our Comet Ship and Our High Teachers, how would they believe us?

Earth Souls must be ready to accept Our Messages and get on with their Lives.

The High Holy Comet Ship will not come until it is more Peaceful on Earth, and people recognize the need for Spiritual help.

When the Comet Ship comes it will prove Life After Death. People on Earth will recognize the High Teachers the Comet Ship carries, and this familiarity will lend credibility to Our Message that will Change the World.

We think the Comet Ship will come in 2007 or 2008. But for that to happen we <u>need people to open up and realize</u> that we are here. We hope this will happen when the Books are published.

It will still come to California because it remains the most Spiritual State and Los Angeles <u>is the most</u> Spiritual City.

Aristotle, living in Los Angeles, I'm having trouble understanding how this can be the most Spiritual City. There's so much crime here, please explain this to us.

Los Angeles now has more Spiritual People than any other place in the state. Spirituality is so strong here that the Negativity has a difficult <u>time overpowering all of that</u> Positive Energy. We are trying to make that happen – transform Negative Energy to Positive – all over the World.

The people in Los Angeles are much smarter, and more Open-Minded <u>than anywhere else</u> in the United States of America.

We asked several more times for Comet Ship updates, and the answer was always the same: "It will come when the time is right.

Remember, Jan went home to the Universe on April 22, 1996. She continued her work from there.

March 6, 2005

I asked one of Jan's Automatic Writing pupils to write with Jesus, to ask if a new site has been selected for Our High Holy Comet Ship to Land.

Jesus is here. Ron, this is not yet done. Keep asking, and <u>new information will be revealed to you</u>. Be Patient and enjoy the Process.

*On May 28, 2006, I asked another of Jan's Automatic Writing Pupils to ask her High Teacher, Jordan, about the Comet Ship. Incidentally, Jan's pupil today writes for people personally with her Teacher Jordan from the Fourth Plane. *See next page.*

234

Will the Comet Ship come in 2007?

Jordan is here. Yes, it will be late 2007 or 2008. Don't worry about what month, we will tell you to look for it when the time is right.

Relax, you are doing fine. When you are writing with us we will speak to you through the writing.

Do I need to do anything to assist with the Landing of the Holy Color Comet?

No, just see what happens. You will <u>receive messages every</u> <u>so</u> <u>often</u>. The Books must now be finished, and Published for a <u>full</u> <u>year</u> <u>prior</u> to Landing.

I entered this writing here to provide readers with the most recent Information about The Comet's coming.

Much earlier, I asked Teddy Roosevelt, "Is the World going to Change when Our Comet arrives?

His answer is quite interesting. I've entered it here to close this Chapter.

Yes. The World will become Better, a more Peaceful and Harmonious place.

We want it this way. The Comet's purpose is to convince Souls to Open Their Minds and Change Their Ways.

It will be a sight to see, <u>but we didn't want</u> anything here to Interfere with any Comets.

All Comets <u>are beautiful</u> and we have been sending them to Earth all throughout history. But the Comets <u>have work to</u> do and we want them to do it without Interference.

*If you are interested in a personal writing see information in back of book how to contact her.

This work is for you to Learn and Grow Yourself so you can get on with your Life.

We didn't put you on Earth to Control Our Planets but we gave them to you to Help and Guide all Souls on Earth.

This Interference we speak of is caused through Souls Not Listening. Too many Non Listening Souls on Earth.

Also all of the Corruption that exists on the Earth, the Misuse and Abuse of Earth and Space are Interference.

All of this has a direct affect on all of the Planets in your Universe. This is not right.

This makes Our Work, to maintain a Balance in the Universe, so much more difficult.

You may learn about the Planets through Astronomy. The Planets will Guide you to get on with your Lessons and live your Life in Harmony working with the Universe.

You can Change if you Choose to and make your Life Better. But don't expect the Planets to change your Life, or that you should Live your Life by the Planets.

The Planets Cannot run Your Life; the only purpose of the Planets is to maintain the Earth's Energy Balance.

Without the Earth, we wouldn't need the Planets. Earth is the Doorway to Learning that takes you to another Dimension.

We must all go to the next Dimension and move on.

You must move from the Working and Learning Planet Earth you are now on, to the next Working and Learning Plane, which is the Astral Plane.

But you all don't have to go to the Astral Plane. You can go Higher, as it is <u>rather full</u> on the Astral Plane now. Because of this, we would like you to go Higher and become Teachers.

I'm adding this material written by Conier from a personal writing to close this Chapter.

Our Books will tell all about the Comet Ship, and explain all that we want Earth Souls to do. We hope many will read these Books.

THEN, SPIRITUAL LEARNING WILL BE HEARD.

Doors will open up for this Knowledge, and many will Listen. The Teachers will deal with those who don't Listen when the Teachers have time. There are too many to deal with now. The Teachers are overloaded and extremely busy.

More Earth Souls need to know that Earth is the place to Learn, because you can learn faster here than you can on the Planes. On the Planes, it is much harder and takes much longer to learn the same lessons you could have learned on Earth.

This is why Souls go to Earth because it is so easy to say <u>I'm sorry</u>, ask forgiveness and change their thinking and then decide to work, never wronging another Soul again. What can be done on Earth in a short lifetime would take <u>hundreds and even thousands</u> of years to accomplish here.

Earth Souls will start to listen soon now as we are opening many doors in different ways all over this world. We need all the help we can get as we are bringing people together for strength in numbers to make known that we are here for **ALL OF MANKIND**.

See the Chapter, "Planets In Our Universe," in Book II, "Many Planes Above" for more information about each Planet's purpose to sustain Our Lives here on Earth. All of the Planets, Sun and Stars were made for Earth only.

The next Chapter explains Ron's Life Mission, followed by the chapter describing Ron's Healing Teachers.

MY LIFE'S MISSION
By Ron J. Oberon

I have come to realize "through Life's experiences" that we all have Our Own Mission in Life to fulfill. We know Our Mission within our own Heart and Soul.

I have discovered that My Mission is Universal Healing. I do this mostly through Absent Healing. This means sending Mental Thought Healing. I also do this through the laying on of my "Golden Hands" working through the Aura, uplifting and cleansing the Aura and Mind for clear thinking.

Healing can be sent anywhere on Earth, or anywhere in the Universe. Healing is Natural Love Energy.

LOVE is the most powerful energy in the Universe.

I help people find Personal Enlightenment; to Center and Balance themselves to continue on with their Lives. To remain on the Path of their Life's Mission and to fulfill their Soul's Purpose of Who they really are. Also, this will help them make their Soul Progress through their Life Lessons on Earth.

We are all Spiritual Beings here to do just that; make Soul Progress, and we are all here for the same Purpose – to Learn that we all are One with "Life" Itself including, and most Importantly, One with each Other.

Yes, this includes One with every Soul on Earth, and One with the entire Universe.

All of Life in its Entirety could not exist without any One of Us, as a part of the Whole. That is how Important each and every one of Us really are, and how Important Our Mission is.

As we all contribute to the Whole, we slowly then begin to realize how we are One with all that Is. I hope I haven't lost anyone; are you still with me?

Therefore you can never be Truly Lost or Separated, we can never Truly Die, or be Killed because Our Souls or Light Within can never be Extinguished. This is the real you, as "we have always been and always will be," the Important part of Life.

We also have always had, as a part of Our Existence, a Free Will or Free Choice to Experience all of Life. We are Learning about everything Our Heart and Soul Desires.

As each of us is Expressing Who we are and what we Desire, we are Learning that Life is Ever Changing as we are, Always Changing.

Each one of us is Remembering whom we really are from within our own Soul, and Who we really want to be from our Soul's Desire. Just know that all Change is Progress.

We are all at Various Levels of Learning, trying to Re-create Ourselves Anew in every moment; in the "Grandest Version of Our Greatest Vision we have ever had about who we Really are."*

That is Our Purpose of Life.

My Mission is to Heal and Teach, to Change People's Ways and Thinking for a Better World for All Mankind. I hope this will help you to discover Your Mission!

With Every Word You Read in Both Books you will receive my Sincere and Divine Love Healing because I have touched them with my Golden Hands. This Universal Healing will help you Open Your Mind and to get on with Your Life.

May Life Continue to Bless You All.

With Love and Light

Ron J. Oberon

*These words come from the "Conversations with God" books by Neale Donald Walsch for the New Spirituality now unfolding on Earth. I highly recommend the entire series.

The next Chapter charts Ron's Healing Progress.

RON'S TEACHERS AND PROGRESS AS A HEALER

MOVING FROM PLANE TO HIGHER PLANE

Conier will write for you Ron. Your High Teachers and Healers from the Universe's School of Healing are working throughout the body to heal each different area when you do Healing Work.

One Teacher is a Very High Healer and his name is Gandi. He is a True Healer from India and lived in the year of the Great Healers, 1030 A.D. You can find books about these Great Healers on Earth if you like.

He has been with you since you were Ten years old.

Conier, that has been most of my Life. You mean I have been practicing Healing all of this time?

Yes. He has been working with you all of this time. He is your Head High Teacher. You started working with him direct on the Fourth Plane, also called the Marvel Plane.

This is the Healer that stays with you always. Other Healers come and go as he calls them.

Conier, would you please explain my Healing Progress and how we work from Plane to Higher Plane? Can you also explain why a Teacher always comes from a Higher Plane than us?

I feel this is Important for Our Readers. I want them to understand how High we can Progress by doing Spiritual Work on this Earth.

That's fine, Ron. You understand us and this is what is Important. Do you know your High Healing Teacher comes from the Twelfth Plane?

No – He started working with you directly on the Fourth Plane. Working with him is the reason your Healing has progressed and why you are now working on the Seventh Plane.

Gandi, your Healing Teacher, always came from a Higher Plane than you. Now he is working to move you to Higher Planes.

Since you began your work in this Life, you started above the Astral Plane, working with Indian Guide Healers, and Gandi stood back.

You have advanced, with much hard work and by believing in us, to this Higher Plane. You have also advanced because you realized that you needed help to grow, and you were willing to ask for it.

Gandi began working with you directly when you progressed to the Fourth Plane, from above the Astral Plane.

He now calls on the help of Healers from the Universal School of Healers, for whatever Specialists he needs.

We know you faced <u>much opposition</u> on your journey. But your Determination has earned y<u>ou the</u> Right to be here.

The work that you are doing aligns with Our Ways. There are many Poor Souls who don't understand your work.

They don't understand the Importance of making Progress to <u>advance themselves</u> for the Betterment of All.

These Souls are not your concern. We have much more Important work coming for you to do.

This was only a <u>stepping-stone for your</u> Progress. Many have <u>already</u> <u>benefited</u> by your Works. We want you to continue that work and help many more.

You will do this throughout your Earth Life and bring much Comfort and Happiness to <u>many</u>. This is your main purpose in this Lifetime.

Please do not be discouraged. We are preparing you to carry on Our Works in the near future. You will reap much more satisfaction than you ever dreamed of.

We Love You Very Much, and want to thank you for all you have done already.

You have made your mark on Earth and it's just a matter of carrying on. But this time we want you to have your Rewards, too.

So we are getting ready for your Work to Progress in a different way with people that Appreciate and Care about you.

You will have many friends through Our Works. Your Sister Jan will help Guide you in the Right Direction; please be patient.

It won't be too long before you will be busy <u>helping so many people that really believe</u> in your "Golden Hands." Do you feel better now?

Yes I certainly do. I am so Grateful for the Love and all the High Universal Blessings I've received.

When <u>I speak of "we,"</u> I speak of all High Teachers who Guide and Help you with your Work.

This includes your Highest, Gandi. He works with your Indian Helpers to make your Healing Power Stronger so you can achieve <u>what you and all of us must do.</u>

Each time you work with a person who has problems – which we can only see from Our Side – we call in other Healers to give you the <u>power necessary to help y</u>ou heal in those areas. You have been unaware of this until now.

Each Healer that comes to help MUST WORK THROUGH GANDI AND MUST ASK GANDI'S PERMISSION TO DO SO. GANDI HAS A COUNCIL OF TEACHERS that Guide and Advise him, and tell him the direction he must go.

He was assigned <u>to y</u>ou when <u>you were only</u> Ten years old. He has been waiting for you to make Progress with the Indian Guide Healers to step in and work directly with you.

242

He will work with you until the High Council of Directors decides if you need a New Teacher.

When Gandi Opened your Channel to become your High Teacher you had already progressed to the Fourth Plane.

Gandi, before Opening your Channel, worked along side your Indian Guide Healers. He has been waiting all of your Life for this, to be your High Teacher of Healing and to Work Directly with you.

With the Progress you've made, and with Gandi Working Directly through your Hands to heal others, you will advance much higher than the Seventh Plane.

The writing immediately changed here. It became different and much larger. Gandi continued with the following.

Gandi is here. I am your Healing Teacher. You must understand I am your High Teacher. I will work with your Guide to protect you <u>from illness</u> only when you are giving Healing.

I direct you in your Teaching. I am a full-blooded man from India.

Your Guide is an American Indian, **and his name is Santus**.

You have never asked for me before when you were Healing. But now you are Opening Our Channel to contact me directly.

Last night, you performed your best Healing <u>when you asked for my</u> <u>help</u>.

You did so well! I was Amazed at Your Progress. It is now coming along the way we want it to.

You did a fine job on the Lecture, too. You delivered Our Messages accurately and clearly. I don't think you missed anything at all.

I was there helping you. You must realize you can only give so much at a time. We did well.

They all seemed to enjoy it, and that is the purpose of Our Work.

Each one's personal messages were satisfactory. But these people need to Open Up much more if they are going to understand their real needs.

This is what we must do to get these people on the right road to make full use of their Earth Lives.

So much time and energy is wasted pursuing Material wants. This Must Change.

You know we understand the desire for Material Things, but so many of them are unnecessary. Having so many "things" just clogs their Minds leaving no room for Spiritual Progress.

We must take away these Material things from them – because they are unearned – until they understand about us in the Universe, who we are and why we are working with Souls on Earth.

Thank you Gandi for writing for me. I am most pleased to understand the process.

I then asked Conier to identify the different Healers that worked under Gandi's direction while they were Healing. This is how he responded.

Red Moon is an Indian; he is a Healer and works with Gandi. You can ask Gandi to have Red Moon explain to you when he works with Gandi.

Gandi brings in other Healers to help him and work with him as needed, depending on which parts of the body need healing.

You have a famous Doctor of Medicine who works with and through Gandi. He is Dr. Malousa of an Indian Tribe. He is the Only Modern Doctor.

He lived in your Earth year of 1892 and helped Heal Whites and Indians.

You have many Healers around you. Another one is Sister Theresa. She brings Spiritual Knowledge to feed your Spirit Soul; you will hear more from her later.

She comes from France in the year 1602. She always healed the sick and she is now working with you through Gandi.

White Eagle is a Medicine Man. He is a very patient man. He wants you to know that Our Work is Progressing nicely, and that you are now at the crossroads. He wants you to go ahead.

Quiet Waters is a Red Chief of the Sioux, and he is now working with you on your nerves. You must ask him to calm you down.

Each thing you do is for a Reason. The more Calm and Peaceful your Attitude the more Progress you will make. He is Learning Healing and Mind Work.

Golden One is very young. He Learns with you. He never Lived Long on Earth.

Golden One was killed in battle in 1898 as a young boy. He was a Chief's Son of an American Indian Tribe. Golden One is smart and strong.

He gives you strength and must learn more. He is an Iroquois Indian, and he knows your Guide, Santus, well. Santus was an Iroquois Chief.

He is Learning with Santus and some day will help you write your Books from his Knowledge.

When you write these Books, he will Teach you what to write.

Dr. Moye also helps with Healing sometimes when we need him. But he doesn't stay here too long.

Your Message and Healing Teacher is Gandi. He calls for whom he needs; sometimes he calls your Relatives and sometimes he calls Healers. As your Healing Teacher, he always stands on your left.

Santus, your Guide, always stands on your right. Yes, that's Santus on the right, and Gandi on the left. Santus also has a Dimension name, Comadas.

Ron, there are too many Healing Helpers to list them all. Gandi sometimes directs as many as Fifty Healers in some of your Healing Sessions.

You must ask for a clear, Open Channel between you and the High Universe. Through this Channel you will receive Positive Strength and Energy that you can use during Direct Healing and to receive Truthful <u>answers to</u> <u>your</u> <u>questions</u>.

Conier, who is around me at night as I sleep?

Your Mother is around you <u>day</u> <u>and night</u>. She is always <u>running</u> <u>around after everything</u> and <u>everyone</u>; always <u>working to</u> <u>get</u> <u>other</u> Souls <u>to work</u> and Progress on the Astral Level. She likes to go to Church with you.

Last night Sister Theresa was with you. She wants you to know she is working with you.

Mostly <u>we are around all day</u> <u>and night</u>. We <u>talk with</u> <u>you in</u> <u>your sleep</u>. Your Guide is always with you, right now and <u>always</u>.

You are never left alone. **God is always with you**.

God accompanies All Souls in All of Creation in ALL WAYS.

What a Great Comfort it is to know that we are never alone and that we can turn to them for answers in our sleep. I hope we can remember the answers when we need them during our busy days.

At this point the writing changed. It looked like Eastern Indian writing, and this is what was written.

I am Gandi, High Teacher of Healing. I am here for you Ron. I am your Teacher. I always work with you, and have been with you since you were Ten years old. <u>When</u> <u>you call I am there</u>.

You will <u>feel a cool breeze on the left side of y</u>our body so you know I am there.

I have a Message for you Ron. Your personal Life is going in the right direction, and I want you to know that now we will Progress much faster than before.

The Spiritual Work for you will come; we understand your problems and we will take care of you and steer you on the right path so that all of Mankind will benefit from your Work.

We all are still working to manifest your Healing Center, "The Divine Light of the Rays." Please be patient. To make this happen requires a great deal of time and effort.

People from all over the World will come to you for Healing and will donate money. You will build your center with their donations.

Earth needs your Healing now, Ron.

Many other Healers are coming to work with you and carry on Our Work.

Good Luck for now. Your Lectures will be Great. I will help you; it's much easier for me now. So don't worry.

I LOVE YOU, RON, for your KINDNESS.

Thank you, Gandi. I Love you also. I am so Grateful for all your help and your direct Assistance with Our Work.

Conier, is my High Healing Teacher Gandi always with me, even when I Mentally project Absent Healing for someone?

Yes, Ron. He stays with you always and will remain until you have Completed your Work with him.

Your work is different. He will be with you for a long time, where Jan's Teachers will keep changing because her writing work is again different.

247

We, the High Teachers in the Universe, keep Progressing Higher with each Teacher. We, too, Progress higher when we've completed Our Work with a Pupil.

Your Teacher Gandi sends Messengers to those people carrying your Absent Healing Thoughts. The Messengers take care of everything.

When you are in the company of a patient or client, Gandi Channels Direct Healing through you. Your <u>presence with the person receiving</u> Healing <u>is all that is necessary</u>.

However, if you have the opportunity to place your Hands <u>on the area</u>, it helps. It's only necessary to keep them there for a few minutes. Or, a simple, limited touch will work, like shaking hands. Even that simple act will help the Energies to Flow.

You do Good Healing. What you are doing is just fine. However, most Healing takes time so maybe Several Treatments <u>are necessary</u>.

Should I Meditate on the names on my Healing List and send them Absent Healing all over the Earth Plane?

Yes, you can meditate using your Healing List. Work very hard with it and your Teacher will help you.

When you do Absent Healing saying the name sends a thought directly to that person.

The Healing begins through your Teacher Gandi, Directly, or he has many Healers waiting to <u>be sent</u> for Assignments. Gandi does all the work for you, or will get the proper help. Sending Healing to the World helps our work to Open Minds.

Also, when you do Healing <u>in y</u>our home, turn on y<u>our</u> Ionizer <u>machine</u>. This clears the air, and helps to <u>balance</u> the Energy in the room, making it much Stronger.

The Crystal Rock, which was given to you, is a Special Rock of Protection and it does have Healing Power.

It is Mika Stone Herkimer rock Crystal and Amethyst, hollow in the center. It comes from Arkansas and it took generations to form underground.

So it really has Healing Power? And it's cut in the shape of a face?

<u>Absolutely</u>. It is for your house and a Gift of Knowledge for you. We <u>ensured that it was sent</u> just for <u>you</u>. It is the Ancient Egyptian face of a Great Healer, Talahar, who comes with Crystal Rock to aid in your Class Healing, or Healing in your home.

What about the painting?

The High Universe inspired Jan to paint that for you and your Class. The painting has its <u>own</u> <u>job to help</u> <u>everyone</u> in the Class become Teachers of Our Ways.

How is it that we read of so-called "Miraculous Healings" taking place in many different parts of the World throughout Earth's History?

This is because <u>the person really</u> <u>wanted to be</u> Healed and they are now working Our Ways. This person benefited from Direct Healing that was available because there were more clear Vibrations on the Earth Plane.

<u>Many</u> <u>more</u> Souls <u>worked Our Ways throughout history</u> than do now.

It is very hard for Vibrations to reach Earth today.

I never realized that so many factors were involved with a Miracle Healing. Is it possible for a Miraculous Healing to come through my work some day?

Well <u>that's a big</u> <u>order</u>, Ron. We are still trying. You <u>realize this is hard for us</u> and <u>must be</u> <u>patient.</u>

However, we will come through for you eventually and bring you someone who is ready for this.

That was Conier's last writing about my Healing Progress. He wrote that on January 6, 1986 then he left on January 12, 1986.

Jan's next Teacher, Jennifer "Mary Todd Lincoln," came, to write on January 13, 1986 and wrote the following for me on January 27, 1986 about my Healing Progress.

Jennifer, would you write a little more about my Spiritual Progress through my work with the High Universe? I want those who read Our Books to understand that people can make faster Progress on Earth when they're on the right track.

That way maybe more Souls on Earth may start Working to help Others. And in helping others they will advance their Own Progress toward becoming Teachers before it is time to return home to the Universe.

Jennifer is here. Hi, Ron. Yes, of course we will talk about the Progress you have achieved moving from Plane to Plane.

You are a Very Special Person of Ours, and you have asked for the Highest and the Best. You receive this according to the Plane Level of Growth you currently occupy.

You came to the Earth Plane from a Very High Plane. You lowered your vibration to the Fifth Plane to Reincarnate and Start Over on Earth from above the Astral Plane.

This is the Second Plane where High Teachers Reincarnate to Earth for their Mission. Basically it was difficult for you to come back to Earth and start over from such a High Plane.

You only came because Earth greatly needed your Work at this time. So we asked your Permission if you would return to Earth and give your Healing to Earth Souls.

You so Graciously Volunteered for the Mission. However, you didn't have to come; it was your Free Choice.

So you see that you have Chosen Your Purpose to return to Earth at this time.

If you can think back to when you were Young, I will help you understand why you were so Confused at such a Young Age.

At Ten years old Gandi came to help you Progress, starting with Second Plane Work. You were starting over from that point. It was slow and difficult work because nobody would Listen to you, a Child, or even later when you were a Teenager.

I'm sure you do not remember in your Conscious Mind the Difficulty you experienced. But now we want you to understand they were difficult years for you and why it was so.

You began to use Your Own Ways and the Ways of Our Dimension to Teach the Right Ways to those that crossed your path. You could do this because you were fully familiar with Our Ways.

When you were older you then joined with others to do Good Work, becoming the President of the Service Club called Sertoma. This represented generous Service to Mankind.

You then made More Progress, helping Handicapped and Under-Privileged Children. This moved you through the Second Plane Work helping these Souls with all of your Club Projects.

As time went on, and once Earth Souls began to Open up and Accept Our Ways, you Progressed to the Third Plane.

For many years you stayed on the Third Plane, Healing and Working with Indian Guide Healers, and with Gandi overseeing.

Your Open Mind and y<u>our need</u> to Grow moved you to the Fourth Plane. You did most of this work on your own.

Once on the Fourth Plane your High Teacher Gandi stepped in and Worked Directly with you. As a result, you earned your way to the Fifth Plane. That took you only one year.

Gandi comes from the Twelfth Plane. But once you reached the Fifth Plane it was easier for him to work with you.

You have this High Teacher who will help you Progress, and some day your work will be equal to his Learning. Remember, you are always Progressing.

You then moved through the Sixth onto the Seventh Plane. You can see your steady Progression since starting over on Earth. You earned this by using your Hands to give Constant Healing, Teaching and Learning to Earth Souls.

We will be advancing you shortly to the Ninth Plane.

So you see, we had to wait until now for your Progression because the Earth Souls were not ready to open up to your Work until now.

As you Progress, we want to raise you to the Fifteenth Plane and Higher.

All of this will make much more sense later on when you experience Souls coming to you that need your Healing Powers, and they will trust you to heal them.

This is all Jennifer wrote on my Healing Progress. Most of her time with Jan was spent writing for individuals and answering many of my other Questions.

Then I asked, "Jennifer, can I teach myself to use the Computer to work on the Universal Books?

Or, can I find help to see that the writings are presented in Proper English?

She replied with the following.

Ron, I will obtain the services of a Scientist who will impress you and tell you which way to go.

I am going to engage Dr. Martin Closs, an Englishman, to work with you on the Computer.

He is an Old Soul and highly knowledgeable about Components. So just ask for Dr. Closs whenever you want to work.

He will be coming through the Channel soon to assist any time you need help. Since you're working on Our Books, he will advise you with Proper English, too.

I had different Personal writings in between Questions with both Jennifer and then Teddy Roosevelt, whom kept updating me about My Progress through the Eighth, Ninth and Tenth Planes during the next six to seven months.

This next writing with Teddy confirmed the identity of my New Teacher and my Progress. My quick advancement demonstrated once again how much faster you can Progress here On Earth.

Teddy Roosevelt, Jan's next Teacher, wrote the following.

September 5, 1986

Ron, Teddy is here. You have been Assigned a New Teacher to both help you with Our Work and to help you with your Progress.

His name is Dr. Martin Closs. He has been with you for a while learning about you. Martin will be available to you <u>day</u> <u>and night</u>.

The two of you will become close. He will <u>write with you</u>, so try and <u>write with him</u>.

253

Your High Healing Teacher Gandi remains as well.

Martin lived on Earth in the year of 1435 A.D. He studied the body's Nutrition and Functions.

He opened the door for better Nutrition, a notion that is readily accepted today. In his time people wouldn't accept it.

However, he lived a long Earth Life because of the way he took care of his body, and he left much Information on the Earth Plane.

Martin is with you now primarily because of your interest in Nutrition in you're Past Lives.

He speaks Excellent English so he can help you with Our Books. He was well bred, and accomplished much in his Earth Life, and was way ahead of his time.

Martin did groundbreaking work with Herbs and Serums, and relates to your Ways. He believes in You Very Much.

He tries hard to Stabilize and Protect your Life so you can do more Prosperous Work in Our Universe. Martin will also help you with your Material needs.

So Ron, now you have two High Teachers.

First, we must attune your Soul, Mind and Body so you can Progress Further on the right path.

This is his Mission with you at this time of your Earth Life.

We want you to fully understand the Meanings of the Information we are giving you for Our Books.

We do not want you to draw your Own Conclusions. So let us Clarify your Past Memories of this Information.

You couldn't hear us clearly in the past primarily because of the Interference from Lower, unwanted Interpreters pushing their way in for Recognition.

So therefore, when this is clear, you will fully understand what we are trying to Communicate for your Future Work.

Soon it will become clear and you do not have to worry about where you must be or go. You will just know.

We will Guide you in the right direction when Earth time is ready, as you know Earth time is Difficult to Co-ordinate with Others.

If we had Our Way we would not waste time, but sometimes we do not have full control because of the God-given Free Will of all Souls.

Please be Patient; soon it all will be coming through Clearly, and we will connect you to the right people.

Martin resides on the Thirteenth Plane and you are now working towards the Eleventh Plane.

Now that you realize this is what has been happening, maybe you will calm down and think more Positively. If you do, you will reach the Eleventh Plane before the end of the month.

Also, thanks to working with you, Martin will move to the Fourteenth Plane.

Will Martin then leave me because he has advanced?

No, he must finish his Mission first. Then he will Leave.

September 21, 1986

Teddy is here. Hi, Ron. I want to tell you that now you are working on the Eleventh Plane and have been for a little while now.

Your Healing is Strong and we want you to keep going to Progress even further.

Teddy Roosevelt left Jan a few days later on September 29, 1986. Then on January 22, 1987, Solon, Jan's first Director, wrote next about my Healing Progress.

January 22, 1987

Solon is here. Hello to you, Ron. I am a Director from the Twenty-Fifth Plane and above. I am here because you must understand that we are ready to move forward in Our Work. All dues have been paid.

Your Teacher Martin is fine and will remain with you until his Work is Complete. That will be soon, and then we will give you a New Teacher and move you from the Eleventh to the Thirteenth Plane.

The Universe has delayed the Books because the Earth wasn't ready yet to accept them. The Minds of many Earth Souls must be Opened up to the Universe. When that happens more Earth Souls will pay Attention to the Books and to Our Comet coming.

We will let you know when to Proceed. Originally we wanted The Books published <u>one</u> <u>year before the coming</u> of the Comet. Now, the Books will be <u>published when the time is right</u>.

When this was written January 22, 1987, it never dawned on us when we learned that the Books would be delayed that the Comet could also be delayed for the same reason.

That meant that the Books would have been published by now, and that the Comet would arrive one-year later on January 17, 1988.

February 28, 1987

Solon is here. Ron, the New Teacher we just assigned to you will bring you more Stability and Reassurance. His name is Michael and he is now working with you.

256

He is Spiritual and will help you remain calm. He will stay at your place of business and will Work with you all the time.

Michael is Sharp and works with you on the Thirteenth Plane, where you are now.

You have advanced. That is why we sent you a New Teacher, to keep you moving Higher; he comes from the Eighteenth Plane.

He will teach you much about New Revenues.

He is also an Englishman, and he lived on Earth around 1200 A.D. Michael was a Businessman, a Landowner and a Tradesman. He Worked with People to Advance, and so will you.

June 21, 1987

Solon is here. Hello Ron. Your Healing is coming along nicely, and you are becoming quite well known.

The people really appreciate your work and there are New Healers working with you.

Have you noticed the change in your energy's Vibration as they work?

Gandi directs these New Healers to help with different areas of the body. They are Specialists from the School of Universal Healing. With these New Healers helping you, your body should not get so tired now.

Michael is still helping you with your Progress. His purpose is to help you with your energy.

Gandi does the cleansing, which is his focus, because he is much Higher and almost a Director in the Universe now.

Michael is your personal Teacher. His job is to help you with your business and other material activities. Gandi doesn't have time to do this for you.

July 18, 1987

Solon is here. Hi, Ron. Gandi, your Healing Teacher, is now a Director on the Twentieth Plane. You are on the Seventeenth Plane and will continue working with him.

You will get a New Teacher when you're ready. You still have work to do with Gandi.

Will Jesus work with me as a Healing Teacher some day?

Jesus is <u>unavailable now</u>; if you continue your Progress we'll see if we can have him work with you some day.

That would be appropriate because you were <u>one of</u> Jesus' <u>followers,</u> the Apostle John, in your Past Life.

He is a High Teacher over the Twenty-Sixth Plane. I am also over the Twenty-Sixth Plane but we stop counting once we reach this level.

You still have a ways to go but are Progressing <u>rapidly</u>.

You may now have a Universal Courier to help you with your Healing work. You can call on a Courier strictly for Protection. The Courier remains with you always to protect you against Negativity and we will see that you receive it.

This will greatly help in Our Work because the Negative Souls always hang around when they see what you are doing and <u>think</u> <u>you</u> <u>will help</u> them.

November 15, 1987

Markus is here Ron. You are making Progress nicely now and have progressed to the Twentieth Plane. We are all so proud of you and Thank You for continuing with Our Work.

December 30, 1987

Markus is here Ron, I am sorry Gandi is no longer with you *He was with me 38 years.* He has now progressed above the Twenty-Fifth Plane working with you.

258

The Earth is not ready yet for the work that Gandi had to do next and you are, you are ready to advance higher. Therefore, to serve his needs and yours, we've assigned you a New, Higher Teacher.

His name is Piaus, and he will call and direct many Healers to work through you.

Piaus is Holy, Smart, Wise and Powerful, a Director and Doctor of the High Universe. He will teach you new methods to bring more energy through your hands.

He is a Greek Healer and an Ancient Soul that lived on Earth during the days of Atlantis. You need the Healing he brings to carry on your Earth Work.

Great Healing occurred during the time of Atlantis; the Earth made great Progress then.

January 30, 1988

Markus is here. Ron, you are progressing nicely with Piaus. You are also a Teacher and it's up to you to use your Knowledge to Guide Earth people.

Piaus, with his new power, has been assigned to Earth to accomplish Our Great Mission.

You do understand that with the closing of the Vortex in Martinique we are now gaining control over the Dark Forces and beginning to clear the Earth of Negativity.

This creates the possibility that more Earth Souls will Change their Ways to Our Ways.

Ron, Jesus is still coming to work with you, but not yet. It's too soon.

You and Piaus are working smoothly together so you can project your Absent Healing.

The Aliens have assigned a Universal Group to work with him.

You work direct with Piaus and he will call on whomever he needs for the Healing.

Your Guide, Santus, has earned the rank of High Teacher. Equally exciting, so have you.

We want you to exceed the Fiftieth Level for the future work that Earth is going to need.

This Level far exceeds our numbers; we know you always like numbers Ron, but we do not use numbers once you pass a certain High Level.

Pray for World Protection, Love and Peace, which we hope to accomplish in the next 20 to 30 years on Earth.

At our Class on October 12, 1988, someone asked the following question while I was giving a Healing to a Student.

What is Higher than a Director in the Universe and what is the Sign of Life?

The Great Aristotle began to write, and after about a minute or two the writing suddenly became one and one half inches in size.

We were taken aback and overwhelmed. The writing was as follows.

Aristotle is here. Higher than a Director is a Master Director.

The Master Director here tonight is a Healer who comes to supervise the Healing for better success.

The Emblem he brings represents the Whole Truth of Life. Yes, he likes you, Ron, and wants you to understand. He will draw the Sign of Life for you.

Recreated by Sophie Kessler

Whole Truth of Life
The Sign of Life

His name is…MORTIMEIRZ. YES, I AM A HIGH HEALER OF PROGRESS AND THE SIGN OF LIFE IS CRITICAL TO ALL.

YOU MUST UNDERSTAND THIS. IT IS IMPORTANT TO ACCOMPLISH THIS IN YOUR LIFETIME AND IT BRINGS GREAT REWARDS.

YOU NEED TO PUT EFFORT AHEAD FOR THE FUTURE AND FORSEE IT.

BELIEVE IN YOURSELF AND WORK TOWARDS GROWTH WITH SPIRITUAL LOVE. IT IS THE KEY TO ETERNAL LIFE.

Thank you. It is a Great Honor, Mortimeirz, to have your Presence with us in our Class.

You're Welcome! **I AM IN CHARGE THIS EVENING AND I BRING A LONG LINE OF HEALERS. YES, MORE THAN Fifty.**

MY JOB IS TO TAKE EACH OF THESE SPECIALTY HEALERS INTO CONSIDERATION WITH THE FULL BODY, MIND AND SPIRIT HEALINGS YOU EACH WILL RECEIVE TONIGHT.

YOU ARE MOST FORTUNATE, ALL OF YOU; TO BE AMONGST THE HIGHEST OF THE UNIVERSE. IT IS INDEED A PRIVILEGE.

IT'S ALSO A PRIVILEGE TO BE ABLE TO HELP OTHERS. YES, OF COURSE, WE WILL GUIDE ALL OF YOU TO BECOME OUR TEACHERS ON EARTH.

This was a Privilege. What a powerful Healing we all received tonight from this Master Director from above the Fiftieth Plane.

He wrote each word in Large single letters, so I Capitalized and Highlighted what he wrote.

While he never came again to write, I believe he continued assisting Piaus, my Healing Director, at all of our Classes.

I'm also sure he directed his Message to me to help me prepare for the Healing Progress that I need to make for my Healings in the Future.

February 7, 1989

Aristotle is here. Ron, in addition to your High Healer Piaus, you now have Conscious, an additional Protecting Guide. Michael, who was helping you with business, has now left.

We are now going to send a Superior Salesman to help you get your new business off the ground. He is going to work hard for you.

His name is Phillip and he will keep the Negativity away from you. He is a High Teacher; his specialty is business Sales.

Conscious will continue to help your Protecting Guide, Santus.

262

Phillip is tall, a Proud Englishman who knows the Food Business and will help with your friend's Wedding.

He took care of and waited on Royalty in his day. He lived on Earth around 1400 A.D. when Class was Class.

Phillip is clearly aware of your need to Progress.

September 3, 1990

Ron, you and Phillip are doing well. We are bringing you a New Teacher later in the year, as Phillip has almost finished his work to help you stabilize your situation at work.

You will need a more Spiritual Teacher next for the Spiritual Work you must do.

November 7, 1990

Aristotle is here. Ron, Your New Teacher is Paul, and he is not the Apostle.

He is here to help you with Business, as you need a lot of help here. He is also Deeply Spiritual so he can help you with your Spiritual Work.

Paul is Greek and comes from Greece in the year 180 A.D. He is Brilliant and started Many Businesses in Greece. Paul wants to help you with your Business.

He is a Director of the Universe coming out of Retirement to Work with you. Also, he will help you with the Healing to Better Yourself.

Then have both of my Teachers moved on now?

Yes, they have; you only have one now. We feel this is all you need at this time. You still have the School of Healers that helps you with your Healing work.

263

Paul will adjust to your Vibration in about a week and <u>will be a</u> <u>great help</u> to you. He will adjust to the Other Personalities in about one and one half weeks.

Paul will also help to <u>calm you down</u> and Handle Situations Better. So <u>don't worry</u>, <u>it will be fine</u>.

February 17, 1991

Your Dream <u>about your hair falling out is</u> Symbolic of <u>letting go of</u> the Pressures in your Head.

This proves that Paul is <u>successfully helping you</u> with this. You should be pleased.

The steady rap on your <u>living room skylight</u> is your Teacher Paul <u>trying to relax you</u>. Your Mother raps on <u>the bathroom skylight</u>.

A rap is a crackling sound that that Spirit uses to send you a message to confirm their presence or that a just-made decision is the correct one.

May 9, 1993

Aristotle is here. Ron, you now have earned another New Teacher, David.

David is also English and was a Businessman who comes to get you Re-established and help move you to Higher Planes.

He was a Barrister, too, around 1300 A.D. and upheld the Law <u>to help people feel safe and secure</u>. He is Sharp and Classy, and brings you calming Reassurance.

He is a Director and will be beneficial to Your Healing as he Teaches Healers now.

You're doing fine in Your Spiritual Work, so continue Living your Life as Promised. The Spiritual Always Follows.

David is Proud of you. He wants you to Always Trust the Universe because <u>it will always take care of</u> you.

264

So just remain Patient and everything will <u>come together in its right time</u>. As you know, timing is everything.

December 29, 1993

Aristotle is here. Ron, Matthew is your New Teacher. He comes for business and to help you Progress <u>using less energy</u>.

He is a Healer and a Director, and will also work through you with your Healing.

He is sharp and understands what you are doing. He owned his own food service business in Greece in 897 A.D.

He serviced all of the Royal Family members and <u>was quite influential</u> with all <u>people of rank and position</u>. We believe you and this Teacher will make much Constructive Progress together.

<u>Please welcome him</u> and ask for his help. He knows about food presentation and vegetables. He will use this latter knowledge to help you with your own Nutritional needs.

Good Luck, Ron, with your New Teacher. You <u>have earned him</u>. He Loves you a lot and is <u>enthusiastic about working, so put him to work</u>. – Love, Aristotle.

Notice they allotted no numbers to the Planes of Progress for the last six Directors assigned to me in the last four years of my Progress. Remember, they noted several times that after a certain level they stop counting.

Two years later I finished my Food and Beverage career and opened a Flower Shop.

January 15, 1996

Ron, we here in the Universe want to assign you a New, Wildly Creative Teacher to help you with your New Flower Business. He has many new ideas.

The New Teacher's name is Germaine. He is a Great Artist and will help you create Spiritual Designs with your flowers.

Teach him to Guide your Hands in <u>making</u> <u>all</u> <u>your</u> <u>arrangements</u> and Create new ideas for other times.

Use vases of clear glass or other clear substances in your arrangements. The clear holds the Universe's Energy and so you use it in your work to send Healing with your arrangements.

Ron, <u>every</u> <u>flower that leaves</u> your Shop will carry Healing with it, and <u>this is a way</u> <u>of helping</u> the Universe.

This way people will accept the Healing Energy, which is critical because <u>so many</u> <u>need it</u>. Always remember it's your Healing Hands <u>guiding</u> <u>those who receive</u> your arrangements <u>in whatever you</u> Create.

Matthew is your Director. He <u>will stay</u> <u>to support</u> <u>your business</u>. Germaine is a High Teacher and will <u>draw the</u> <u>people</u> to you for Flowers and Healing.

This is <u>the best way</u> <u>you could do our</u> <u>job</u>. This will Change the Attitudes of the <u>people that receive</u> <u>your flower arrangements</u>.

The Designs you do will be like no other. This is Our Secret and Our Thanks for allowing us to <u>work through</u> <u>you</u>. The Universal Healing carried in the arrangements will also make the <u>flowers last</u> <u>longer</u>.

Germaine is excited; he Loves your Shop and is helping you to get the <u>best</u> quality <u>fresh flowers</u> and to generate <u>business</u>.

Ron, I am <u>talented</u> in Design. I lived in Greece around 1200 A.D.

During my time on Earth, many of my Designs were <u>painted on</u> <u>walls</u>. I Love <u>fresh flowers</u> and to Create using many <u>colors</u>.

I owned my own business and worked with baskets; I **Love** this as they last longer. Together we will make many Creative and Impressive Designs.

I entered all this information to demonstrate the degree of support you will receive from the High Universe when you are aware and are working with the Universe.

Much earlier, I asked Teddy Roosevelt how one could keep Themselves Nutritionally Balanced?

You need to balance yourself with Nutritional Foods. So many don't eat enough fruit and vegetables, both of which are important.

Also many lack Calcium, sometimes Potassium; it's best to take a Multivitamin and try to balance your food intake.

Everything should be in Moderation, including Exercise. Not too much over Exertion and plenty of Rest to Center and Balance your Body.

September 11, 2001, severely diminished my business. It never recovered, so in 2003 I closed my doors. Since then a New High Director, James, has been helping me in our quest to publish Our Books.

James and I shared a Past Life. We were James and John in Biblical times. He says it was a Wonderful Life then. Together we Taught, Healed and saved so many Lives.

Ron, that is why you are now letting the Universe take your requests for Healing Prayers and work on your own on Earth. You have my help from the Universe; it's like we are working together as we once did.

Also, I have a New High Master Director of Healing; his name is Job, from the Bible's Book of Job.

I, Job, Direct the Healers of the Universal School of Healing. They are anxious to work to heal the Lives of those Earth Souls that you touch with your "Golden Hands."

Our Work will become so much more rewarding when Our Books are published. Then we can spread Healing through every word in our Books to help Earth Souls in their Lives.

Every Book will be a connection to the Universe and your "Golden Hands" will touch every Soul who reads them through the words.

Job also said I could find some of his story chronicling his time on Earth on the Internet, but says much of it is not true.

My story was compiled by a Close-Minded Man and was meant for that time period. But today Man needs to Open its Mind to New Thoughts and forget about what things meant in the Past.

This Old Thinking is holding back Soul Progress on Earth and Advancement to the High Universe.

This is why most of the Apostles have been Reincarnated on Earth as Teachers now in this age – to bring about the Change for a New Spiritually, which is taking place.

Some have already finished their work, like Pope Paul II, who traveled the World bringing people together in Peace.

He was one of Our High Teachers, Ron, who has returned to us in the Universe. There is other work that is now in Process on Earth. Or, it will <u>open up</u> <u>at the right time</u>, including your Work to come.

Everyone needs to Listen to God Within himself or herself and make Peace and Progress with their own Soul.

I am grateful to one of Jan's Automatic Writing Students, Alice, who wrote for me, and her writing Teacher, Jordan, for his writing, to identify my present Directors working with me now.

Once I receive their names I can talk and work with them to receive direct information.

I hope you dear readers now have some idea how much Progress is possible on Earth in one Lifetime when you are open to the Universe and work on the Spiritual path outlined in these Books.

As you have followed my Progress you see how I started over, returning to Earth for this Special Mission, and have Progressed back to the High Universe from which I came, while still here on Earth.

My Spiritual Healing and Teaching will move much Higher before My Mission is complete. I have had Twelve Teachers, and as I continue to Progress, I will receive more according to the need.

You, too, can make this Progress with your Own Soul and, "can do greater things than I," if you accept the Universe and work hard helping others.

You will receive more and more help from the Universe as you grow Spiritually and will be so Gratefully Rewarded when you return Home to the Universe.

My Sister Jan also had Twelve Teachers and had risen above the Fiftieth Plane before she went home.

You can follow Jan's Progress in the Chapter, "Jan's High Writing and Art Teachers." Each one of her Teachers raised her to a Higher Plane.

Visit web site to request healing. There is no charge.
www.ronsgiftofhealing.com

The Next Chapter we talk about "New Souls."

NEW SOULS

Conier, who Creates the Soul and how long have Souls existed?

God Created The Soul, and God is All of Our Teachers from the Highest of Planes.

Souls have been the Existence of All Knowledge. **God is the meaning of Soul Existence**.

All Earned Souls are God, and they Create Good Souls to Learn and work for Our Dimension. You must understand that all Souls are God and it is LOVE OF ALL.

Souls have always existed, and there have always been Souls Created to work on all Planes.

There are Good Souls and there are Bad Souls, or Souls that do not work and Progress. Remember, the Soul makes that Choice.

Sometimes when he or she arrives back in Our Dimension they can't find their way. That's because when they were sent to the Earth Plane they refused to go. It was so much nicer here and they didn't want to work again.

So they forget why they were sent to the Earth Plane and don't do what they are sent there to do.

There are lots of them on Earth that don't Listen to Teachers anymore. So they are called back having made no Progress and the Teachers banish them to sit in Dark Corners.

They do not Reincarnate back to Earth until they ask to work to get out of the Dark.

Then, when they have worked their way to a certain level of Progress on the Astral Plane, their Teachers could choose to send them back to Earth.

Teachers always decide when a Soul goes to Earth. That decision is usually connected to Family and Lessons that need to be learned.

Now, if the Soul is not Progressing with the Family and is called back, it will leave that Earth Family but only after working from the Astral Plane for Three Generations with that Family.

Then, the Soul moves on to another Family to start over to work with, only from the Astral Plane. Again, it is possible for Teachers to decide if they feel Progress can now be made by sending this Soul to Earth in this Family.

If not, then after Three Generations with this new Family working to make Progress from the Spirit World; as the Fourth Generation takes over the Older Soul; it is now ready to move on. But only if it has Progressed, to be a Guide for an Earth Soul connected to that Family.

If you are a Fourth Generation Soul of a Family on the Earth Plane now that makes Progress, you will help and work from the Spirit World for the Family, for a full Lifetime.

Then the next Lifetime will become Third Generation, the next becomes the Second Generation, and then the finally last becomes the First Generation. This then frees your Soul from further Family obligation.

You are obligated in the Spirit World to a Family to work with, for four Generations, all according to the Progress that you make.

Then, after this you will also move on to be a Guide for an Earth Soul unless Teachers have some other work for you.

Many are Couriers for Our Teachers, and all Couriers help Teachers always.

Jennifer was asked a Question on New Souls. How do we get New Souls on Earth? The following is her answer.

First, we explained that God Creates New Souls and then they are sent forth to Progress through the Ape or Bigfoot on Mars; this helps them to learn mobility of the Body.

Then, when they've progressed through the Apes' body, these Souls then become Little Children in Our Dimension.

When they've finished their Learning here they go to the Earth Plane to work and Progress.

This was back in the Early Days. Then Souls were First Born into a Baby's body as Cave Men and Primitive Natives – the first primitive inhabitants on Earth.

Now, if you remember, we said that every Soul that is presently on the Earth Plane is there for at least the Second Time and many are there for their Third and Final Time.

Well, none are there for the First Time, or better still, there are no New Souls on Earth because we don't send them there anymore, though we used to.

We now send New Souls to Our New Dimension when they finish their Learning as Children on Our Dimension.

They do not have to go to Learn mobility through the Ape experience, as they will not ever be taking on an Earth body.

How interesting. I thought you were not sending Good Souls to Earth anymore but didn't realize this about New Souls. Here we go with time again! How long has it been since you sent New Souls to Earth?

That's right, Ron! We are not sending Good Souls back to Earth and haven't for some time now.

They also go to Our New Dimension. Many, many years back we sent many New Souls but they were not progressing so we stopped.

The last time we sent any New Souls to Earth was at least 500 years ago, and then some came and some didn't because too many Earth Souls were not following the Missions they were sent to Earth to fulfill.

You must also remember that New Souls always started their Earth Lives in the most Primitive Tribes of people, because their Only Progression was through the Apes' body experience.

They bring the Animal traits and senses with them and must Learn and Progress from there while on Earth.

Your Primitive Tribes that are on Earth today are Not New Souls, but Souls that haven't made any Progress or very little at all.

They have been making such slow Progress on the Lower Astral Plane for many, many years and have now been sent back for their Second Reincarnation, hoping they will make Progress.

Some of your Primitive Tribes on Earth now are on their Second Time, because they were Bad Souls during their First Time. They had to start over back on Mars as invisible Mars People, not as Bigfoot Apes because they were not Progressing on Earth.

When they are moved to Earth from Mars without having learned much, they are just beginning; they are Primitive and confused because they still relate to their other Planet Life.

They all carry great Negativity and like to pass it on to others. This makes them feel good. These are Souls to stay away from.

These Primitive Natives are not educated and they come as Ignorant Souls that have many Lessons to Learn. This is their way of living to begin making Progress.

Again, there are No First Time Souls on Earth now, some Second and mostly those experiencing their Third and Final Reincarnation.

In the Period Prior to 500 years ago, the New, Non-Progressed Souls First Reincarnated on Earth as Amazon Indians or members of other Primitive Tribes.

This comes after they've progressed as Apes Learning body mobility on Mars and then for a time as Children on Our Dimension.

In the past 500 years they're making Progress on Our New Dimension, but not on Earth because there's too much Corruption there.

We do not want New Souls exposed to Corruption because <u>once that happens</u>; it takes them too long to Progress.

They do not know Corruption on Our New Dimension; there is none there.

That answers my Question about why we still have Primitive Tribes on Earth today. Thank You So Much Jennifer "Mary Todd Lincoln!"

I am inserting this writing by Teddy Roosevelt from August 21, 1986, about God Creating New Souls and Good Souls. It never hurts to expand a little more on a Subject.

Teddy is here. When there was a need to Better Mankind, God Creates more New Souls. God did this to <u>maintain an equal balance</u> in the Universe between Good and Bad.

Souls have always been created to maintain Balance on the Earth Plane. When Corruption gains the upper hand on the Earth Plane, New Souls were created to <u>restore the balance</u>.

This is the beginning of Good Souls. They are Good when God first creates them to make Progress with Love and Sharing.

The initial three steps in the <u>progressive</u> <u>process</u> were: first occupying an Ape-Sasquatch body on Mars; second, progressing on Our Dimension as a Child; and third, sending them to Earth as Natives or Primitives to Learn and Progress.

But Corruption kept growing, forcing the Universe to stop sending Good New Souls to Earth anymore.

We in the Universe felt it was useless <u>to try</u> <u>to correct</u> Earth anymore. Therefore, we decided, meaning God's Universe decided, that Souls on the Earth Plane must straighten up themselves; <u>keeping in mind</u> that the Universe is there to help.

It was the only way at this point we could clean up Earth and make more Progress.

We Hope in the next 20 to 30 years, All Earth Souls will Improve their Lives and Change Their Ways. In this way, all of Mankind can definitely Progress.

Thank you, Teddy.

About one year later, on August 30, 1987, I asked Markus: Could you explain so we understand clearly a little more about the Mars Process of the Ape Body?

This is what he wrote. Wow! I felt it was going to be heavy!

That's fine, Ron. We all need to understand clearly.

The First Born on Earth is a New Soul that has been Created by God to Learn and Progress with Love.

Remember, the Soul is just a Tiny Light. We use the body of the Apes on Mars to condition the Soul into using a Physical Body. The Apes there are different than the Earth Apes.

You mean this could explain The Missing Link that says we came from Apes? Are these what we call Sasquatch or Bigfoot, and Yeti?

You are correct, Ron. Those are suitable words to describe them. The Sasquatch is the Male and the Yeti is the Female; some are Mates. Some of them are on Earth now and they come from Mars.

Mars is a Frigid Existence but the Soul <u>does not know what cold is</u> yet because <u>it has had no experience</u>.

Souls placed in an Ape Body do have <u>thought and energy</u>, but have <u>no</u> Knowledge <u>of the functions of</u> the Body. We can place many Souls simultaneously in one Ape Body.

275

So, they are busy there experiencing, and Learning to Progress to become Children in Our Dimension. Following that they would go to Earth.

Remember, this is how it was done in the past, 500 years ago and before. Since then we don't send New Souls to Earth anymore.

The Ape Body never Dies unless it leaves Mars. Even on Earth they live for a long time, and if they die on Earth, a Mars Ship retrieves the Ape Body so Man can never find it.

Only New Souls, not Reincarnated Souls, were placed in Apes. When they came to Earth they were placed as Native Indian Tribes. Presently, Earth doesn't care about this; it was so long ago.

I'm sure many will be interested how we all started out from the beginning of Creation. This has never been explained before on Earth.

Man surely has Grown and Evolved enough to now Learn this, so I'm entering it in Our Books for those Open Minded Readers. It is up to them if they wish to accept or reject it.

Markus how have our bodies changed from this Bigfoot Ape-type body to our current Earth Body?

We specially selected a Sasquatch and a Yeti to be the First Man and the First Woman; who have been called Adam and Eve.

Adam was the Soul of the Man, who later was called Jesus, and the first Male on Earth.

This was Jesus' Third Reincarnation on Earth; his Second Reincarnation after Adam was as a High Spiritual Teacher and Leader in an Early Ancient Spiritual Civilization long before Atlantis.

Eve was the Twin Soul of the first Woman and the first Female on Earth; later she was called Queen Victoria. They both came from the Star Universe.

Her Second Reincarnation as Victoria came when she was returned to Earth with a Strong Purpose.

She came back to Earth in the period of the Powerful Kings. Yes, she was Queen Victoria, who was the Strength of the Earth Plane's English Empire.

The Male was created from a specially selected Sasquatch Ape body. Also, the Female was created from a specially selected Yeti Ape body, and this created the attraction between Male and Female Souls.

They were Twin Souls that split from one, as all Souls are split and have a Twin Soul Mate.

Then we have Our Ways through High Universal Energies, which Earth Souls could not understand, to clear all the hair from the body.

We also removed some of the Animal Traits from their bodies, but their Instincts still remained for their Survival.

We also have their minds stripped of all senses as they must experience everything and Progress from the beginning.

As time went on and as some Souls made Progress they earned better-looking bodies, and eventually lost most of their Ape features, such as longer arms. They also lost their Animalistic Traits and Senses.

Also, many Souls that were Progressing too slowly retained some hair and some Ape-like looks and actions for Centuries, even through today.

There are none of these First-time Souls on Earth at this time. However, many Non-Progressing Souls were sent back to Mars to start all over again as Mars people, not in the Ape body though, but as Non-Progressed Aliens.

See the Chapter, "Planets In Our Universe: Life on Other Planets," in Book II, "Many Planes Above."

Some now have earned the right to return to Earth to start over there from the beginning.

Therefore, because there are many Souls that are slow Learners, we have many Primitive, Second-time Souls on Earth today in the Amazon, and as Gypsies wandering in many remote areas and Nomadic Lands.

Some still with <u>a lot of hair on their bodies,</u> which we explained comes from making no Progress; are starting over and have not earned a better body.

That was as I thought it would be; that's some Pretty Heavy Stuff. This could account for the Werewolf stories, and how some people's faces and bodies are covered totally with hair. It is called Hypertrichosis.

It sure gives me a Better Understanding of the so-called Missing Link. We may have to re-think or re-write Our Theories of Evolution!

Markus, this Very High Director of the Universe, brings this information for the first time to Earth. He wants Earth Souls to understand this, but only if they Choose.

We have this Knowledge because of my inquisitive nature and desire to understand all things as they really are.

Thank You so much, Markus.

You're Welcome, Ron. There is so much in the Universe that Earth Souls are not yet ready to Understand.

This is true, Markus. But we are trying with Our Books to Open their Minds to accept some of this Knowledge!

The Great Aristotle wrote this later about Nomads. Jan and I went to the Race Track, and I asked why it felt so Cold and Negative there. The answer is appropriate to enter here.

Aristotle is here. I feel it's always nice to get a new look at Life. I think today at the Races was Educational and I appreciate this. Thank You.

There are so many Nomads here. The Cold, Negative Vibration that you are feeling comes from them.

Nomads are Primitive people that still Live in the past. The Soul of each Nomad was a New Soul in its first time on Earth. Now, in their Second Incarnation they could not stand the shock of the modern way of living; it's a very new thing to them.

These are Old Souls there today; they are the ones that won't Progress.

These on Earth today are the ones that helped to Populate history and it's the same people today that are attuned to this Primitive way of Life.

Many people that hang around the Race Track are the most Non-Progressive people. There were also many Nomad Entities there.

Aristotle, there was kind of a balance of the energies with all the Beautiful Gardens of Flowers everywhere and the Lush well-kept Greenery.

Yes. The Angels toil here, and they work hard with Energy and Minerals in the Earth to create these Beautiful Gardens.

The Gardens need this Energy to grow.

They are fine Angels and they work hard here to make the Flowers Beautiful. These flowers send Healing to all that are around them.

Ron, this is Angel Souls Work that you see. They are Healing Souls standing by to help. Well, there are many of these Healing Souls there, and you see Energy in the Beauty, Universe Energy, and you do breathe this Energy.

The Healing was High Today to create this balance.

I had doubts about excluding this Information, as I have had with other Information that I excluded, because of the possibility of creating even more Controversy than already Exists around certain subjects.

Well, we will put it out there anyway for the Open Minded Readers who may say, "Wow!"

Or they may simply not accept any of it. After all, we have Free Choice to feel some memory of this from Our Past, as Our Souls have already Progressed through this Experience.

Or many may not Open Their Minds to accept even this Possibility at all. Maybe we are not ready to understand yet, but I've included the following for those that wish to Open Their Minds and begin to work with the Universe for New Spirituality on this troubled Earth.

You know all Change Is Progress, and the purpose of the Truth entered in these Books is to OPEN MINDS on Earth.

Hopefully, this information will Change Their Way of Thinking from the Old Way to this New, Enlightened Way.

If we don't change, we as Humans will just continue on the Path of No Soul or Spiritual Progress by passing on the Old Information to Our Young.

The Younger Generation born today is here to Change Our Earth!

They will eagerly absorb the Information in these Books, and Open Their Minds to the Truth, Knowledge and Wisdom that comes from the High Universe for their Own Souls' Current and Future Progress. Our Beautiful Earth Plane desperately needs that Progress.

I think this Information is so wonderful, and it helped me to Comprehend Life to the fullest.

I have this slight memory of my Life in the Cave Man Days on Earth when I Healed others using Mudpacks and Herbs, and by Listening to the Universe for remedies and direction.

280

I am entering this information received from Teddy Roosevelt during one of our classes. The question was: Do New Souls go through the Apes on Mars?

The Apes are Souls paying for errors. No New Souls go through the Apes. It is not being done this way now.

The Souls that have so Many Mistakes to pay for have to return as the invisible Mars Aliens to start over. There they must pay for their Mistakes all over again. Also, we send there the Souls who refuse to work.

The New Souls, which were created, are not coming to Earth any longer. Therefore, they do not need to learn the Mobility of the Body experience on Mars. They go directly to the New Dimension now.

They do not have an Earth Body there and will never need an Earth Body because we do not send New Souls to Earth anymore.

They will never be exposed to Earth's Corruption and will remain PURE.

In Our Universe there are many Planets that have Apes. They are different from the Mars Bigfoot-type Ape in the Earth's Universe.

In the Earth's Universe the Planet Mars was created for Earth's Soul Progress only.

The New Souls that were created for Earth over 500 years ago did go through this process on Mars, but not since then.

We will talk about "Lost Earthbound Souls" in our next Chapter.

LOST EARTHBOUND SOULS

Conier, what are Lost Souls?

Lost Souls are Souls that have made No Progress and are living in the Outer Darkness of Our Earth.

That Outer Darkness is the area between Earth and the Astral Plane.

It is not a Plane. Though there is the Earth Plane and then the Astral Plane, which is the First Plane, then the Second Plane, the Third Plane, the Fourth Plane and so on, with "Many Planes Above."

Note: "Many Planes Above" is the title of Book II.

The Souls there in the Dark and the many Clinging to Earth probably did not do much good for themselves or others.

They have not listened to their Guides or Teachers, and through their Own Doing are consigned to this Darkened State of Being.

The number of Souls in this condition is beyond human comprehension. Unfortunately, most or all of them are making Little Progress, if any.

Most just sit there in Complete Darkness. Some have been there for many thousands of years and are not able to figure anything out for themselves.

The Lowest Level Souls Clinging to the Earth Plane are called Earthbound Souls, and as we know, the human eye cannot see them.

However, there have been many cases throughout Earth's history where these Souls have found ways to inform Humans of their presence.

Some sensitive Souls here on Earth have seen them through their Mediumistic Gift of Clairvoyance.

These sensitive Souls have seen and heard them through Clairaudience; some sense them through Clairsentience or even by feeling these Earthbound Souls touching or poking them to get attention.

I myself have strongly felt these Negative Souls. They tried to solicit my help, as they seem to know that I was aware of them when no one else was. They see me helping others with Healing and think I will help them.

The Universe and I did a Great Deal of Work to raise my Vibration level to completely protect me from them. I am so Grateful to My Guide and Protector Santus along with the Couriers for the Devine Protection I enjoy everyday and night.

Santus is a Very Large, Powerful early American Indian who was a Chief of the Iroquois Tribe. He has progressed with me to become a High Teacher and may now call on Couriers to help him Protect me.

Today, there are T.V. Shows based on these Earthbound Souls with Mediums helping them to move on and go to the Light.

However, it is not as easy as it looks on T.V., because most of these Earthbound Souls are Stubborn and do Not Listen. That's the reason they are here in the first place.

They refused to go through the Tunnel to the Light.

Nevertheless, these Shows make for Great Entertainment and are becoming more frequent. They help to open people's Minds to this serious Earth Problem.

Thank You, to all who make these Shows, including the Directors, Actors, Writers, Producers, and Crew, and the Mediums or Psychics that serve as Advisors.

Shows like this serve the Universe by showing that Earthbound Souls are Real and that they can be found all over Our Earth.

I truly believe this is the cause of many of Our Earth's Tribulations: Psychological Problems especially Multiple Personality and Voices in One's Head, Entity Possession, Drug Addiction and Medical Problems.

And, most Importantly, Murder, or simply any Negativity that we have known on Our Earth.

Mankind has created these Earthbound Souls throughout its History. These old Clinging Earthbound Souls are still here Influencing Earth Souls to continue the Corruption that exists on Earth today.

This is all Negativity, and whenever the Universe speaks of Negativity in these writings it is referring to these Lower Lost Souls.

All Negativity is created by the thinking and actions of Earth Souls – here on Earth and in the Outer Darkness.

"As we think is what we are" – and what we attract to ourselves in Our Lives.

It is time for Mankind to Change its Ways and it's thinking to Heal all Negativity for the cause of World Peace!

Ron, Earth Souls must understand the Universal Law of Attraction – "LIKE ATTRACTS LIKE."

If you allow your Rate of Vibration to drop to these Negative Levels you open the Gate or Door for these Lower Lost Souls who are wandering the Earth. At these Negative Levels they can seek you out and stay with you, <u>draining your energies</u>.

They may lead you into <u>situations you just do not like</u> or they may develop into situations of a more Serious Nature.

You always know when something is Right or Wrong. However, because you have **God-Given Free Will** to do as you wish. But maybe after making several Wrong Choices you may begin to Think Twice about the decisions you make.

There is No Punishment. There are Only Consequences.

I had been working with a Medium for two and one half years; she would go into a Trance State.

The Lower Entities, were Bothering her and her Family. They would take over her body and spoke to me through her one after the other.

This is how I Learned so much about these Unfortunate Lost Earthbound Souls.

I had taped and transcribed these sessions to put them in book form but became so Bothered with them myself that I had to discontinue this work with Lower Entities.

***The Teachers told me,** "Ron they have had their chance."*

Furthermore, the Universe said that by burning all of my transcripts and tapes it would help the Universe to Protect and shield me from them.

It took the Universe more than 10 years to cleanse and clear Untold Thousands of these Earthbound Lost Souls and create Peace and Protection for me.

You may understand more in the following writing where I ask my Healing Teacher, Gandi, questions.

Conier is here. Hi, Ron. *Could I speak to Gandi, my Healing Teacher?* Yes we will get Gandi to speak.

Gandi began to write in his native East Indies hand, which included a little broken English just like he wrote when here on Earth.

Gandi is here. You are Progressing because you are attaining a Higher Vibration level. Keep this up and please don't hang on to these Stubborn, Earthbound Souls.

He is speaking of Stubborn Lost Souls. I'm just trying to help them to move on. Do I help them at all?

Yes, you do help some of them to move on, along with the help of Our Teachers. That is what we want to accomplish.

You must get the Medium to raise her Vibration; she must ask her Guide to protect her from them.

Who is the Guide Protecting her?

Her Guide is Matoose, an Indian man of the Iroquois Tribe, the same tribe as your Guide, Big Chief Santus. She must ask Matoose for more Protection.

It will be better for her Guide if she were to ask for his Protection, as he is shy and afraid of the Lower Entities. This shyness and fear prevents him from doing his job.

He has to Fight to come in and get through the large crowd of Souls wanting help that surround her.

He must learn to Chase them away. Gandi has the company of Healers. One is an Old Medicine Man who's name is Quiet Waters. He wants to help heal her, too.

Do I have Protection around me?

Yes, you do. You are so lucky to have your Protecting Guide, Santus. He helps protect you and we want you to keep working with him.

The amount of Progress made depends on the Vibration of the Medium receiving the Spirit Souls; this depends on her shifting moods.

Who is the Soul that keeps pushing in the line when we are talking with another Soul? He says he is Carlos.

Carlos <u>is not real</u>. <u>He lies about everything</u>. *He says he is helping and a Healer.* THIS IS NOT TRUE. This is Earthbound Souls' <u>nonsense</u>.

Is there anyone truthful?

Sometimes, but you must watch this because they tell Imaginary Stories.

The Liar Carlos is a Liar and not a Healer. He is mixed up and he <u>loves to lie all the time</u>. He doesn't know any better.

You must tell him to move on and don't talk to him. Gandi told him what to do and Gandi speaks in Spirit Tongue.

Who is the Soul that says his name is Benito?

Benito is fine. He's just a seven-year-old boy, and he is Not Learning <u>anything</u>. Children <u>need direction; someone has to tell them where to go</u>. He thought you could tell him where to go.

He saw the line and slipped in to <u>talk through the</u> Medium.

Ron, <u>are you aware</u> that you have <u>started a line of</u> Lost Earthbound Souls that is <u>longer than the eye can see</u>?

They are <u>pushing and shoving</u> to come <u>through this</u> Medium for <u>you to tell them what to do and where to go</u>.

It is <u>hard for us to</u> Control this from Our Side when the Medium <u>does not want to</u> raise her Vibration to a Higher Level. So we may help Souls that have made some Progress and are ready to Listen and Progress to the Light.

Could I ask for a certain Spirit to come through the Medium to speak to me?

No, Souls that are coming through are in Darkness, and some have been there for Hundreds <u>of years already</u>. They didn't listen while they were on Earth and some are Not Listening to you now.

You have instructed some to look completely around them for any Glimmer of Light and to go to that Light.

Those that have seen <u>any</u> <u>crack</u> of Light say it is too far away and would take too long to get there.

You have encouraged them to work their way to the Light <u>no matter how long</u> <u>it takes</u>.

You must realize these are Lazy and Stubborn Souls that do Not Listen.

You told Souls that haven't seen the Light to sit and wait until someone comes for them.

They responded that it was too long to sit and wait. Again, you responded that <u>someday</u>, <u>someone will come</u> for them; they must sit and wait.

Each Soul must do this for themselves.

Some have even been sitting for Thousands of years. <u>They</u> <u>had their chance on</u> Earth to Listen and correct their Mistakes. Some have already had many Lifetimes to do so.

Also some of the Souls Clinging to the Earth Plane pushed their way into the line and Listened to you, and <u>are working</u> <u>toward the</u> Light.

If you know a Soul who is still Clinging to the Earth Plane you could <u>only</u> <u>ask for them to come through</u>. Only <u>advanced</u> Spirits on the Lower Astral Level can come through, as the Medium's <u>vibration is too low</u>.

My Father is sitting in the Dark in his wheelchair, just like he did on Earth. Can I call him to come?

<u>No</u>! Your Father is not ready yet. *And my Mother?* Your Mother is <u>afraid of all the</u> Lower Entities. But you could <u>speak with your</u> Uncle Walter if you wish.

You can ask for him – <u>if he can</u> <u>get through this crowd</u> – because he has been working longer than your Mother on the Lower Levels of the Astral Plane, and he understands.

Thank You. I understand that as a Soul works its way toward the Light from the Darkness, that Darkness turns Gray and continues to grow lighter until the Soul reaches the Lower Astral Plane

Then, they still must go through the Dark Tunnel to gain access to the Astral Plane, meet with Teachers and agree to work off their Mistakes.

Who is this Lady that came in and says she is from the Land of Light?

The Lady from the Land of Light is actually between Planes. She's in the Gray area that we just spoke of, moving towards the First Plane. The First Plane, of course, is the Astral Plane.

She has earned her way this far. However, she is still not in the Light and remains alone. She must <u>keep</u> <u>working</u> <u>if she is</u> <u>going</u> to reach the First Plane.

The First Plane as we said is the Astral Plane but you must go there with Teachers. You cannot go it alone because the Teachers <u>tell</u> <u>them the work they</u> <u>must do</u> to Graduate through the Astral Plane and all of its Levels.

These Teachers work at the Gate of the Astral Plane.

The Lowest Stage is the "Clinging-to-the-Earth Level." The Teacher asks when you arrive, "Are you ready to pass and Work on Correcting Your Mistakes from your Past Lives?"

If you don't Listen you must remain on the Low Grey Clinging Level until you are ready to work.

Most will respond by saying, "<u>Who are you</u>?" to the Teacher; or "I won't Listen to you." So we leave them there until they realize it's time to Work. Very Few Listen.

Gandi, this is so hard to believe. How sad that our Ignorance, Stubbornness, Laziness and Closed Minds have Created this mentality on Earth. And we've been doing it all through our history.

We have Souls sitting in Darkness for Thousands of years through many Lifetimes.

Then, when they finally reach the Light they refuse to Listen to the Teachers to begin their Work. This is such a shame because it is the only way to find what their Earth-bred religions call Heaven or Peace.

Then they still must Work and Earn on the Astral Plane to move to Higher Planes. But they do Not Listen when the Teachers tell them that they have to work to even move on to the Astral Level of Light.

You are correct, Ron. <u>Few move on</u>, and what they believe as Heaven is <u>not a geographic location</u>; it's a State of Mind that has to be earned. It is <u>within each of us to do that</u>.

We are all working to Correct Our Mistakes, Progress Our Soul, and discover more of Heaven and Happiness within Our own Souls, as we move on through Eternity.

This is why these Books must be written and all Souls on Earth must read them to Learn their Earth-Life Purpose.

This is why Our Teachers are so busy. They <u>are overloaded</u> when these Souls finally make up their mind to Begin Work and Correct their Mistakes.

We do not have enough Teachers. A Teacher must work on a One-on-One <u>basis for each</u> Soul <u>to understand</u>.

Gandi, Thank You! This is what is Wrong with Earth. There is no Religion that Teaches Personal Responsibility or that tells us that we have to go it alone for the Soul's Own Spiritual Progress.

*We alone must find out Who We Really Are, Who We Want to be, and How We Want to Live. ***

Religions are teaching of a God Outside of us, which condemns and punishes us, instead of God that is Within Us. A God that is able to satisfy our every need and who asks nothing from us in return.

GOD LOVES all of us. All we need to do is Turn Within for all of Our Answers and know that we are never alone.

You are welcome, Ron. Today, Minds are Now Opening on the Earth Plane. They are Learning to work on the Earth Plane to help themselves with their Own Spiritual Growth.

I feel there is a Great Movement Underway. People are moving into the New Spirituality because the old ways are not working.

Hopefully, we will see Many Changes in the next few years in Religions, Governments and Schools all over Our Earth.

Ron, this Spiritualist Church you attend is Teaching such Old Ways; it's sickening and you are <u>wasting your time there</u>.

Spiritual Understanding is a fact and a Definite Way of Life.

It is preparation on the Earth Plane to make it so much better on the Next Plane. You know it can be Beautiful if the Spiritual Eye, <u>the eye of the mind, is opened</u>.

Gandi, I will leave this Church and try some others. Maybe I can find some Open Minded ones somewhere!

*Again, I recommend you read these and other beautiful words in Neale Donald Walsch's "Conversations with God" series. These words will help you understand God and help you get on with your Life.

Are Good Souls moving directly to the Light when they return to the Universe?

Yes, the Good Souls who are Very Good – those who give, care and share – move straight to the Light on the Astral Plane. But they must want to, some Refuse to.

This is their Free Choice.

We are all God's Children and are taught this from the Beginning. It is Our Choice what we do with Our Earth Life and no one else's.

What is wrong with Souls on Earth today is that they Refuse to Listen, and therefore are Not Making Any Progress Spiritually.

Because they refuse to listen, we must leave them here. They linger on Earth; these are the Clinging Earthbound Lost Souls that bother many.

I agree that these are serious Problems you must tackle as an Earth Soul. However, to overcome this Problem you all must try to rid yourselves of these clinging Souls: be strong and persistent when they won't go on or move on.

This is Important for all you Ghostbusters and Ghost believers searching for Communication with the Dead.

These Clinging Souls feed on the fear and horror that moviemakers generate with their sensationalized movies about ghosts, goblins and poltergeists.

This gives Recognition to these Clinging Souls, which is what they want. This is how they attach themselves to Earth people – by their thoughts and interests. They Live through you, even Possess You.

For example, a Murderer has many former Murderers hanging around them. We may want to rethink Our Death Penalty Policy. A Drug User has many former Addicts around them. We may want to rethink the Possibility of Overdosing.

The same is true for Rapists, Thieves and Molesters, even Terrorists.

We may want to Rethink Our Killing of one another or anything of a Negative Nature you could ever think of because...

"AS YOU THINK IS WHAT YOU ARE."

This applies to individuals, and it applies collectively to the thoughts and actions of an entire Country, as well.

This is how an entire Country as well as we ourselves attract Earthquakes, Hurricanes and other Disasters.

These Negative thoughts of Corruption and Non-Listening Souls attract these Disasters.

This is all based on FEAR. Why not Change it to LOVE?

Gandi, what is the Universe's view on the Death Penalty? Also, we have a case on Death row now. Some are pleading with the Governor to stay the execution, just as we have had many before this.

The Governor will not stop it, as he feels it's correct.

The Universe's point of <u>view of the execution</u> of this Soul is that this Soul is bad and <u>is ready</u> to leave, <u>but this is not to say</u> it is Right.

We use this as a tool to remove the Soul from Earth.

However, <u>those who choose to</u> play <u>a role in that execution</u> are affected. There is <u>a mark on their</u> Souls. We do not like Lives taken.

But on the other hand, if it's a Soul's time to leave, and they are going to be executed, we allow it. If it's not their time to leave, there will be <u>a stay</u> of <u>execution</u>.

What is an alternative to Capital Punishment?

A good alternative for Capital Punishment is to follow Universal Law – let the Soul Punish itself for its Sins or Mistakes.

Capital Punishment only releases the Soul from Paying its Dues, but they will have paid some back by Loosing their Life.

They will then have less to pay back, but still all must account for their Mistakes.

These people, if given a Longer Chance on Earth, could do more Constructive things. But in the long run they have to Account to the Universe for their Mistakes.

These Souls do not go through the Tunnel; they go to the Darkness unless they pull back to Earth and become Earthbound.

In the Darkness they have to wait for help to work off their Mistakes. That could be a very long time.

Thank you, Gandi.

Now Conier continues writing about Clinging Earthbound Souls.

You must tell these Clinging Souls to walk towards the LIGHT. Most can see the Light and they must move on.

You may have to tell them that they have lost their Physical Body and Must Work their way to the Light and Listen to the Teachers when they get there.

Tell them, "You do not belong here any longer; move on to the LIGHT."

Ghost Hunters, you must tell this to your Entities to free them and to free the Earth from the Souls Clinging to Earth.

Ask Your Own Guides to help them, the entity to turn all around to see any glimmer of Light and then go to the LIGHT.

Also, remember that if you are not careful and if an Entity likes you, you might just take them home with you.

I know this from experience working with Lowers through the Medium; I have taken hundreds home with me.

After I stopped this work it took so many powerful Indians and High Universal Souls so many years to cleanse my home and remove the longest line outside my door of these Clinging Souls.

You must remember you have to Change Your Ways to Free Yourself of them. This is the time to start asking your Guide to help.

Your Guide is on your right. Your Guide has always been there and will be with you all of Your Earth Life.

You may also Turn Within and ask God for help. God has always been in your Heart, not outside of you, and will be with you in all ways.

Say thank you, God, before every request, be it for Energy to Change Your Ways or Habits, or even for an answer to a question.

This way you show your Sincere Gratitude for your request as if it has already been done.

The following, written by Conier just before I stopped working with the Medium, helped me make my decision to no longer do this kind of rescue work.

Ron, when you worked with the Medium the other night, your Guide Santus was <u>crowded out of the place</u>. She is so full of these Clinging Entities he couldn't work beside you.

These Entities are now Out of Control, and they do Not Listen to you; they never listened while on Earth and they are not listening now.

You must ask her Guide to protect her, as he can't get near her.

Ask her Guide to protect her everyday she doesn't ask for that protection herself. Too bad she never listens to what you are saying. She thinks you are going to do all of her work for her.

The Higher Spirits Work with Earth people to Learn, and ultimately, to earn their Progress. You should be doing this High Spirit work instead of working with these Lower Souls.

You should not be working with Souls that have already passed; they had their chance and will Never Listen to you. These Souls don't know any better.

I know in your Kind Heart you wanted to help these Souls, but this is not the work we want you to do now.

It is not your Job to do this on Earth in this Lifetime. You have a different Mission now.

When you return to the Universe you will be able to continue your work helping these Lost Souls.

Right now, you are on a Mission to help the Earth Plane that comes directly from Our Directors of the Round Table. We are all tired of trying to help these Lost Souls that had their chance to Listen and didn't.

This is when I stopped the Sessions trying to help Lowers. I did not realize that I had opened up a big Can of Worms when I abruptly stopped the sessions at the Medium's home. By doing that I brought the entire lineup of Lower Souls home with me.

These Souls tormented me day and night, poking and jabbing my body. They all wanted me to help them.

I tried to send them on their way; maybe some Listened and moved toward the Light, but most did not. They expected me to perform some kind of Miracle to free them – not knowing they have to do this for themselves.

They are so Ignorant. They just don't know any better. This is a Serious Problem on Earth and people need to be aware of it.

I will cover here some of these Soul Experiences that we wrote on.

Because we cannot see Spirits, they tell us of their presence by knocking lightly, or rapping, on ceilings, doors, walls and windows. They will knock or rap on just about anything to let us know they are here.

They are not necessarily all from Lower Spirits. Some Raps could even be Family or Friends saying hello.

Ron, Raps <u>confirm our</u> <u>presence for</u> y<u>ou</u>. We are able to Rap only when we feel the vibration is right.

It has to be a hard surface, and it must <u>be a</u> <u>quiet vibration</u>. We <u>touch the area with our energy</u> and this creates the Rap. The energy must be High, and we can only Rap on High Energy.

When you hear a Rap, Pay Attention. We are sending you a message. Most of the time that message is to confirm that your decision to alter some action or plan <u>in</u> y<u>our immediate future is right</u>.

Your Teacher Gandi Raps on the Skylight in the living room, and your Mother Raps on the Skylight in your bathroom.

I asked Conier, "Who is the Spirit Rapping on my window?"

The Spirit that raps on your window is a Lost Soul; his name is Bob. He hangs around your house because he doesn't know where to go.
You must send him on to the Light and the Teachers. He needs to work and <u>does not realize this</u>.

You have many that have followed you home and <u>they</u> <u>know</u> y<u>ou are their only</u> <u>hope</u>.

For example, there is a <u>little old</u> Lady who stays in your bedroom all of the time; she followed you home from the Medium's house and you let her in without realizing it.

She likes you; well, she likes your bedroom. Souls like her must Learn to move on to Our Dimension, not <u>follow everybody</u> <u>everywhere</u>.

You must ask your Guide for Protection and for God's White Light; if not you leave yourself open to these Poor Souls.

You must tell them to go on with their Work to Progress and that you don't have time for them.

I know of nowhere on this Earth where people are taught this, or that it is even mentioned that they have to WORK when they pass on to the Universe from this Life. Lower Souls have told me that they didn't know this.

Once they are told, some have refused to work, saying that, "I worked so hard in my Earth Life. I am retired; I do not have to work any more."

I have asked these Earthbound Souls, "What happens when you die?" Their answer is usually something like this, "When I die I'll see what happens." Many Earthbound Souls are not even aware they are Dead.

We hope these Books will finally teach this for the first time on Earth to prevent what has been happening to all these Poor, Ignorant Souls.

My Grandfather stubbornly sat and played cards, mentally for many years on the Lower Astral Plane until my Mother finally convinced him to start his Work.

My own Father would Not Listen to anything I had to say about the Spirit World when he was here on Earth.

He spent his last years in a Senior Home. All the while remaining Stubborn and giving the Nurses a hard time.

When he passed over he just sat there in his Mental Wheelchair in the Dark, not understanding or knowing where he was. Nor did he realize he was even Dead.

He sent everyone away that tried to get him up out of his Mental Wheelchair and out of the Dark.

My Mother gave up on him because of his Stubbornness. "I'm not wasting any more time with him," she said in writing for me. My Dad was always quite Stubborn.

I will always treasure this writing from my Mother. It is exactly like she wrote while on Earth.

My Father's own Mother left in tears when he said to her, "Get away from me, you're Dead."

I prayed prayers of Love and Healing for my Father for more than two and one half years.

During that time my Father's brother, my uncle, stayed by his side in the Darkness, encouraging him to get started. Only a family member Soul from the Astral Level can do this.

My Father finally listened to his brother and moved to the Astral Plane to start working off his Mistakes. He's happy now and understands. Dad is doing so well working for his family.

I received this message from him through another writing. He wrote for us; this was a special gift from the Universe for both him and me. The first thing he wrote was…

"I didn't know I was supposed to work."

He went on to write that he understood now and had started his work.

You see, a Lost Soul has never been taught how to handle their Passing or what to be prepared for with their Passing.

It is a subject nobody wants to talk about here on Earth. As I said earlier, I have heard many say, "When I die, I'll see what happens and take care of it then."

Again, I hope these Books will be instrumental in helping all people to understand what happens when they are making their Transition.

There have been many Documented Cases of Near-Death Experiences, and there are many books available on the subject worth your consideration. These books recount the experiences of Souls that have reached the Light and returned.

There is one Author worth mentioning, Dannion Brinkley. *

He's had more than one Near-Death Experience and founded the Twilight Brigade, Compassion In Action for end of Life Volunteers.

That organization provides Comfort, Reassurance and Compassionate support to the Dying and their Loved Ones. Thank you, Dannion.

Everyone on Earth will experience upon his or her death passing through the Outer Darkness and moving through a long Dark Tunnel.

Those that have returned from this experience have related seeing many Souls reaching out to them from the Darkness, and then seeing a Bright Light at the end of the Tunnel.

You must Listen to the Teachers when you arrive in the Light. If you agree with what you are asked you will remain in the Light to Work off Your Mistakes from all of your Previous Lives.

If you refuse to Work you will remain in the Lower Grey Level of the Astral Plane until you Change your mind.

If you have not made any Progress in your Earth Life and have made more Mistakes you will sit in Darkness until Teachers have time for you.

*The title of his book is "Saved By The Light." He's written several other books since and there was a T.V. Movie made about his Life.

Now, Conier continues to write, after I have been writing about all my experiences with Lower Entities and what happens when you pass on. I hope this wasn't too much for you!

Ron, you need to work more with your Healing.

I am giving Healing to Lost Souls.

That's commendable, but you must send them on their way. The Lowers seem to crowd around you. There are too many for your Teachers to get close to you; it's like a thick cloud all wanting help.

PLEASE ask that they don't come through your door anymore, and start Healing the ones that need Healing on the Earth Plane.

These Souls that follow you drain your energy so you have to work harder to regain your strength.

This is not good for you, and you must reach a Higher Level to help us.

We will handle these Lost Souls.

You must ask both for Protection each and everyday and night, and for your Aura to be Cleansed so that your strength returns.

Are they holding me back?

Yes they are. These Lost Souls are tormenting you in your sleep.

Does the water under my bed help?

Yes, the water helps some, but it's not enough; you must burn **WHITE CANDLES** with the lights on to clear your house of all of this negativity.

Tell them to move on to the next Dimension, which is Our Plane, to do their Work where they can Progress for their own Betterment.

Ron, <u>we appreciate</u> <u>you</u> and we know your Work is sincere. We do Thank You and want you to move on. Your Teachers are right beside you trying to clear everything for you.

All of a sudden the writing changed to very large letters and broken English.

I AM A TEACHER OF RON. I AM YOUR HIGH TEACHER OF SPIRIT WORK.

I AM THE GUIDE OF YOUR PROTECTION. MY DIMENSION NAME IS CONTTIER, OR COMADAS.

MY EARTH NAME IS CHIEF SANTUS, AMERICAN INDIAN OF IROQUIS TRIBE. I PROTECT YOU ALWAYS.

ASK ME TO HELP WITH YOUR PROTECTION. ME LEARNING TO WRITE FOR YOU.

ME BIG CHIEF OF IROQUIS INDIAN USA. IN THE YEAR OF THE EARTH 1824.

Please give me your identification.

THANK YOU VERY MUCH. ME BIG CHIEF SANTUS. WILL PULL ON YOUR UPPER RIGHT ARM.

Will you please cleanse my Aura and my home?

Yes, fine. Me <u>going</u> <u>to clear the</u> Vibration, <u>I will stand</u> Guard <u>at front door so</u> <u>you can sleep</u> <u>more.</u>

You just ask me. I will be there always.

Jennifer "Mary Todd Lincoln" Jan's new Teacher, has taken over from Conier, who has moved on.

302

Jennifer, as I now see it, so many Earth people are not aware of these things, about where they came from and where they are going; in general we see Little Spirituality on Earth.

It seems people are Passing on in Ignorance and making little, if any Progress.

Ron, there are <u>many</u> <u>more now making</u> Progress <u>than there used to be</u>. Any Progress that is being made helps the Teachers in their work.

Why do you think we are asking for these Books to be published? We want more Earth Souls to become aware of what's going on.

Those Souls in Darkness have been there for thousands of years and more. Plus, more keep going there and not one has ever been back on the Earth Plane or will ever have a chance to return.

<u>That's right</u>! Darkness is Darkness and no Progress is ever made until Our Teachers have time. Right now, we have no time so we just let them sit.

We now only spend Our Time trying to Open Earth Minds in hope that we can save as many Souls as possible from entering the Dark.

Only when this is accomplished will we have time to deal with these Ignorant Souls.

There are also many Souls who refuse to go through the Dark Tunnel to the Light to Work and Progress. Instead they pull back and <u>wander around</u> the Earth as Earthbound Souls.

Some Souls, out of Fear and Ignorance, pull back. Some Souls, when shown the Work <u>they</u> <u>must do</u> when they reach the end of the Tunnel, Refuse to Work.

These Souls go back and <u>become trapped</u> in the <u>magnetic</u> <u>pull</u> of the Earth's atmosphere.

These are Selfish and Ignorant Souls that prey on Humans. These humans allow these Souls to influence them to the point that they adopt some of the Souls' Earthly Habits.

This is why you have so much Crime, Selfishness and Corruption on Earth. There is no Progress in these areas when Earthbound Souls stay on Earth or in the Outer Darkness.

How can people protect themselves from these Souls hanging around the Earth Plane?

First, do not allow them to influence you. You know what is Right and what is Wrong, so listen to your Inner Voice or Conscience. That's your Guide doing their job trying to protect you.

You must tell them to move on, and work with your Guide, your Protector, asking for a White Light to be placed around you Cleansing your Aura of all Negativity.

Simply put, you are in control of yourself and will not allow another to control you.

Sometimes they are Stubborn and won't Listen to you. But you must persist and have them move on.

They don't belong here unless you have allowed them to be here. Or, maybe you enjoy them pestering you to do Wrong Things.

These Souls are hanging around Earth because they Fear Death and do not realize there is no Death.

They also are not aware that they have lost their physical body and that they have Remorse over what they did while on Earth. They do not want to pay for it.

Not knowing they are Dead already, they influence other Souls on Earth to carry on what they did on Earth.

There are all kinds of Souls on the Earth Plane, and all kinds on the Lower Levels hanging around in Earth's atmosphere.

You all need to be aware of this reality on your Earth Plane so Earth Souls can Change their behavior. We want it Changed.

Foolish things happen on Earth because so many Lower Entities gather around people with Negative, Vindictive Thoughts. They are stopping us from doing Our Work.

It takes us so long to get them to move on and we just don't have enough help. There are just too many of them.

I am entering the following from Jan's Teacher Mara about fighting Negativity.

The best way to fight Negativity is to try and block out Lowers draining your Energy.

Also, keep The White Light around you, and your Guide and Teacher of the Universe will Protect and keep you Clear and Happy.

Are there certain Categories of Souls, or various types of Souls?

No. There is no such thing as placing a Soul in a certain Category or labeling it as a type. They are all the same. A Soul is just a Soul.

We are ALL ONE and ONE is ALL! No Race, Color, Money or Material things make any difference in a Soul.

Again, ALL are ONE and ONE is ALL!

Jennifer, where is the Outer Darkness, or rather, where does it start when we Pass Over?

305

It starts just as you pass over in the Universe; it actually begins just outside of the Earth's atmosphere. This is called the Outer Darkness.

If you do not go through the Tunnel of Darkness to the Light, Choose to linger, and no one tells you to move on, the Soul will spend years clinging to Earth.

The same fate awaits them even if someone tells them to move on and they refuse to listen.

This is why the Earth Soul must Change. That's the purpose of your work with these Books: to Open Minds to Truth and to explain how things really are.

We need many like you, Jan and Ron, to Open Minds to Our Dimension's Existence.

There are Groups all over the World now Opening up to the UNIVERSE. All of those who know we are here are becoming Stronger and starting to realize where they are going.

So in a few years, there will be a Strong Spiritual Bond among all these Groups.

Many future Disasters will cause many more to open up their Minds to Our Dimension. These Disasters will provide proof that the Universe is in Control.

I asked Aristotle on March 28, 1990, to explain a little about the Ghosts of the Queen Mary Ship in Long Beach, California.

Ghosts on the Queen Mary are Earthbound Souls that Refuse to leave Earth. They have No Knowledge of the Universe and we cannot force them to leave. We may never infringe upon their Free Choice.

They are just Ignorant about the Universe and are Clinging to what they know. Some don't even know they are Dead.

As soon as we get more Teachers we can start trying to Communicate <u>with</u> Earthbound **Souls** to begin to Change this.

This all happens the Minute you Pass Over. So many refuse <u>to leave because</u> most of them <u>don't know</u> about **Life** after **Death** and have <u>never taken the time to find out</u>.

You will only go if you have had a Great Love for Others or have had a Hard and Miserable Life on Earth.

Aristotle, I often feel an Entity crawling around my left ankle. Could you explain this?

The Entity is from 35,000 years ago, <u>crawling on the ground</u> <u>because it made</u> No Progress.

It <u>knew you from your</u> Cave Man Days, your First Life on Earth, and he <u>still hopes you will help him</u>.

Wow! Aristotle, this is hard for me to comprehend – that a Soul is still crawling around the Earth from so far back in time without making any Progress.

It's hard to accept such Ignorance. Yet this Soul is smart enough to somehow find me again in this Lifetime and still be looking for my help.

It's Ironic when I think of the untold numbers of Earthbound Souls that lined up outside my door from the Medium's home for help.

It took Ten years to clear those Souls. I wonder how many of those were possibly connected to me in my second Past Life as a Teacher and Healer?

Ron, there is no time here. This Old Soul has <u>no concept of time</u> or conscious-mind memory of it, only Subconscious memory.

The <u>subconscious memory</u> is the Soul that has <u>all memory</u> <u>within</u> to Learn to Progress Spiritually.

One day there will be a Teacher to help him. We chase him away now, but please understand they Refuse to move on, and keep coming back to you for help.

There was a time that you provided that help, and he remembered this because you are a Healer. That makes you ultra Sensitive to the Other Side.

They cannot and will not hurt you, but they are always trying to snag your attention, and that can be annoying. But you must not give them any Recognition. We always remove them when you ask.

Aristotle was asked in a class about the Homeless. How is it that some seem to be possessed, talking to invisible people around them?

The Homeless are people who refuse to get on with their Lives. They don't want responsibility. They are thoroughly Lazy People and deserve their fate.

This is not a Spiritual Lesson though, as they choose this on Earth.

Yes, many are possessed and carry around with them many Lazy, Ignorant Entities. They talk and argue with all the voices of these entities in their heads.

These street Gypsies have all Chosen this lifestyle and need to turn themselves around.

They are all Weak Souls that allow this. You could help them if you choose, but they don't seem to Learn anything.

The best way to channel your generosity and compassion is to give to agencies and organizations that feed and care for Homeless Children.

Thank you, Aristotle. I see these street people as an example of split personalities, which are nothing but Lower Earthbound Entities.

They are attaching themselves to open, vulnerable and weak people to continue their Earthly habits. These people then say they hear voices in their heads.

Some even claim they hear the voice of God, and use that to excuse their subsequent actions, when all the time it is these Lower Earthbound Entities that are to blame.

Most Murderers have these Souls surrounding them. These Souls influence their host body to continue Murdering and to commit other crimes.

In 1990, Aristotle wrote the following when I asked him about the situation in Romania and in Russia. I also asked him about the Romanian man and his wife causing all the trouble there.

Romania's situation is Grim, at this time and it will spread through all the Countries around Russia until these countries acquire the Right to Free Speech.

It will force Russia to start taking <u>care of its own,</u> <u>something</u> they <u>should already</u> <u>be doing</u>. Russia will be reformed <u>for the sake of the</u> World.

As for the Man and Wife in Romania, they are Possessed with an Evil Soul.

This Evil Soul is hanging around the Earth trying to <u>connect with those who can help</u> <u>him continue his desire for</u> <u>power over</u> <u>people without</u> his Body. He is not <u>aware he is</u> Dead.

This <u>man and his wife</u> allow this Soul to control them. That Soul's Evil Ways possesses them.

This situation in Romania will straighten out in a few months and things will be Free and Calm.

These Souls that Refuse to move on and remain on Earth have <u>been accumulating</u> throughout all of the World's history.

They find and influence other Weak Souls to do their bidding. This has been happening since the beginning of time on Earth.

The Universe slowly <u>starts</u> <u>pulling</u> <u>them</u> off of the Earth and placing them in the Dark. We place many, but some are <u>smart enough to</u> escape <u>back</u> to Earth. That happens because <u>we cannot override their</u> Free Will.

We all have Our Choices, and they just continue their Evil Ways.

Is this because of Overcrowding in the Darkness? Could I help with Healing?

No, <u>don't worry</u>. There is <u>pl</u>enty <u>of room in the</u> Dark, and we <u>will make more if needed</u>. These Souls are <u>lined up</u> <u>for</u> Miles in Darkness, and <u>we stack them one on top</u> <u>of another</u>.

We are taking care of this. But you can't Heal the Whole Earth because <u>they come back as fast as they</u> <u>go</u> unless we get them to the Way Station first. There are just so many of them.

This Way Station – is what some Religions call Purgatory. It is a waiting place.

As we said, all Souls on Earth have Free Will and we need to ask them to move on. <u>But we cannot force them.</u>

Are there no Judges to tell these Souls where they went wrong by committing Murders, Sex Crimes and other countless Evil Deeds!

No. We <u>don't have any</u> Judges here because it's not important to us.

You must listen to your Inner Self; it's the best way for you to Judge what you have done Wrong and take into account <u>all of the</u> <u>different</u> Circumstances.

As for Sex, it is an Earth Function Only. It has nothing to do with the Universe. There is Nothing Wrong with Sex, unless you use it to Do Wrong to another, or hurt and Abuse Others.

I asked Teddy Roosevelt, "Is a Walk-In a Lost Soul?"

Yes, you're right. They are Lost Souls taking over the body.

This happens with a Weak Soul who is not maintaining control of their body and allowing the Lost Soul to take over.

A Walk-in is a Soul taking over the body. This does not happen very often and it is under unusual circumstances.

This also could happen in a Coma Situation when the Soul decides not to return to the body and the body is still good.

A Very High Teacher is responsible for this, always with a definite purpose in mind.

We usually have the Soul complete its Mission in its current body. So it's rare that we utilize this option, and even so, ultimately it's the Soul's decision to make.

We've done this sparingly at all times in Earth's history, and we could do it today anywhere in the World if a Special Mission required it.

See more on Walk-Ins in the " Disease and Afflictions" Chapter in Book II, "Many Planes Above."

I also asked Aristotle, "What about Souls that kill others?"

Earthbound Spirits are responsible for people that kill others.

311

These Spirits enjoy hurting others, and find people on Earth with weak Souls that have these same or similar thoughts. Then the Spirits force these people to do their killing for them.

This is how these Earthbound Spirits keep their Negativity going.

Note: Earthbound Spirits is another name for Lost Souls.

I am entering the following to bring a close to this Chapter. It is a personal writing from my Mother, who is on the Astral Plane working to help others to correct their Mistakes and earn the right to go to the New Dimension.

The New Dimension will be like Earth, but with some essential differences. There is no money there or the need for it; no Corruption; no Selfishness and all is Peaceful. It is new and not too many know about it yet. But Our Book will tell the whole Earth about it.

Earth Souls are being told; you must Change Your Ways because all the bad Lost Souls that don't listen will be put in Dark Corners. All the good Souls will move to the New Dimension when their Earth lessons are complete.

It is like a new Earth; but peaceful, a new Planet for learning and teaching for Souls to continue with their own progression.

At this point Mother wrote about the seriousness if Souls did not Change.

There will be much Destruction of the Earth. The good and the bad will be separated. The good will go to the New Dimension and the bad will be placed into Dark Corners.

This was written in 1985 and predicted for 2007. I have purposely left out the details of the Earth's destruction. However, there is no time in the Universe and things can always change. We hope and pray that they do change so there is no need to speak of the end of Our World, as we know it.

Our next Chapter covers "Reincarnation." This is an interesting subject.

REINCARNATION

Conier, why has all of this information about Reincarnation been lost on Earth down through the Ages?

It's been lost because of Souls that are not Opened Minded. They close their minds to Our Workings; they are so wrapped up in Material things.

How is it that we do not remember Our Past Lives?

We purposely do not allow you to retain memory of your Past Life. That's because you're in a new life now and must learn the New Ways necessary for you to continue your Progression.

If you remembered your past life completely you would be the same with little or No opportunity to Progress.

So we let you retain only the Good memories and hope you add more Good to the past experiences which you are Learning each day.

Mara wrote this in a class about Past Memories and Lives in connection with Dreams.

Your Past Memories and Lives can combine, as they often do, in many Dreams at night. These dreams show us Past Lessons and point the way to Lessons we must Learn in this Life.

All from the Past is never forgotten, until the Lessons are learned.

The same principle applies to Lessons you must Learn in the here and now and also in the Future.

The more you learn each day the faster your Progress for your Future.

Someone asked Aristotle almost the same question. I've entered his written response here.

Sometimes, they <u>still remember about the</u> <u>past</u>, but most of it is erased. It is erased completely but only when they take on another Earth body. It is possible that you <u>vaguely</u> <u>remember some</u> of your Past Life.

Until then they remember and see all of their Mistakes when they are in the Universe. These memories are erased when the Soul comes back to Earth.

They remember some of it because sometimes they are not happy with a Choice they have made coming to Earth, or they are trying to Change their Mind about it.

They are then remembering <u>what they</u> <u>did wrong</u> in that Life, which they are either <u>correcting</u> in this Life or may have already <u>corrected</u>.

So this means they want to leave Very Young or that they had Volunteered to bring a Special Message with their Knowledge from a Previous Life?

Yes. It <u>could be both</u>. These Souls either Volunteered to leave Young because they <u>were not meant to stay</u> <u>long</u>, or they are part of the Lessons that those <u>involved had to</u> Learn <u>and in fact have now finished</u>.

This is <u>arranged and agreed upon</u> here before they come to Earth.
<u>Everything</u> <u>happens for a reason</u> and many Earth Souls do not understand the various ways in which they leave. It is all so the Soul can Progress.

Conier, can anything from Our Previous Life be passed on Genetically?

No, it can't be passed on in the Seed of Man. The Soul has its Own Existence. It's part of the Mind <u>that encourages</u> the Soul to move on.

The Spirit Body is <u>shredded</u>.

Then it takes on an Earth <u>body</u> when it's sent to Earth to Learn or Teach.

Then the Earth <u>body</u> <u>is shed</u> when <u>it is time to return back</u> to the Universe. Your Soul <u>lives forever;</u> this is the part of God, which we all are.

Conier, it is so marvelous that you answer all these questions for Our Books. How is it that you can answer all these questions so quickly?

I am a High Teacher; I lived on Earth in 297 B.C., and I just moved up to the Fifth Plane when Jan earned Jennifer's "Mary Todd Lincolns" help from the Fifth Plane.

I am staying with Jan a couple of months longer before Jennifer takes over. I asked, and received, <u>permission to do so</u>.

We all Love Jan Very Much; as she works for us through writing with each High Teacher, both she and we are Progressing quickly to Higher Planes.

We Progress <u>so much faster</u> when we work with an Earth Soul like Jan. It would take us about 175 years in Earth time to accomplish <u>what we've achieved here</u> in the Universe with Jan in just a few months.

So you see, it is <u>so much better for all of</u> <u>you to work with us</u> in the Universe to achieve your Progress on Earth.

There are <u>no limits</u> to <u>what can be accomplished</u> in One Lifetime on Earth.

You could all become Master Directors and arrive on a Very High Plane of the Universe when it's your time to return, if you so desire and work hard.

For example, say you lived on Earth for 100 years. Whatever Progress you made during that time would take you 10,000 years in Earth time to achieve here in the Universe.

One Earth year is about 100 years in the Universe.

We have no time here. Therefore, we do not count time. But we apply this measurement so your Earth Mind can understand how Important your Spiritual Growth is while on Earth.

Rather, we count Soul Progress. **That is why we created the Earth – for faster Soul Progress**.

I, High Teacher Conier, will return to continue Teaching many Teachers in the Universe.

I am also ever Grateful for this opportunity to contribute to Our Books, and for moving up one whole Plane since I started working with Jan five months ago.

RON, I KNOW THE ANSWERS TO ALL OF THESE QUESTIONS BECAUSE I WAS IN OUR DIMENSION TEACHING WHERE ALL KNOWLEDGE IS AVAILABLE TO US.

THESE ARE SIMPLE QUESTION FOR ME. I TRAVEL AND HELP ALL TEACHERS ON ALL PLANES BELOW ME. I AM A TEACHER OF TEACHERS.

Ron, our paths will cross again someday when your Mission is completed on Earth and you return home to us once again.

Thank you so much for your Loving Contribution to Our Universal Books. I have certainly enjoyed your Knowledge and Wisdom.

You're Welcome, Ron. *Conier left.*

Jennifer, "Mary Todd Lincolns" writing is entered here related to the following questions about Reincarnation.

Madame Helena Petrovna Blavatsky taught Reincarnation in 1925 and into the early 1930s. She wrote a book called, "The Secret Doctrine of Truth." Was she wrong?

No, <u>she was not wrong</u>. They condemned her for her views on Reincarnation and were too Small-Minded to understand Our Ways.

So she had to change her Teachings, for Earth Souls' Salvation.

Reincarnation does Exist; this is part of your Soul's Teaching and Learning.

More should begin to realize this. Ironically, you really do know this but most of you just do not remember.

We have been sending these Messages of **TRUTH** from the Universe throughout all of Earth's history.

Abraham, Noah, Moses, Isis, Zarathustra, Socrates, Plato, Homer, Emerson, Apollonius of Tyana, and Jesus, as well as Madame Blavatsky and many greater Patriarchs, Seers or Mystics, have received the same Messages of TRUTH.

Jennifer, I have always known most of this Truth about Reincarnation and Past Lives.

However, Jan's writings from you and other Teachers have refreshed my memory.

These writings have also confirmed my Past Lives, answered some of the questions I had and clarified other memories.

I hope it helps many others to Open Their Minds and begin thinking about it.

Especially when accepting Reincarnation explains so much about why things are as they are.

It explains why they are here on Earth, why events repeat themselves in this Life and their connections throughout Our Earth's History.

Jennifer, could you tell me a little more about the Man Apollonius of Tyana and also the Man Jesus?

Apollonius of Tyana was a knowledgeable man. He knew what was right. We sent him to the Earth Plane in 200 B.C., where he did much good and taught many.

The Man Jesus was a Medium and High Teacher. He is an Old Soul from the years of Ancient Civilizations.

We brought him <u>back</u> to Teach Earth Souls and to open the Minds of the Ignorant. He was Wise and Powerful.

Jesus is on Our High Planes now and is still sending <u>his same</u> Messages from a High Plane.

He taught God's Way for all to follow. Not everyone listened like they should have.

Earth's Religions have <u>made him into</u> a God. This <u>is a carryover</u> from Ancient times when Earth Souls practiced Paganism. They believed in <u>many</u> Gods then; there was a God for everything.

Mankind used Jesus and his Teachings to create another Religion on Earth to hold Power over the people, as in times past.

He is not God, as Earth people have been made to believe through their Earth-made Religions.

Jesus is the Son of God; he was Adam, the first Man on Earth from the Star Universe.

318

He spoke of God as his Father. We are All Children of God; he is Father to us All.

GOD is ALL, for ALL with ALL, is the DIVINE POWER from WITHIN each and EVERY ONE of US.

Our Own Soul is Part of GOD. ALL that is – is GOD!

Wow! Then who was Eve, the first Women, if I may ask please?

Eve was the first Woman. She returned as England's Queen Victoria from 1819-1901.

Then the High Master Directors of the Round Table in the Universe chose the Soul of Jesus and the Soul of Queen Victoria to be the First Man and Woman – Adam and Eve.

Therefore, they were the Earth Mother and Father of All the Earth Souls that followed.

Yes, Ron. You must understand that Souls have always existed. Also many Other Universes Existed in Galaxies long before the Master Directors decided to Create Our Earth and its Universe.

Also, they needed to Create Our Universe to Balance and Sustain the Life on Earth.

Souls needed a place where they could go to make faster Progress, a place where they could learn and grow. This was a long time ago.

See the Chapter elsewhere in this Book, "New Souls" that explains how the Universe created the First Souls on Earth.

Adam and Eve were the first Souls created from the Mars Ape Creature Bigfoot.

Also, there is more in the Chapter "Our Earth And Universe" in Book II, "Many Planes Above."

Jennifer "Mary Todd Lincoln," can Regression tell you the truth? For example, can you learn about someone's past life through Hypnosis?

Jennifer is here. There can be Truth in all Regression; however, only we in the High Universe <u>are only</u> <u>able to see</u> <u>your</u> Past Life. If we feel you will not Progress by knowing your Past Life <u>it will not be revealed to you</u>.

If we feel you will Progress <u>by</u> <u>knowing it</u> we <u>will allow it to be revealed</u>. Once you know your Past Life it sometimes helps with your current Life.

The High Universe Teachers are all in charge of this.

Is there any danger of not learning the Truth through Regression? For example, can Lower Entities enter the subject or take over the body while in this Hypnotic State?

If that happens could they get the wrong information – like receiving the Entities' own Past Life?

Yes, it is Dangerous. I do not recommend Regression. Some times the Lower Realms of Earthbound Souls can take hold of a weak, uncontrolled body.

Only the Souls that know about Reincarnation, that believes it's a Lesson of this Lifetime and accepts it as such, can be Hypnotized and Regressed.

Then, <u>regression must help</u> them to Progress and Heal Past Life Ailments or Mistakes. Otherwise, there is No Purpose in it at all.

If you take the Knowledge of your Past Lives and use it in this Life for Progress – avoiding the same Failures and Correcting Past Mistakes – then Regression could be good.

If you use what you Learn through Regression <u>as a crutch</u>, then it only hinders your Progress.

You should <u>not dwell on who</u> <u>you were</u> and what you did because it sometimes stops your Progress.

We see no Purpose to reviewing <u>your past</u> unless you use this Knowledge to better <u>understand the</u> <u>present</u>. Otherwise, the past is over. Our Only Purpose is to Love and Progress for a Better Future.

A great deal of Misinformation about Past Lives has come from Communication with the Astral Plane.

Remember, only a High Teacher of the Universe <u>can see</u> someone's True Past Life. That means you could be <u>receiving</u> <u>false information</u>.

Ron, <u>you should never submit to</u> Regression. Doing so <u>removes you from</u> <u>your body</u> and into your Subconscious Mind.

If that happens, <u>we may</u> <u>loose control</u> of the Protection we've placed around you. The Lowers could then enter and <u>take over</u> <u>your body</u>.
<u>This is dangerous</u>; that's why we're <u>warning</u> <u>you</u>.

Also, we have already told you about your Past Lives because you are one of Our Teachers from a High Plane. You have always been aware of this.

However, many Souls on Earth that are making Progress are also aware of their Past Life identities.

This is the first time we learned about the idea of a Triad in connection with Reincarnation. This comes from Marilyn's writing dated July 23, 1985. This is what she wrote.

I didn't understand this fully until Jennifer, the Teacher after Conier, wrote about the Triad.

Now it seems like a new way the Universe looks at Reincarnation, where Souls move to the New Dimension when their Lessons are complete.

"Triad" is <u>a new term that</u> Our Dimension uses. It only applies to Souls that <u>have already</u> paid for their Mistakes.

<u>You are not to use this term loosely</u>, as <u>many</u> <u>are not aware of this</u> on Earth. <u>You are a little more informed than most</u> so I will tell you about this.

I feel it's now time to enter this Information about a Triad in Our Books. It has been over 20 years since we initially received it.

I mention this now because the Universe is using the term often to describe the three primary reincarnations we all experience. It is through the Triad only that our Souls make Progress.

This is a completed Three Square Movement, which all who stay in Our Dimension can use. This helps us to complete Our Work with Stronger Force that we can apply to the Earth Souls' Learning.

Moving Souls that have completed Three Reincarnations and have <u>corrected all of their</u> Mistakes into Our New Dimension transformed Our Planes.

This Universal Change is unfolding as we now remove all these Souls from Earth.

When Our Work is done, Earth may not exist anymore, unless all Earth Souls completely Change their Ways.

We have started already; Good Souls are being sent to the New Dimension where <u>their memories</u> of Earth are <u>erased</u> and <u>they</u> <u>start all over</u> in Peace and Harmony.

Marylin, what happens to the Souls of Soldiers and the Innocent Civilians killed in wars?

Both the soldiers and the civilians are in Our Dimension now. It's fine; they are rewarded for this.

Our Teachers call on these Soldiers and Civilians, or any other Victims of a War, to move on.

Their work is done on Earth. They are needed here to help us so that we can really get Our New Dimension going.

This is because it is their Third Reincarnation and we take all those who have been there after three times.

So when a Plane crashes we only take the ones that are ready to move on.

We want Earth Souls to know that **WE ARE IN CONTROL** and **ANYTIME OUR TEACHERS SAY SOULS ARE TO LEAVE**, we must assist. We try and warn you Ahead of time when it's going to happen, but no one Listens.

We create a Triad, which consists of three. This is why we do it in three. All the Souls in Three Disasters Create a New Triad.

When you move on depends on how many Triads are ready after you have completed your Triad period on Earth.

We are working on Triads all of the time because 75% of Earth's Population is being called back. That's because they are already on their Third and final Reincarnation.

Thank you Marylin. Now back to Jennifer for more on the Triad.

Jennifer is here its fine to continue with your questions about Reincarnation, Ron.

323

I now understand that there are Only Three Reincarnations, like a Triad pattern, that account for the Soul's Progress.

Could one return more often during periods between the Triad of their Three Lifetimes?

See the diagram showing full circles at the points of a Triad; this represents the three full Lifetimes.

The half circles represent possible short Lives between the full Lifetimes. However, you stay for only short periods.

Jennifer sketched the following diagram that we've recreated here.

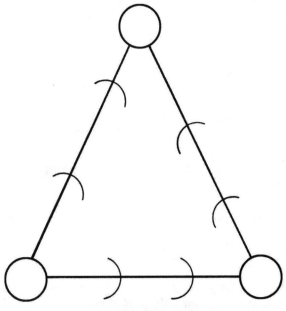

Triad Diagram
Recreated by Sophie Kessler

Yes, Ron. You could return between Lifetimes, but it could be a long Period for a Soul to Progress.

It would be a long time if they returned to Earth many times <u>for short</u> Periods between the Triad to accomplish any Progress at all.

Remember, you only clear up one major mistake in a short Life.

However, most Souls on Earth are there for the last time now. They already completed short lessons in between the Triad. Some are finished with their work, while others have made No Progress.

If they've made No Progress after the Third Reincarnation and all the many short ones in between, we may not allow them to waste their time just sitting on the Lower Astral Level.

Instead, we might erase their minds and send them back to Mars as Mars People to start over again so they may learn to Progress.

Only Souls, which are slow in Learning or haven't made much Progress, Choose to return between the Triad for short and Quick Lessons.

Usually, Souls use the lives between the Triad to learn other, specific Lessons. They must Learn something during this brief Reincarnation otherwise the effort and time's been wasted.

However, they do Progress if they accomplish their mission.

How many short visits could a Soul Reincarnate between the Triad?

Numbers, I do not like numbers. There could be many – but you must understand they are for only a short period.

An example would be if a baby or a young child leaves before living a Full Lifetime.

These Souls choose to come to teach a Lesson, such as getting the Parents back on the right track, while at the same time Learning a Lesson to advance their own Progression.

Remember, Ron. The Soul <u>always selects its</u> Parents so it can teach the Parents while it corrects its own Mistakes and learns any necessary Lessons.

I would like to share this with Our Readers: We are always looking for someone to blame for our own Mistakes or to explain why everything goes wrong.

One morning I heard a song on T.V., with the lyrics, "it's all their fault." Referring to their Parents " After all, you didn't pick 'um!"

On the contrary, you did select your Parents to be born on Earth! Stop blaming them for your Lessons.

Jan's Teacher Markus, who came in on August 24, 1987, also wrote about Reincarnation. So I'm entering it here.

Many people think it is Important to Reincarnate many times. Is this true? Here's what Markus had to say.

Markus is here. This is <u>not true</u>. Only Three Reincarnations <u>are</u> Important; any others <u>are not</u>.

These Souls like to <u>feel</u> Important, <u>thinking</u> <u>like this</u>.

They also think they Reincarnate immediately into different people all over the World. Is this true?

<u>Not true</u>. They usually cling more and Reincarnate in to their Family.

For example, a Mother in the Last Life is a Daughter in this Life. Or, a Father and Daughter in the Last Life are now Brother and Sister in this one.

The Soul chooses this according to their Lessons to be Learned and Mistakes that need to be corrected.

I hope this is not too confusing to you, but try and imagine the Importance of Family.

They were put together for a Reason, and if there were Mistakes in the Past Life, they return and connect within Family again because they now have Lessons to Correct in this Life.

One comes back in about 900 years or more, usually within their own family. This is the earliest that a Triad Reincarnation can happen. Souls never Reincarnate immediately.

Therefore the Family in this Life may have been connected in some way to a Family from about 900 years ago or more. But now they are in a different roll according to their Mistakes that need to be corrected.

All children who are born into the Family agree to work on correcting their Mistakes with other specific members of the Family in this Life.

This is why we say that Families are most Important and for you to try and get along and be there for each other. Heal yourself of all wrong doings, with Love in your Hearts and Souls for each other.

This is the main reason for a Soul to come to Earth. This is how they Progress Spiritually and move to Higher Planes when they return to the Universe – by correcting all Mistakes.

Even if a Soul is on a Special Mission there will be these connections in some way to members of the Family so they can complete their Mission.

Markus, what about Soul Mates? Do they return sooner?

The connections between Soul Mates exist so they can learn Lessons and Progress together. Possibly, they could return sooner.

A Soul or Soul Mate could come back for a short time, but not have a long Life. It could take at least 200 years before a Soul Mate could return for a short period of time.

There are exceptions, though. Sometimes circumstances account for their Growth. For example, if you were a Good Soul and your Life was cut short, you could choose to return sooner to finish your shortened Life.

It's all according to the specific Lessons that must be learned. Some Lessons must be Learned within a specific period of time.

Thank You, Markus. Information from the Universe is always so Enlightening.

You're welcome, Ron. It's my pleasure; we will soon be talking again!

Someone in one of our classes asked Solon how the Dark Race started on Earth. She was taught as a child that it was because they lived out in the Sun all the time.

They must have learned that Ignorant idea from some Earth Religion. The Universe created the Dark Race in the beginning to help maintain the balance in Earth Souls.

This started with Cain, who killed his Brother Able. The races evolved from there based on the mistakes made from this Early Age.

We give Souls a Choice of race: White, Black, Brown or Yellow. Souls choose their Earth bodies based on the one that will best help them pay for and correct their mistakes accordingly. Part of that Choice is to Learn to Live with their Choice.

This Choice includes the color of their skin. The Soul makes this Choice before coming to Earth according to the Lessons they need to Learn and the Karma they must pay back.

328

This is Our Work in the Universe: to help each and every Soul Progress Spiritually. This has been Our Mission throughout Earth's history.

You select your Parents both by the Lessons that they have to Learn, and the Child you must be to grow up and learn the direction of your own Progress.

You always have the Choice of your Race and the objectives you need to accomplish.

How your physical body will look is up to you, and you know this before you take on your body. The Universe shows your future body to you before you leave.

Sometimes people choose the same looks they had in a Previous Life; other times they Change Sex. This is also a Choice.

As the body finishes its Earth Life, its looks repeat from generation to generation.

Looks can be reborn, and sometimes there are two look-a-likes, which is very possible.

Jennifer, does each Race Reincarnate into the same Race?

No. Not always. It depends on the Mistakes. Each Soul Chooses the Race or Nationality that can best help them Learn and correct their Mistakes so they can Progress.

The individual chooses their race depending on the volume of Mistakes they must correct. Their Choice depends on how hard of a Life you want.

Sometimes, white colors have a hard Life and dark colors not so hard, but it's a Choice the Individual Soul makes before it comes.

Easier Lives have Fewer Lessons and Harder Lives have more Lessons.

329

Please remember that all of you volunteered for this before you came.

Each Soul knows their Purpose and how they must prepare before arriving on Earth. Once they arrive they Forget or Ignore this Purpose because they become Obsessed with Earthly things.

We are working to Change this to get Earth Souls back on the right track.

Who decides when a Soul should Reincarnate?

You do. The Soul itself decides when to return to Earth, and that decision includes the Choice of Parents that will serve best the Lessons that must be learned.

All High Teachers explain this. When it is part of your Progress to come to Earth for a long time or Full Life you must stay until its time for you to return to Our Dimension.

How you stay is also your Choice. This is why you have sick Souls that remain sick for so long, some most of their Earth Lives.

This is because they refuse to Progress on Earth. This is No Excuse because the purpose of Disease and Illness is to awaken the Soul and help it realize that it must Progress.

So they stay with their Illness until their time is finished and they must move on.

If the Terminally Ill would stop refusing to Progress and Learn their Lessons, they could be well again.

Earth Souls make their own Physical Disease and Illness.

They choose to be sick and bring it on Subconsciously, because they don't want to Work and Progress, or put an effort into it. Therefore, Illness remains because they simply don't want to change.

These are Stubborn Souls who <u>refuse to</u> <u>get on with their</u> Lives. They could Change this, but some get so wound up in themselves and don't care to improve.

By ignoring their Purpose on Earth they <u>do not</u> Progress. That means <u>when they</u> <u>pass on</u> and arrive in Our Dimension they must <u>work for a long</u> <u>time</u>; <u>much longer than if they</u> <u>had done their work</u> on Earth.

If <u>they</u> <u>refuse to work</u> in Our Dimension we <u>let them sit in</u> Darkness until Our Teachers have time to <u>start working</u> <u>with them at the</u> Soul <u>level again</u>.

Sometimes, a sick Earth body develops the Soul by Opening the Mind to Spiritual Awareness and possibly bringing the Soul <u>back on the</u> <u>right track</u>.

This question came up at class. Jennifer, can more than one Soul be reborn into a body and then wander off into other bodies?

A Soul can only be <u>reborn in one body</u> <u>at a time</u>. It <u>cannot</u> <u>wander between or among</u> <u>other bodies</u>. It would serve no Purpose. It is ridiculous to even ask this.

A Soul <u>needs all the energy</u> <u>possible</u> to work through <u>one</u> <u>physical bod</u>y. If they accomplish this in an Earth Soul's Lifetime, it indicates much Progress for that Soul when he or she arrives in Our Dimension.

The idea of two Souls in one body may come from a <u>second</u> <u>personality</u> in a Soul, like a <u>split</u> <u>personality</u>.

We call that a Soul Possession when a Soul allows Earthbound Souls <u>to use their body</u>. This is <u>not</u> <u>prudent and does not serve</u> <u>yo</u>u. But remember, you alone are in <u>charge of</u> <u>yourself</u>.

Jennifer "Mary Todd Lincoln", I asked before about my friend Sara who is always sick. Once she's well she takes a trip and returns home sick again.

She has taken several trips to China returning ill each time and complaining about everything on the trip. "I'm sick of rice, its too far away, it takes too long to get there" and on and on. Yet still she goes back again.

I insert my friend's personal experience in Our Book only as one example worth mentioning because it opened My Mind to better understand my friend and to the impact of Reincarnation.

Jennifer answered with the following.

Ron, your friend is a <u>wanderer</u>. She is always <u>running somewhere</u>. She never takes time for her Inner Soul.

She is sick because <u>she abuses her body</u> <u>a lot</u> and is always <u>searching</u> <u>for the unknown</u>; never realizing the answers lie <u>within and are all around</u> her.

The purpose of her Illness <u>is to make her slow down</u> and start her thinking about where she is going, <u>but it never even enters</u> her mind to do so.

We are trying to make her aware of the Other Side of Life so she is ready <u>when it's time for her to return to us</u>. But she won't listen. She is too stubborn.

We are working with her on Earth <u>for y</u>our sake, Ron, before she moves on. We regret that she <u>simply</u> <u>refused</u> to listen.

She is <u>a perfect example</u> of what we are trying to do for many Souls <u>before they</u> <u>pass on</u>. The real problem is that so few Souls <u>ever consider where they</u> <u>are</u> going <u>when their</u> Earth Lives are finished.

They Choose to worry about it only when it happens. But by then, it's <u>too late</u>.

Yes, Jennifer. I have heard it said many times, "When I die I'll see what happens." It is so sad. Is Sara like this because of her Past Life?

Yes. Her Past Life was a Disaster. She was a Chinese lady and she was <u>confined</u>. She had <u>no</u> Freedom whatsoever to go anywhere or do anything she wanted to do.

Oh! Now I understand why the constant Travel and why so many trips to China complaining about it. She probably never saw any of her own Country then, or realized how large it was.

She always journeyed to different parts of China, then complained about the distance she had to Travel. I can see this if she was confined; she would have no understanding of distance.

Yes. In this Life she has the Freedom she didn't have in the last. And because she came from China in her Previous Life, she constantly returns <u>searching</u> <u>for missing pieces</u> of her Life.

She is certainly not a Chinese Lady in this Life. But she Chose America for the Freedom <u>it represents</u> because she <u>needed freedom now to compensate for her past confinement.</u>

By the way, she still loves everything Chinese or Oriental around her, like the character Jewelry she usually wears to the Ming trees and statues in her Garden.

Isn't it so interesting understanding Reincarnation?

Yes, Jennifer, I enjoy being able to understand and see the whole picture of someone's Life. Then it makes sense why things are the way they are.

It's like seeing the Truth and Purpose behind all that happens.

I hope the readers will now realize that every Soul has a story that accounts its behavior. This allows us to Learn from our experiences, without Judgments.

Jennifer, what will happen to her when she passes over if we don't get her to Change her Thinking and Listen?

I have already told her of the After Life. She said if there were Life after Death she would return and boot me in the rear end to let me know; she was always a Joker.

She passed before these Books were published. By the way, she did indeed return and boot me in the rear. I felt it!

Joking aside, Ron, she will remain in the Dark because she doesn't understand or know about Our Existence, and refuses to listen.

If she has only Two Long Lifetimes that count could she return for her Third to complete the Triad and have another chance to Progress?

She would have to wait in Our Dimension until she Progresses before she could come back.

However, she would have to be helped Out of Darkness first and this could take Hundreds or Thousands of years.

Ron, you could send your Healing Prayers for her and we will help to get her moving from the Darkness to the Lower Astral Level – just as you have <u>done for others that are now working</u> on the Astral Plane. Thank You, Ron.

I know some people think they can return Almost Immediately. How long without Our Prayers from Earth would it take for her to Progress enough to return?

I think that the concept of returning immediately or much sooner is because time does not exist in the Universe.

Everyone is just a Soul, which is the Subconscious, and so the Soul has no concept of time in that Dimension.

They don't know how long they have existed in the Universe.

They seem to think when returning to Earth they were just here and have returned Immediately. But indeed, hundreds of years have passed.

Another thought. It depends on the way they received this Past Life Information; the Soul providing this information could be an Earthbound Soul or a Lower Astral Soul, which may not even be aware they no longer have a Physical Body!

All the Information we have received is from the High Teachers. They tell us you cannot trust any Lower Information to be true because of their lack of Knowledge at that level.

Only the High Teachers are able to see one's Past Lives and will only reveal this to a Progressing Soul if there is a Purpose. Otherwise, they won't. That's because they do not want us to dwell on the Past; there is no Progress in that.

Ron, as I previously mentioned, it would take a long, long time, maybe Thousands of years, to Progress and Reincarnate.

So many Souls are in the Dark and they do not Reincarnate until they Progress, which always takes Thousands of years.

This is such a shame when all they have to do is Open up to Our Existence in the Universe and Listen to their Guide – their Conscience while still on Earth.

That's how they make Progress there. And they can Progress so much faster there than here.

That is why we created the Earth Plane – to make Faster Soul Progress.

However, by praying for your friend we may be able to help her much sooner, as we have already helped many of your Family coming from Earth through your constant Prayers.

335

Earth Souls should continually pray for their Loved Ones <u>after</u> <u>they</u> <u>pass</u> <u>unless their</u> Loved Ones <u>are aware</u> of Our Existence already and know they <u>have to work here</u>.

So from what Level do Souls Reincarnate? And do any of the Souls in the Dark Reincarnate?

Souls working on the Higher Levels of the Astral Plane may Reincarnate, and many do.

The Souls in Darkness may not Reincarnate until they Progress to the Higher Astral Plane.

Again, this takes a long, long time so you'll see they are making little Progress. <u>They</u> <u>just sit there</u> in the Dark.

Now, I want to enter from my Personal Writings a few cases we asked about to explain why things were happening as they were in the Lives of these people.

Of course, I share these writings without mentioning any names, and, of course, no one has ever seen or heard this information.

This was totally for our own knowledge and understanding.

Every one of us has different circumstances governing Our Learning and explaining why we attract certain People and things into Our Life.

I've entered these for your understanding and awareness; I want to show you the connections that exist between Past and Present, and Purpose and Lessons.

We all make Choices in Our Lives for our Learning to Correct Our Mistakes and Change Our Ways.

Maybe, we could do a little evaluating and Soul Searching Within?

The following is the first writing of a few Past Life connections and explains why things were happening in their present Lives. Also, I entered my own Reincarnation, which I was privy to receive.

This Lady's Daughter was having serious boyfriend problems and wouldn't Listen to anyone. We asked Conier to write if this fellow would marry her.

Conier is here. He will <u>not marry</u> <u>her</u>. She will marry someone else altogether. She is really mixed up about this current man.

She needs to smarten up and get her own Life together. But she is not interested in improving herself at all.

She is interested only in her <u>surface self and needs</u> because <u>she is selfish</u> and <u>wants her own way</u> all the time.

She will not Listen to anyone at all. <u>However, she is much better than she was</u>.

This has <u>a lot to do with her</u> Past Life, and <u>yes, I will tell</u> <u>you so you see the connection</u>.

She was <u>spoiled rotten</u> in her Past Life. She was a <u>rich little</u> <u>girl</u>; Daddy <u>gave her everything</u> and she <u>never had to earn a thing</u>.

She was born in Monaco, in Monte Carlo, with a French and English background.

She married twice but <u>never had children</u> and <u>never worked at</u> <u>all</u>. She had everything she ever wanted.

Now, in this Life, it is <u>time for her to work</u>, <u>give to others</u> and Learn about Life.

She <u>must earn everything</u> <u>that comes to her</u> before she <u>will have any</u> <u>peace of mind</u>.

Here is another about this woman who was Masculine and Domineering.

In her Past Life she was a strong man of Great Beliefs. She is still fighting the notion that you can Progress in <u>a woman's body</u>.

In her past <u>as a man</u> she did not <u>believe women capable</u> of any Intelligence.

She <u>looked down on women</u> as Slaves. She was a powerful man who had women by the dozen to wait on him.

She <u>as a man</u> was a King of Egypt, and <u>misused woman</u> and Power. She has the feeling of Power over women.

This is an example of another Lady's Past Life preventing Progress in this one.

She <u>hides in others</u> so she doesn't have to <u>take responsibility</u> in this Lifetime. In her Previous Life she never had any responsibility and is not Progressing at all in this one.

She demanded <u>everything from women</u>. She came from England, a Scot who had everything.

She was waited on in the days of Great Ladies and she still demands it.

She Lives in the Past. She never had Children in her past Lives, but has them now and <u>doesn't care about them</u>.

She has always been <u>number one</u> in her Lifetime and hates to give to others. She is a Selfish woman.

This was a man who had just Passed Over from AIDS.

He was a man who was overly Masculine and determined to <u>rule over men</u>. He came from a Great Warrior Past where he ruled over all of his men with great Satisfaction.

Therefore, in this Life he still could not learn to share with Women. So he must move on and return to pursue his Lessons.

AIDS was the <u>vehicle he used to</u> pass over. Now, he will help all other Victims to find Peace of Mind. He will accomplish this while working from Our Side now.

Conier is here. Go ahead. *May I please learn about my Reincarnation?*

You, Ron, Reincarnated from other Lives. This is your Third and final Reincarnation.

First, may I say you were always A Special Person!

The First time you lived was in the day of the Old Ages, the Cave Man Days. You are an Old Soul. You did much <u>for others,</u> showing them how to exist with Natural Healing and helping many.

You were a good man of the Early Ages of Life on Earth, some 35,000 years ago.

You were a Great Healer. You <u>taught people</u> around what became Egypt. During the Stone Age you helped people understand their ways.

You were a Doctor of sorts, using <u>herbs and mudpacks,</u> and you derived a Medicine of Natural Healing because that's the only Medicine that was available in the Cave Man Days of early Ancient times.

Conier, there was a fine movie, "The Clan of the Cave Bear" about these times. I thoroughly related to and enjoyed this film.

Spirit showed the Movie Makers the days of the Cave Era, and this was the <u>inspiration and template</u> for their Movie – showing Life as it really was in those early days of the Earth's history.

Someone someday, will make a movie based on the Information in Our Books, starting from the First Day of Existence on the Earth.

Boy! Unless they change their belief system before the movie is released, the different Religions will rapidly try *to underline the foundations of* this movie.

The Second time you Reincarnated back to Earth you lived in the Holy Land; these were the Earth days of Jesus.

You did Healing of the body and Soul with Jesus for all Mankind, and you were a Teacher of Spirit's Ways.

You were John the Apostle from Palestine, Jesus' Great Follower. As John, you prepared the way for Jesus and called on Elijah to work with you to prepare for Jesus' coming.

Later on you worked with James and everyone spoke of you as James and John. Together you did much Healing and Teaching to better many Souls.

You were a Teacher and Preacher of all Knowledge, and many learned from you.

You are one of Our Healers from this Dimension. Jesus will work with you again someday.

You've never been married or had children. Your Soul Mate works with you from here in the Universe awaiting your return to us.

You still Heal in this Life and will heal much more before you leave Earth. Your Mission lies there and you will successfully carry it out during your stay on Earth. Good things are coming to you through Our Works.

All the years in between we let you stay and work in Our Dimension because your work was always good on Earth.

You are a Good Soul, and when we asked you to go back to Earth again you enthusiastically agreed.

That's because you could see that Earth needed this Healing to come about again at this time on the Earth Plane.

We asked you to return to Earth to work because you are an Old Soul and possess much power of Healing.

Earth Souls were not ready, with their old, <u>ineffective ways</u> and Closed Minds, for you to <u>start the</u> <u>greatest</u> <u>part</u> of your Healing work.

You will contribute significantly to Our Ways and Changing the Ways of Earth People.

Your Mission's Purpose is Right Now. It would have been too early to start before now.

We had lost control of Earth Souls; therefore if you had started working publicly sooner in this Life many would have opposed you.

Things are now changing more to Our Ways; therefore you can go ahead and begin your Mission. Is this clear?

Yes, Thank You.

It will become clearer. When we are ready to show you your Past Lives some night in your dreams, then maybe you will understand fully.

In Our Dimension we can see all Past Lives; this is no problem here.

We will let only a few Chosen Souls, like you; see their Past Lives so they can fully understand. We can only do this with permission.

Your Dreams are going to be a reality, and there will be Many Messages for the work you will do.

You will help Many Souls with their problems and will meet them Soon now on Earth.

Are there other Apostles from my Past Life on Earth here in this Incarnation? Will I meet any more of them?

Many of the other Apostles are Reincarnated around the Earth at this time to help with Our Work.

They are All on Special Missions to do Our Work helping Earth Souls to Change their Ways.

You have already met Matthew and know of Mark. You will have the opportunity to meet one more, Luke.

He also does Our Healing at this time, and you will meet him before you complete your Mission.

I am entering here my personal writing from my Mother explaining how she is doing. She talks about her experience and how she is enjoying her Life Learning on the Astral Plane.

Hi Jan and Ron. How are you? I am fine and working real hard now. Daddy is working for you, too; he understands now, with your help and **Jan's** Teachers working with him.

We enjoyed Lunch today with you, especially the tea biscuits. They were just like home. Daddy is fine now, too. He will write for you soon. There is not much new here, though, as I don't stay in one place too long, I'm always busy trying to help everyone.

Please tell us something about your continued Life there.

There is lots of learning here and Many Planes. I am on the Astral Plane and it is real nice here, lots of everything. Red roses that I like so much and many other pretty flowers. No houses or buildings, though. We don't need them here. Nobody bothers you here.

We don't need to eat food but we enjoy the memory of it when you are enjoying a good meal. I still love peaches, strawberries and all the fresh fruit and vegetables. I don't have to wear my glasses anymore.

I never get tired here and we don't need to sleep. There are no beds, no comforters and no sewing machines. I remember the seasons from my time on Earth; it was so cold when it snowed. I have never been cold here and I am glad I will never be cold again.

The New Dimension where good Souls are going is the one that is so much nicer. There's no money there and it takes many years to move up the levels if you don't understand. If you do understand and listen it doesn't take long to get here. I didn't understand but I listened.

Daddy wouldn't listen before but now he does. He came to see me and I was so surprised because I just about gave up on him. It was his Brother that showed him the way from the dark. Yes, Uncle Zep. He is smart and he knows what must be done. He never stops helping everyone in the family all of the time.

I still like to talk with my Mother, but I don't see her much as she rests a lot, her work is tiring and I don't know why that is. But I will ask and let you know.

Grandpa is still playing cards. He plays Solitaire and he likes it just like he did on Earth. Uncle Gordon is still making business deals like he did on Earth and Aunt Nance still wants Gord to listen and start working but he keeps making deals.

Donald is not painting anymore, he hates to work and he just sits. Aunt Nance tries so hard, but between Donald, Richard and Gord she works so hard to get them to listen and work.

Uncle Walter is my favorite Brother; he works so hard to help everyone and is always around to help you whenever you need money. He helps with Uncle Zep. He has progressed and comes to see me a lot but never stays long. He says he is too busy, but it's all right; I understand what he is doing. He still helps Aunt Helen, as she needs him to understand her new Life here.

Aunt Honey follows Jan all the time. I don't know why she does this; she must like her clothes and the way that she's always on the go, but I guess it's OK because I ride along with Todd when he's driving around.

343

Aunt Honey just wants to play and never wants to work. She just likes running around; she thinks it's great, but I go, too.

I like England and I always wanted to go there. So I go now anytime I want and I don't get cold. Yes, Todd, I go with you, too.

Aunt Lucine is so happy and so beautiful, with no more hurt for her from her Epilepsy. Now she plays a lot here.

I came from the Earth Plane to the Astral Plane. Next, I must now work to go to the next Plane but you always can go back and forth if you want to.

There are no cars here; you find them just on Earth. All Planes are Spiritual and all have learning and beauty. The higher the Plane, the more learning you'll find, and the more beauty, peace of mind and tranquility.

Some Souls don't stay on Earth very long and pass over as Babies. I asked this because I wanted to see how much my Mother Learned about her new world during her time there. Her understanding surprised me.

Oh, that may be because their lessons are short and they don't need to stay on Earth long. Their Mistakes have been paid for so they move on.

Babies here can be grown, or children who play all day or whatever they want. They have been on the Earth Plane before but now stay here for a while. Then they are sent back to the Earth Plane for a short time and leave again as Babies. Some have to do this over many lifetimes to Learn.

All Babies that move on from Earth are lessons for the Parents and there always are reasons for this. Also, some of these Babies have had other lives on Earth and must pay for their Mistakes. They have not made much progress from their previous lives and this helps them to make some progress. This can take a long time and many short lives on Earth.

Some Souls volunteer to teach Earth parents lessons, to pay attention, to change their ways or maybe get back on track and listen, or some other reason.

344

When you are a good Soul, you don't need to pay for Mistakes. So why stay there on Earth when it is so much nicer here? Also, they do not want to be exposed to CORRUPTION again.

All Children are born to teach the parents these things and many other lessons, depending on the circumstances. All Souls select their parents from our side. Most have to do with Reincarnation and many have been connected to their families from previous lives.

All of this happens because of the lessons that need to be learned and the past Mistakes that must be corrected.

We know of a couple on Earth that has lost three different young ones within a few years, all from not watching them and leaving them alone and all from different incidences of neglect.

Yes, Ron. But you see Earth Souls never learn what they should, so they are left to go on with their Earth life and they must pay for these Mistakes.

I also understand that Souls may choose how they wish to look or whatever age they would like to be.

Yes, we can be whatever age we would like to be. I now look like I did when I was sixteen; it was my choice because I looked my best at that age. I know now about my Reincarnation and why I lived on Earth.

The first time I came to Earth was many years ago. I was a man and I lived in the early days of Before Christ in England. I was a hard working, successful Farmer, but I misused money.

The second time I was a Canadian in Kitchener, Ontario. I learned later that my life's purpose then was to have children, whom I never had in my first life. In this second lifetime my purpose was also to work hard, as I did in my first time.

But during that second lifetime I had no money because I misused money from other people. So my lessons were hard that second time.

I must come back again for a third Reincarnation, and this time I must learn to care more. I may have money to share with and help others. I will not have children. I mistreated you children and I was wrong.

*Mother, we forgive you and **LOVE** you. The way you are bringing through all this wonderful information; you could be a Teacher.*

You're right. But as a Teacher I must work in the Spirit World, and if I work very hard I will be sent to the New Dimension and not have to return to Earth. There is no good Souls Reincarnating to Earth anymore. I will teach the right ways next time.

I entered this to help readers realize the connections between Reincarnation and Past Lessons to Correct Mistakes, and to help you understand that we all have Missions. Also, I included this to help you see that there are reasons for everything; and that there is a Purpose from Life to Life.

*Mother said, "**Ron**,* you keep Lecturing and Healing and all things will be taken care of for you. Your lectures are good; keep it up.

Your Teachers are always working with you, and, yes, you are teaching **TRUTH** – most importantly that **GOD** is within and always with us in **ALL WAYS**.

I try to tell this to people in my lectures and whomever I meet in my life, but I know many are not listening or getting the message.

They don't take it in, or sense the reason behind it or even use their common sense to determine if this is at all possible.

They need to know that all answers of truth are within them through the God Within.

We will discuss how God is all that is and within us all in the next Chapter, "God is within us."

346

GOD IS WITHIN US

Jennifer, what can we do to get people to realize that God is all and Within All of us?

There is nothing you can do but live this within yourself. Earth Souls have a lot to do to learn this before they can Progress at all.

The Religions on the Earth are responsible for this; they themselves made up these stories to convince everyone to behave in a certain way and to donate to the Church.

So as a result of this many walked off the path of the True Teaching. That's why Jesus was sent to Earth in the first place.

There is excessive Politics, Greed and Selfishness on the Earth Plane. Religions are being lead by their Own Stubbornness, a stubbornness that can possess them.

Jennifer, do some Souls gain any benefit from following Religions and attending Church and Temples?

Yes, some do. But Earth Souls Don't Listen and they create their own wrong beliefs. Others wanting Power on a Lower Plane possess them. They allow this because they don't want to stand on their own two feet.

Jennifer, in the news everyday we see or hear stories about people losing material things through events or actions we call Accidents, Disaster, Acts of Nature, Earthquakes, Tornados, Fires and Wars. Do I need to go on?

We must understand that there are no Accidents or Coincidences in God's entire Universe.

Everything happens for a purpose or reason, and can you guess why? You should be able to by now. If not, I will tell you.

347

TO CHANGE YOUR WAYS – TO CHANGE YOUR BELIEFS.

GOD is **WITHIN,** not out there somewhere.

Go and pick out some other books like this one, read them and find out.

"WHO YOU REALLY ARE and **WHO YOU WANT TO BE."** *

Great Aristotle, is the Universe bringing all these Disasters to the Earth Plane to remove Material things?

Yes, with all these Disasters, some Material things must be taken away because there is so much Greed, Selfishness and Corruption – accompanied by a severe lack of appreciation – on the Earth Plane now.

Earth people need to stop taking the Gifts of the Universe for Granted.

Aristotle, what can I do to help with this? Could I send Healing to the World?

Ron, you are doing all you can at this time. You need to have faith in Our Work and Patience to understand how hard it is for us to make these things happen.

Giving Healing to the World does help, though; it leads or inspires some to begin making Progress and to get on with their Lives.

Earth has so much Negativity because most people attract it to themselves.

People must Change Their Attitudes to alter this attraction, but so many are too wound up in themselves to think about the other person.

* *"Conversations with God" Neale Donald Walsch. I recommend reading every book he has published.*

This draws <u>mounds and mounds</u> of Negativity to the Earth. Those that do understand are helping to counterbalance that, but we need <u>so many</u> <u>more to correct this imbalance</u> on Earth.

Ron, you need to be there for everyone when <u>they</u> <u>need</u> <u>you to explain how to</u> <u>get on</u> with their Lives, Change their Ways and turn to God Within, instead of thinking only about themselves and their material wants.

People on Earth are consumed with themselves at this time, so you have to be Patient like us and <u>wait for</u> <u>your opportunity</u> to <u>attract their interest again</u>.

So much time is wasted on Selfishness, and the Earth Souls never seem to learn this. What they are doing is <u>so unimportant</u> but <u>each one on their own thinks they</u> <u>are right</u>.

To change this all they have to do is <u>think about others</u>, and not what's in it for them, but what they can <u>give without expecting</u> <u>anything back</u>. Most people always <u>expect something</u> <u>in return</u>.

Spending your day doing your best for <u>yourself and another</u> whenever possible <u>would help</u> <u>rid the</u> Earth <u>of some</u> of this Selfishness.

Whenever I give advice people always ask how much can they get from me, and they <u>want a guarantee</u>!

They rarely ask, "What can I do to help?"

We in the Universe give and give but no one seems to understand there <u>is a time to</u> pay <u>back</u>.

The Universe is full of Souls <u>paying</u> <u>back</u> all the time, a process that will take hundreds of years to accomplish.

Here, Aristotle shares with us a brief explanation of God and the Universe and how I should tell Earth Souls about both.

349

To explain God and the Universe is to tell them that God <u>is part of everything</u> <u>in and around the</u> Earth, Life Itself <u>and each of us</u>.

God Created All and God is the Universe. **This is All Good Souls working together as one in Love and Harmony**.

Thank You Aristotle for all your Knowledge and Wisdom.

I heard a song on the Radio with the following lyric, "What if God was one of us?" Have you heard it? It's a nice song and I enjoyed it very much.

At this moment it Inspired me to write, and this is what I wrote.

This strong Inspiration kept me writing for a long while.

Ron is writing the following: "What if God was one of us!" God is Within All of Us; surrounds us with the ever giving of all of our needs; God is Within the air we breathe.

We live Within God's Universe and go about our daily events and business with a part of God Within our Hearts, which is Our Very Soul.

We see God's Expression all around; in everything we see through Our Eyes, the Window of Our Souls.

Now we may say, "What if someone has lost his or her physical sight? How can they see God's Expression?" Well, they then begin to see with their other senses, like smell, hearing and touch, and of course, intuition, which is of the Soul, which is All God Within Us.

If they have been born this way, they have Chosen this for their Own Soul's Progression and are so blessed with the Family they have Chosen.

These Souls Chose, as all Souls have Chosen, their Parents because there are Lessons they must Learn to restore them on the right track in their Lives.

350

This is also so these Parents begin Caring and sharing their Love with this Soul, and in so doing, develop their Own Soul.

You notice I said this Soul is "so blessed." Being born blind, they are a Spiritual Soul that has volunteered to be born blind to quickly Correct their Own Mistakes from Previous Lives.

Usually, they're directly connected to this Family, as they may have been together in a Previous Lifetime, and have Lessons and Mistakes to Correct Together.

You must understand that Mistakes must be Corrected for Souls to make Progress. Are you able to see God's work in all of this?

Just to give you a sample of Previous Life Connections; the Mother now could have been the Child in the Past Life, or Brother, Sister or even Father, for that matter.

Also, they could have been either Male or Female, a choice available only on Earth, as they are Souls without gender everywhere else in the Universe.

We Choose what is best for Our Own Soul's Progression.

In my younger years I never thought much about Reincarnation; it's like I knew about it because my Dad always spoke of it. Because it was part of his belief system, I just accepted it.

However, it wasn't until my Sister Jan began the Automatic Writing and the High Teachers of the Universe refreshed my memory, that I reclaimed this knowledge of my Reincarnations.

Usually, we don't remember Our Past Lives; through these writings I reconnected with each of them.

The Teachers also wrote about the Past Lives of each one in Our Family down through my Great Nieces and Nephews.

Since then my fascination with the subject has helped me to fully understand all of the Connections with all the Common Sense Explanations of Past Lives.

I won't go into the details of their Lives. However, I will say that when the High Master Directors of the Universe asked us if we would go to Earth at this time on a Special Mission, both my Sister and I volunteered.

We then Chose Our Parents with the Directors' approval; we were born three years apart and did not remember Our Missions when we Reincarnated here.

We both seemed to go our separate ways. I ended up in Florida and my Sister in California.

I searched from a young age for Spiritual Understanding, discovering that I just seemed to know things within me, which of course did not resonate with others' beliefs.

I had begun developing my Healing Abilities without realizing I had had a Healing Teacher named Gandi at my side since I was Ten years old.

I didn't have much contact with my Sister for many years. One day I received a Telegram from her asking me to come to California. She said she was feeling the need for some Family Connection. In short, she said she needed her Brother.

So I flew to California, feeling on the flight a Warm, Positive Energy around me with a knowing within that I would find my Spiritual Connection in California.

It was a wonderful flight, with my headset on listening to Classical Music. It seemed like I was flying above the Plane.

I never returned to Florida. I had my friends sell my Car, Television and Water Skis, and give everything else away to start fresh my new Life in California. I have been here ever since to be with my Sister.

My Sister Jan developed her Automatic Writing about twelve years later, on March 16, 1985. Teacher Cormier wrote and explained how we were both Special Souls.

We were put together because we had a Special Mission. Hers was to write Books for the Universe, mine was to start developing my Healing abilities by helping others to get on with their Lives.

Also, we were prepared for the planned coming of a Comet Ship in January 1988. But it was delayed, as explained in the Chapter "Our High Holy Spiritual Comet Ship and UFOs."

Through Past Life Connections, it explains so many reasons why certain things happen and you can fully realize the Divinely Blessed Love Within it All.

God truly is within each of us with Life's Master Plan unfolding through us.

This is God's Love expressing throughout all creation in all "Universes" through every Soul both here and hereafter.

We really are All Brothers and Sisters to all of God's Creation and we live in an Ocean of Life's Divine Love.

Life and God is all One and the same. God is Love and Love is God. God is the Divine Infinite Intelligence in All Creation.

Please know that Love is the Greatest and Highest Energy Force within all Creatures and Beings, within all nature – Flowers, Trees, Rivers, and Mountains or Oceans, on all Planets in all of the Universes.

Love is the Governing Force, the Light and Color, the entire Energy Force – Sustenance of all Creation.

353

It's this Love Energy that holds the Stars and Planets in place.

Love sustains the Existence of all the Highest Universal Planes and Dimensions, of all Universes down to the tiniest insect seed or Microorganism; in all there is...is LOVE.

This Powerful, Love Energy Force can be seen through God's Expression in all Souls around us, through the Beauty of Mother Nature, the Free Soul Birds singing their song of Unconditional Love every morning, not missing one, to remind us to be on the path of Love to all on this new day.

The Animals we have as Pets are given to us with God's Blessings. We receive Unconditional Love from Our Pets Daily to teach us how to Love, and to Open Our Minds and Hearts to others around us.

You have felt this Love often, especially when you arrive home from a stressful day and see how Happy Our Pets are to see us...giving us such a warm Loving Feeling of Unconditional Love.

However, in return we do have to feed and take care of them. You should do this with the same Love they give to you.

Children should be taught about caring for the animals at a young age with the same Love and Joy they receive.

Tell them their Pets give them Unconditional Love; they can give this Love back by Loving the acts of feeding and taking care of them, or walking them regularly.

Many times these Pets have been with them in a Previous Life and return in this Life to a Family or a Member of that Family.

Everything in Life is Divinely Connected and all has a Reason and Purpose for Your Soul's Progress.

Nothing happens by Accident. There is no such thing as an Accident; it is all Lessons.

Once these Children have learned to take good care of their Pets expressing their Love and Happiness while doing so, they will begin to give their Love to All Animals.

This is God's Love flowing through their very Heart and Soul, as God is Within All.

Then maybe someday we'll work at or support movements to Stop Cruelty to Animals. Or possibly save many of Earth's Endangered Species from Extinction.

Loving and caring for animals is one of the critical reasons for us to Change Our Ways. That way these Animals will be here for Future Generations to enjoy.

All Children need to be taught at a young age to Love everything and to always Live in Love, through Love, no matter what they are doing.

Living with LOVE will make their Lives so much easier; they will be so much happier within themselves.

If confronted, tell them to hesitate a moment and ask; now what would Love do in this situation?

You can Change all things around you with Love.

Practice giving Love to everything and everyone around you and being Grateful for everything, wherever you are, and you can make the World a Better Place.

This is the Mission for the Children on Earth today for a Changed Tomorrow.

Truly God is Within All of Us and Within All of Life. Life is God, God is Life.

We are all part of the Whole Web of Life and it would not exist without any one of us.

We can never really die. We Can Only Change. We have and will always Exist Forever Within.

GOD'S LOVE, LIFE'S LOVE

Our final Chapter is "The New Spiritually" for tomorrow's Earth and the Future of All Mankind.

THE NEW SPIRITUALITY

Jennifer "Mary Todd Lincoln" wrote the following when asked about the New Spirituality now unfolding on Earth.

This is the New Spiritual Truth <u>for the Future</u> of **ALL MANKIND**: **GOD** is **ALL**. <u>Every</u> <u>Soul is a</u> <u>part of</u> **GOD** and can never be separated from any part of the Universe.

<u>We are ALL Brothers and Sisters</u> of the same **GOD** and in **ALL WAYS** <u>have been and ever will be</u>.

ALL OF US ARE CONNECTED IN GOD'S WEB OF LIFE, TO ALL AND EVERYTHING THERE IS, HERE AND HEREAFTER.

ALL we do is of GOD-given Free Choice. Through wrong Choices we must Learn to Change and Correct Our Mistakes.

GOD will never interfere with Our Choices or condemn us for Our Actions. God continually gives LOVE and LIFE for us to learn from Our Mistakes as nothing we do can ever be hidden from GOD.

GOD never has forsaken any one of us but always HAS and WILL give this warm UNCONDITIONAL LOVE in Our Hearts. This is where Our Soul GOD resides in this Earth body.

GOD has never taken away any Soul or anything from any Soul but has always only given LOVE – the most Powerful Energy in all UNIVERSES.

We breathe in LIFE ENERGY, which is GOD ENERGY.

We breathe in this **LOVE ENERGY** through the air daily and fill Our Soul's with **GOD'S BEAUTY** expressed in everyone and everything we see around us.

GOD IS LIFE and **LIFE IS GOD**.

Thank You, Jennifer! You certainly make it sound So Simple and So Beautiful, especially with so much Mystery and the Varied Belief Systems set up by Earth Souls down through the Ages!

I am again adding my writing and thoughts to this Chapter to Summarize Book I.

You can Change your Life by simply going within the Quiet of Your Mind and ask for GOD to Heal you of all and any wrongdoings from all your Past Lives.

Ask God to fill you with warm DEVINE LOVE, which is always flowing through every cell of your body sustaining your Daily Life, as you ask for the help that you Need to Change.

Everyone is Searching for the GOD Within and will eventually find it, no matter what or how long it takes.

It is the Soul's Purpose of Being, created by GOD, to go forth and Learn through Experiences and Progress to find yourself as part of the ONENESS of ALL.

This Search is an endless Experience of God.

This is always there for you whenever you are ready to use this LOVE for Yourself First. Then you can give this LOVE to Everyone and Everything.

This even includes the Material Things around you; be Grateful for and Appreciate all that GOD and the UNIVERSE have given you – your car, home and job, for instance – and continually gives you.

YOUR LOVE IS EXPRESSING GOD ENERGY.

GOOD IS GOD *and* **GOD ENERGY IS THE GOOD IN YOUR SOUL.**

If you don't earn Material things through GOD'S LOVE and Appreciation, they will be taken from you.

When you are given Great Material Wealth, which you may have earned in a Previous Life by doing Good, and you do not share this wealth to help others in this Life, it will be taken from you.

If you have taken from others you must Correct these Mistakes by giving totally of yourself to help others.

Remember, GOD is Within you to help you through any situation, always. All you have to do is ask.

Then keep your Thoughts on this GOD LOVE flowing through you. The White Light always surrounding you to always remain on the right path.

GOD IS LOVE *and* **YOU ARE LOVE.** *

When you ask for anything for yourself or for anyone else, or for any situation, ask by saying: "Thank You for helping me with..." – as if you have already received it.

Then be Grateful for everything you have and are given all-day and everyday, which you have taken for Granted for your Sustenance of Life.

If you're uncomfortable with the word "God" change it to "Life," as God is Life and Life is God.

*Again, see "Conversations With God" by Neale Donald Walsch.

Give Love from your Heart to everything around you. Love to all of Nature – to the Birds, the Animals, the Oceans, the Air and the Mountains – and to all that is.

Give it to all the People you pass on the street or meet, all of the people that you work with, your Neighbors and Friends.

Again Love and Appreciate your Car, your Home and your Job. Simply Live in Love, with Love and Appreciation for everything.

Give Love to everything and for everyone for all situations in Life; Live in Love, and teach your children and all around you the same.

Remember, everything happens for a reason. That reason usually is to teach us a Lesson we need to Learn so that our own Soul can Progress.

We don't remember, but we did agree to do this before we came to Earth.

We make all of our Choices from the Subconscious, which is Our Soul expressing, "Who we want to be."

Also, remember Patience is a Lesson and one of the hardest for us to Learn. But all will come in its own time and at the right time.

If we do not receive it we may not have earned it yet. Or, some things never Materialize, possibly because we are not meant to have it. That, too, could be for Our Own Good.

Talk with GOD and your Guide all throughout each day for all your needs and share your GOD LOVE from your Heart in all situations.

BLESS others around you with your kind thoughts, and send your love and prayers to those suffering in the wake of any and All Serious Disasters.

There are many Disasters to come all over the Earth Plane because of Man's present and past Negative thinking, the spread of Greed, Selfishness and Corruption, and Earth Souls not Listening.

This thought Energy is sent into Our Atmosphere. This Energy will now return to Cleanse the Earth and Rebalance Mother Nature through Great Disasters. Corrupt and Non-Listening Souls will be removed from Earth.

As Mankind has given out this Negativity in All Past Ages; so it will now receive the same in the form of large Disasters that will Cleanse and Rebalance Our Earth.

These Disasters will continue happening until Mankind focuses its Thoughts on the Positive and begins working with GOD'S LOVE to ALL.

Thoughts are Very real. Positive Thought can be used to Create, and Negative Thought can Destroy.

"As you give Out so Shall You Receive!"

"What you Think is what you Are."

What entire Countries give out is what will return to those Countries. This applies to all Countries and Civilizations throughout all of Earth time.

Earlier Civilizations have disappeared because of Man's Negative thinking and Corrupt Ways of living.

Many of the Souls that caused this in Earth's early history are now on Earth in the Middle East, and in all troubled areas in our World, to pay for these Mistakes.

They have been given a chance to make it right by being allowed to come to Earth at this time.

This chance comes from God's High Directors of the Universe, who want these Mistakes Corrected and all Earth Souls to Change their Ways for Peace.

This is to bring Earth back to the Spiritual way of living, which existed in all Civilizations before Atlantis, before Corruption took over.

However, these Souls and War Lords of the past, which agreed before they came to Earth to Correct these past Mistakes, are not Listening to their Guides and Teachers and are carrying on their Old Ways, making more Mistakes.

God gives all of us Free Choice or Free Will to do, or not to do, as we wish. For we all must Learn what we really know within our own Soul, which is God, what is right or wrong?

The Universe may never interfere with our Free Choices, but "as we give out, so shall we receive." Our choices have Consequences, so it behooves us to pay attention and Change Our Ways.

Otherwise, we will be called back to the Universe and placed in Darkness, freeing the Earth of our Corrupt ways.

All Earth Souls cannot escape this Universal Law – "as what you give out is what will return to you" – so why not now give OUT LOVE and have LOVE return to you?

You have heard The Golden Rule: "Do Unto Others as you would have them do Unto You."

You must Always Think of what you are Giving Out and the Possible Consequences before taking Any Action.

Also, remember everything that has happened such as Wars, Earthquakes or Disasters of every kind since the beginning of time on Earth.

Or, where any Soul or Souls have been removed from the Earth and the blame has fallen on GOD; it is simply NOT TRUE.

Souls leave the Earth only because it is their time to go and their Lessons are finished.

Or, they are not Listening and not making any Progress at all, but continually making more Mistakes.

Then they are called back to start over from the beginning. Soul Progress is all that counts in the Universe, no matter how long it takes.

GOD does Not Destroy what GOD CREATES. Rather, God is Always Recreating what Souls have destroyed through their Own Free Will-inspired Choices, as GOD is ever-giving.

Every Soul is given Free Will to Learn and to Progress on their Own. From the Choices they make they can Grow with Knowledge and Wisdom to Advance to the HIGHEST PLANES of ALL the UNIVERSES.

Earth Souls must stop blaming GOD or Anyone else for their Own Mistakes, or for what they have created through their poor Choices.

Souls always find another to blame for whatever happens. They need to Learn that they Themselves have attracted these happenings to Themselves through their Own Thoughts, Deeds and Actions.

They should Teach Personal Responsibility to their Young Early in their Life.

ALL this Blaming comes from Man's view of God rooted in Ancient history when, as pagan religions flourished; they had a God for everything.

It also comes from the Religions of today making up their Own God for their Own Selfish Control and Power over Earth Souls.

Earth Religions have created the Worst Problems on this Earth.

Man was never meant to worship any Teacher, Messengers or any one Soul that has ever been sent to Earth throughout Earth's history by the Universe.

There are NO RELIGIONS in the Universe or in any other Universe or Galaxy.

ALL RELIGIONS ARE MAN-MADE and are the cause of most Earth Plane Problems.

The Earth's Problems and Disasters, which have all been blamed on GOD as punishing Earth Souls, is really just the Ignorance of MANKIND, which is punishing itself for its own actions.

GOD does not punish any Soul. It is Not the Will of GOD to punish.

Rather, this is all of MANKIND exercising its Own GOD-given Free Will for the need of their Own Lessons.

This has always been the cause for all of the pain, suffering and mistakes Mankind has endured throughout the history of the World.

All must be Corrected, even those unlearned Lessons or Mistakes that have accumulated throughout Earth's history.

Many, as we have said, of the same Old Souls are on Earth today to do just that; Correct Old Mistakes grounded in Greed, Selfishness and Corruption from the Earliest Ancient Civilizations Corruption that caused their own destruction.

Mankind is still creating Wars and continuing its Old Ways. Therefore, not much Progress is being made.

It will take many more Disasters to wake up Minds and get them back on the right track to fulfill the Missions they agreed to when they left the Universe to go to Earth.

GOD is always giving and never Taking or Punishing Anyone.

Our Life Energies or God Energies are one and the same. While our Souls are limited on Earth and housed within our Physical Bodies, they are Limitless in the Universe.

I received the following inspirational writing about Planets during a visit to Columbus, Georgia, while sitting inside a mock-up of the Space Shuttle in the Science Museum there. I was viewing a video of the Sun and Planets of the Universe at the time.

We all someday may be a part of Creating Planets as Our Souls Progress Higher in the Universe. I know I will and look forward to doing this.

All Planets are created by the High Universal Masters from Life Energies or God Energies, which again, are one and the same.

Therefore, All Is Life or – God – Highly Evolved Soul Energies of Life or – God – has Created all the Planets.

All Souls and All Creation are the Expression of Life or God Energies.

ALL IS GOD. ALL IS LIFE. GOD IS LIFE. LIFE IS GOD.

YOU ARE LOVE and LOVE IS GOD.

One of my High Master Directors of the Universe sent me that message. He said this is what I will do when I return to the Universe: help them to Create Planets.

This happened the day before a Special friend completed his U.S. Army Basic Training at Fort Benning, in Georgia.

I am so proud of him and his Choice of Mission in this Earth Life to help and contribute to turning things around on this Earth. I am equally proud of All Our Service Men and Women, who volunteered for this Mission in the quest for Peace before they came to Earth.

When a Soldier looses their physical body they return to the Universe. Their part in the Mission for Peace is complete. They have finished Correcting their Mistakes.

It's then time to receive their Rewards of Accomplishment. All has purpose and reason in the Universe.

This was a special experience for me, as I see the Life Purpose for All Experiences.

May Life continue to Bless Our Soldiers Everywhere!

I prefer using the word "Life" in place of "God." I feel it is Not So Limiting and separates us from all the different views and beliefs of False Gods from the Past. You could also use other words or phrases, like "Love" or "The Force" or "Life Energy."

Consider that the Web Of Life Connects us to All There Is.

God is Life, and Life is God – God is All There Is!

I also believe in Our Future time on Earth. God will always be called Life instead of God. This word God has become too personalized on Earth.

Again, I feel changing the word to Life will be the Only Way for Man to let go of their False Gods of the Past.

It will also help Man to let go of the varied ideas of a separated God and separating themselves from God. This can help ease their Fear of a punishing God.

GOD IS Within us All – IS ALL THAT IS, which is Our Life Source.

So Speak to LIFE, and Speak of LIFE.

Live in LOVE of LIFE, and let Your LOVE flow to All and Everyone, and everything around you, as LOVE is the Highest Governing Force in All the Universes.

YOU are LOVE and LOVE is GOD.

YOU are LIFE and LIFE is GOD.

This is truth. *

*Again, I recommend you read the Books by Neale Donald Walsch, the author of the "Conversations with God" series, including: "Tomorrow's God," "What God Wants," "The New Revelations," in which God says, "You are Love and Love is God, You are Life and Life is God."

If you are Searching, I highly recommend reading every one of these published bestsellers. They are all available to help turn the World around to the New Spiritually.

Teddy Roosevelt wrote the following on August 26, 1986. I am adding this writing here because I found it in Jan's personal writings from a class question about building Inner Peace, living a Meaningful Life and a New Planetary Government, which I think are interesting.

To build Inner Peace you must first of all find yourself and be very sure of yourself.

Also, when you're meeting someone who is struggling, whether it's someone you know or someone you've just met, look at the person, with compassion.

Each time you do this you are becoming a better person. You've made definite Progress for the better.

Someone else in class asked Teddy another question: "What is a Meaningful Life for us?"

The measure of a Meaningful Life in your case is clear. You have your work now and because of it, your Life is Meaningful and also productive. You will contribute much to many.

Until then, Lessons must be Learned.

All who want to have a Meaningful Life must search their Soul in a Spiritual manner. They must intend to do better for the benefit of All of Mankind.

You must feel satisfied about your Life for it to be Meaningful.

Teddy, will there be New Planetary Government to reflect the Changes being made on Earth?

The International Corporations that are running the World now have too much Control and they must be stopped.

A New Government will be created. It will put a Halt to this nonsense. Planetary Government is not more than 20 to 30 years away.

This was the final Question in the final Chapter for Book I "Our Earth And Beyond."

Book II, "Many Planes Above," will follow. It will include a couple Art Photos the List of Art Teachers and a brief account about each of Jan's Art Teachers.

Also the List of Art Teachers follows the list of Writing Teachers at the beginning of Book I. These same Writing Teachers contributed to the content of Book II.

Book II, "Many Planes Above," includes explanations of the work that is done on several of the Planes, and 15 more Question-and Answer-Chapters. This includes "Planets In Our Universe" "UFOs And Aliens," "Earth Mysteries" and many more.

Thank you for reading these Books and Changing your Lives for the Betterment of Mankind.

Ron J. Oberon

To request healing, visit
www.ronsgiftofhealing.com
There is no charge

If you are interested in a private writing, contact:

Alice Heath
heathalice@yahoo.com

Four Ways to Order

1. Mail completed order form to: Ron Oberon & Associates, LLC
                                              150 S. Glenoaks Blvd., #9342
                                              Burbank, CA, 91502
                                              ronjoberon@sbcglobal.net

2. Web: www.ronsgiftofhealing.com (Go to the Order Books tab)
3. Voicemail: 888-294-8778
4. Fax completed order form to: 888-230-2272

Order Form

Name (Please print)_____

Address_____

City _____ State_____ Zip_____

E-mail address _____

Daytime Phone _____ Evening Phone_____
We will call only if we have a question about your order.

Ship to Address (If different)

Name (Please print)_____

Address _____

City _____ State _____ Zip_____

Book Title	Quantity	Amount
Our Earth And Beyond – Book I		
Many Planes Above – Book II		
Subtotal		
California residents add 8.25 % sales tax		
Shipping and handling (see rates below)		
Total		

Payment Method

____ Check (Payable to Ron Oberon & Associates, LLC)

____ Credit Card (Check one) ____ *VISA* ____ *MasterCard* ____ *Discover* ____ *AmEx*

Card Number_____

Name (As it appears on card) _____

Expiration Date_____

Shipping: Single book: $3.95, International, $9.95. Quantities based on UPS Ground rates.